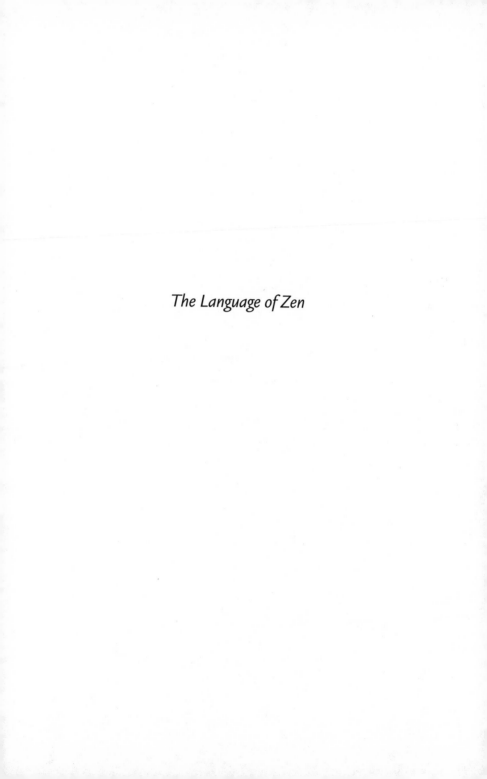

The Language of Zen

EVERY DAY, PRIESTS MINUTELY EXAMINE THE LAW
AND ENDLESSLY CHANT PROFOUND SUTRAS.
BEFORE THIS, THOUGH, THEY SHOULD FIRST
READ THE LOVE LETTERS SENT BY THE WIND AND RAIN,
THE SNOW AND MOON.

(Zen Master Ikkyu)[1]

The Language of Zen

Heart Speaking to Heart

Richard Burnett Carter

STERLING

New York / London
www.sterlingpublishing.com

STERLING and the distinctive Sterling logo are registered trademarks of
Sterling Publishing Co., Inc.

Library of Congress Cataloging-in-Publication Data

Carter, Richard B. (Richard Burnett), 1931-
  The language of Zen : heart speaking to heart / Richard Burnett Carter.
    p. cm.
  Includes bibliographical references and index.
  ISBN 978-1-4027-4701-4 (hc-trade cloth) 1. Rinzai (Sect)--Doctrines. I. Title.
  BQ9368.7.C37 2010
  294.3'927--dc22

                              2009028380

10 9 8 7 6 5 4 3 2 1

Published by Sterling Publishing Co., Inc.
387 Park Avenue South, New York, NY 10016
© 2010 by Richard Burnett Carter
Distributed in Canada by Sterling Publishing
$^c/_o$ Canadian Manda Group, 165 Dufferin Street
Toronto, Ontario, Canada M6K 3H6
Distributed in the United Kingdom by GMC Distribution Services
Castle Place, 166 High Street, Lewes, East Sussex, England BN7 1XU
Distributed in Australia by Capricorn Link (Australia) Pty. Ltd.
P.O. Box 704, Windsor, NSW 2756, Australia

Manufactured in the U.S.A.

Sterling ISBN 978-1-4027-4701-4

For information about custom editions, special sales, premium and
corporate purchases, please contact Sterling Special Sales
Department at 800-805-5489 or specialsales@sterlingpublishing.com.

Dedication

To that realist poet,
Zen Master Ikkyu,
Whose songs and wit
Brought me to that ringing laughter
That is the golden voice
Of true Zen Buddhism.

Contents

Introduction

How easy is to become learned,
how difficult it is to become human.

(Nur Ali Elahi)[2]

This book is neither a textbook nor a suspenseful page-turning novel. It should be read for pleasure, at whatever times you are inclined to read such a book. The Zen words discussed in this book do *not* automatically link together into anything so weighty as "Zen Teachings" or "Zen Wisdom." A word is a word is a word — even if it is a **Zen** word. So the book only discusses a number of those words that struck the author, a scholar of Zen and reader of Zen books, as potentially difficult for his fellow Western readers to grasp in the way their original Zen writers intended.

This or that reader might, for instance, find the terms *God*, *Dharma*, and *Source*, that are listed in Part I, to be of particular interest; another reader might find the entries "Ego," "Desire," or "Zen & Koans" of particular interest. *So . . . ?* So readers should read the entries *according to what interests them most* — or in whatever order they find most enjoyable. (If it isn't enjoyable, it isn't true Zen.) The reader who has read a particular entry — say, *God* in Part I — might like its taste, but could still be a bit hungry for more about the way Zen understands the term; Part II repeats several of those items. This structure will involve some repetition, but that's the nature of the beast.

In short, in Part II, we will further consider several words from Part I — again and again stressing the message we find so elegantly presented in Zen:

Ignore the finger;
Just look at where it points![3]

As one Zen Master remarked:

"Only when you hear in your eyes will you know."

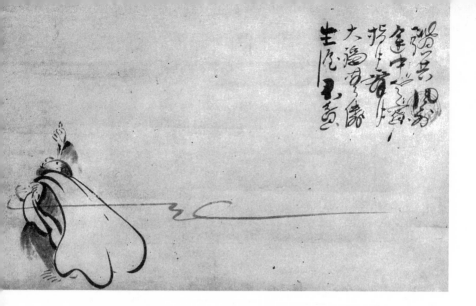

Another said:

> *For explanations without explanations,*
> *one must know that the meaning is not in the words.*
> *If one hears without hearing, one is certain after all*
> *that the words do not contain the meaning.*[4]

I think they are right on. So, the strange text-formatting of a number of the pages in this book is designed to help the reader to "*hear in your eyes*" and to remember that

"the words do not contain the meaning."

For example,

> **While looking at a Dandelion the other day,**
> **it asked me,**
> **"Don't you know that ogling's impolite?"**
> **(We both laughed.)**

Or, as the Chinese poet-sage Pu-erh tells us (in Jane Hirshfield's translation):

> ***Late Indian summer's***
> ***Soft breezes fanning out,***

The sun shines
On the hidden cottage
South of the river.
December, and the apricots'
First flowers open.
A person looks,
The blossoms look back:
Plain heart seeing into plain heart.

But, exactly *why* does this book's text sometimes dance all over the page? Well, we find a sort of explanation in a recent edition of the *Japan Times:*

> Calligraphers may appear still, but in reality they are dancers on the page. To be the best at their art, just as in dance, focused, disciplined bursts of energy are required. Not even a breath can be misplaced.[5]

And, years after I began writing this book with its words sometimes dancing all over the page, I met with this same demand that the readers hear with their eyes and see with their ears. It's in "Jejuri," by the contemporary Indian poet, Arun Kolatkar; he is describing a field with a dozen roosters and hens, dancing a sort of harvest dance —

n

a   d   a   &

Up   do n   n   uP. ..

w   d

for half a page!

Arun Kolatkar knows all about hearing with your eyes and seeing with your ears. (And *what* a poet!)

And, as the poet-monk Ryokan relates:

Late at night, I draw my inkstone close;
Flushed with wine, I put my worn brush to paper.
I want my brushwork to bear the same fragrance as
plum blossoms, ...[6]

Acknowledgments

In my begging bowl
Violets and dandelions
Jumbled together —
I offer them to the
Buddhas of the Three Worlds.
(Zen Master Ryokan)[7]

Those of us who think that Zen practice might have something to offer us have come to it in different ways and for different reasons. I first saw that I wanted to begin its practice in earnest during one hot August afternoon years ago when, sitting alone at my computer, I looked up and heard myself say, out loud:

I hide behind myself. Why?

And, whenever I remember that event, I laugh.

I aimed my subsequent practice at finding out what it meant for me to hide behind myself. And why. I saw I needed to discover who was hiding and who was being hidden, and why it was all so laughable. This involved Zen Sitting (Zazen), as well as reading and reflecting on a number of Zen texts.

It was in the course of that reading that I began to see that there was often a subtle but important difference in the meaning of a number of commonly used English words when I came across them in the translations of Zen Masters. It took me years to tease out how their meanings in the context of their translations differed from the meaning of the same words when they occurred in the context of everyday speech and writing. This present book is my attempt to help others in their reading of Zen texts by sharing with them some of the results of my efforts.

This interest in teasing out the differences between these words led me to visit the International Research Institute for Zen Buddhism attached to Hanazono University in Kyoto, a move that would have been impossible without a great deal of help.

I am particularly indebted to David and Robin Bord, William George Danforth, Anita Tarzian, and to my son, John C. R. Carter, for their unstinting, loving, and generous help and encouragement in preparing me to leave for Kyoto.

Once at the Institute in Kyoto, I met Ms. Sachiko Usami, the institute's ever-attentive, vastly learned librarian. Her grace and kindness were boundless, and I feel privileged to have had the experience of being included in their wide embrace.

Then there was the institute's American scholar-monk, Thomas Kirchner (Shaku Yuho), who helped me contact officials at the university who could appoint me as a research scholar at the institute. When I arrived in Japan, he helped me find my way to his temple outside Kyoto and put me up for my first night's sleep in three days. He took me to the university and helped me find my rooms in faculty housing and helped me unpack. Once I had settled in, the unerring precision of his wide learning, which he freely imparted to me whenever I asked for help, together with the gentleness nourished by his Zen practice, were both greatly encouraging as well as very informative.

Then there was the American scholar and Zen layman Jeff Shore, Hanazono University's professor of international Zen. His great learning and brilliant insights, together with the warmth and generosity of his family, were critically important for my progress.

And there was my roshi (my mentor in my daily Zen practice), Zen Master Kanju Tanaka, chief priest at Kouunji Temple in Kyoto. After he had earned a graduate degree through his studies of the German philosopher Kant, Tanaka became a Zen Master. He has the philosopher's wisdom and Zen Master's insight. Among his immeasurably precious gifts to me were, *"You must seek the seeker!"* and *"You should annihilate everything until you meet your formless Self directly."*

And there was Professor Eshin Nishimura, then president of Hanazono University. A certified master in Rinzai Zen, Professor Nishimura was also a splendid painter in both the classical Zen style and in the style of the more tender-hearted French painters. It was his essay on Hakuin, the eighteenth-century Zen Master, that first opened my eyes to the fact that the Buddha of our age, Siddhartha Gautama, was a prince, and that Zen demands that its practitioners purge themselves of anything that is not noble and generous. The gay, profoundly disciplined exuberance of Professor Nishimura's intelligent worldliness manifested to me precisely that dimension of living Zen I was hoping to experience by traveling to Kyoto. Without his help and encouragement, neither my trip to Kyoto nor this book would have been possible.

I traveled to Kyoto with my begging bowl empty, and returned with it filled with

Violets and dandelions
Jumbled together —

So, this present book is my offering to those of my fellow beggars who think that perhaps Zen's jumble of violets and dandelions can fill their bowls.

Part I

IN ZEN, IF ASKED, "WHAT IS THE BUDDHA?" ONE
SHOULD RAISE A CLENCHED FIST.

IF ASKED, "WHAT IS THE ULTIMATE MEANING OF THE
BUDDHIST LAW?" BEFORE THE WORDS HAVE DIED AWAY,
ONE SHOULD RESPOND, "A SINGLE BRANCH OF THE
FLOWERING PLUM" OR "THE CYPRESS IN THE GARDEN."

(Takuan Soto)[1]

Words

MOON — MOONSHINE

The Teachings of Buddhas & Patriarchs — "Words, Words, Words"

Since Prince Siddhartha's death, Buddhists have written volumes of words. Many of these words have warned us that words, if taken the wrong way, can lead us astray. Words, those books warn us, are tools; if we take them as anything *other* than tools, they can be exceedingly dangerous. Indeed they can, and most certainly have; some have even caused so-called "holy" wars — surely the *least* holy of all human enterprises.

Well, we humans *will* talk, but not all of us are willing to go to war because of the different ways in which we understand certain words. So, how can we learn to use words in such a way that they lead us to the practice of the arts that nourish life rather than the arts of war that are designed to destroy lives?

It seems that we must learn a use of words that involves not only what and when to say something, but also, when to say

nothing.

But *how* can we be taught (using words) when not to use words?

The early Zen Masters most certainly faced this dilemma and came up with a use for words that make us tongue-tied:

Koans.

Whatever else Koans are useful for, they remind us that words are only tools for clearing out thickets that obscure what *cannot* be said in words. Koans use words to reflect the limitations of words, and the cleverer we are in our use of words, the tighter the knot in which a Koan can tie our tongues.

It seems that Zen texts involving Koans are designed to teach us, almost always using words to do so, that there exists a whole realm of experience that is largely hidden from us *because* of words and the opinions to which they give birth. Indeed, a Koan can make a student doubt his or her ability even to use words. And, they do this using words! The response to a Koan is sometimes

s i l e n c e .

But when you get it — or, better, when *it* gets *you* —

LAUGHTER.

Koans do not need to be verbal to teach us something about the limitations of words. They are sometimes word-pictures that work precisely *because* they are wordless. These teach us something about words that words cannot. In such cases, we have,

s i l e n c e **leading to** s i l e n c e .

An example of silence that leads to silence is the word-picture involving Prince Siddhartha, the founder of our Buddhism, as he realized his end was nearing. He is pictured — *using words!* — as standing silently in front of his disciples while he twirls a flower between his thumb and fingers as he considers who is to be his successor. Out of the large group of possible choices, only one monk, named Mahakashyapa, smiled. The story containing this word-picture continues by telling us that the Buddha recognized him as his successor.

This narrative presenting Prince Siddhartha's silence is so sparse, so touching, that its images "speak" directly to us without words, and thus teach us an important lesson concerning the limitations of words. Such word-pictures remind us that the highest order of human speech can involve silent "flower-talk" — that, because it *is* silent, one has to listen very carefully to hear. As one of the Zen Masters counsels us,

we must learn to hear hearing.

We can only do *that* if we learn to hear silence — as when, for instance, a request for a loan is met with silence.

That silence speaks volumes.

Still, whatever we do hear when we hear silence speaking depends in large part on how we listen to words spoken out loud. Because they were so detached, the Zen Masters could calmly gaze on the laughable antics of words as they hop in and out of their meanings and thoroughly confuse those of us who take words seriously. As our own Socrates saw — in perfect agreement with the view of the Zen Masters — words tend to have a life of their own and should be viewed as if they were fleas that must be trained to do their tricks at a carnival sideshow. Otherwise, they will become something whose only aim in life is to annoy us as if we were dogs and cats.

There is yet another reason why understanding Zen's take on words is difficult for us in the West, namely, many of us have been taught to view the words of our holy books as being obvious and unambiguous. This has given occasion for much bloodshed — as if Eternity speaks in words like those found in our elementary schools' primers! This makes it very difficult for us to consider words as mere instruments. Zen Koans provide the perfect antidote:

no word-flea can hang on when scratched by a Koan.

Even if we agree with all this for the sake of argument, mustn't we also admit that there have been a number of truly beneficial words that have been spoken over the ages by great individuals? Just a glance at any one of a number of the recorded sayings of the great Zen Masters reminds us of how rich and precious the utterances of human beings can be. And there are now, and always have been, great poets, law givers, philosophers, and prophets, both Eastern and Western, whose words have been the source of nourishment and delight to countless numbers of listeners and readers. So what could it possibly mean to say that Zen words — or any other words for that matter — are properly to be considered merely as signs and guideposts?

Poets, law givers, philosophers, and Zen Masters are surely more than highway workers painting signposts.

Aren't they?

Not according to what we have been saying.

But think: those who have been really lost and hungry, with night coming on and no place in sight to eat or rest, know what it means to be grateful for the sight of a sign that points them in the direction of food and lodging. When we have arrived, eaten, and rested, we forget that sign.

Entirely!

(If we don't, then that signpost becomes an address.)

In short, for Buddhism in general, and Zen in particular, the world we humans experience as sentient beings is the creation of a kind of *Silence*.

So, yet another possibly useful way of thinking about the term *Word* when we meet it in a Zen context is,

an echo of Silence.

Silence can speak universes, and one of Zen's central practices is designed to teach us how to be silent and how to listen to silence.

Finally, here is what the master poet Basho has to say about these matters:

Do not seek to follow in the footsteps of the wise.
Seek what they sought,

and most certainly, not their words!

Still,

Moonshine is only *Moon-talk*

And,

"Buddha & Patriarch talk" is only "Left at the next intersection"

(But, ask yourself: What would *Moonshine* be without *Moon?*)

Ego

"Who Sez?"
"ME! That's *who!!"*

The Buddha, who preached humility and the need to purge ourselves of Ego, was recorded as having attained his Great Awakening while sitting under a *banyan* tree. We may well wonder, "Why a *banyan* tree? Is there anything about that tree in particular that leads us to think about either Ego or Awakening?"

It turns out that the banyan tree is not a real tree at all. It is formed when birds drop fig seeds on the branches of a tree and the figs grow long roots to the ground for nourishment. In the course of doing this, the figs' roots cross and cross and cross until they completely encompass the original tree's trunk — which is "strangled" by those roots. The host tree dies and rots away, leaving the dense covering of the fig roots as a strange sort of self-supporting tree instead of a trunk. For this reason banyans are often referred to as "strangler figs."

The Buddha is said to have reached Awareness sitting under a ***"Strangler"** fig?* Isn't that the last tree in the world Prince Siddhartha should have been sitting under when he was Awakened?

Well, that choice of trees is so strange that it is more than a little unlikely to have been made by chance. So . . . ? So, if not by chance, why *might* it have been chosen?

It is at least possible that the banyan tree was chosen as a warning against what our Ego does to us — *encases our receptive core within a web of illusions:*

I'M A *VERY* IMPORTANT PERSON.

IT FEELS JUST RIGHT TO ME

SO

IT MUST BE RIGHT FOR ME.

BECAUSE I SAID SO!

But there is yet another obstacle standing in our way of understanding either what *we* mean by the term *Ego* or what the *Zen texts* mean when they use the term.

To begin with, the term that is translated as *Ego* in some translations of Zen texts is translated in others as *Self,* and this can be confusing. In our everyday speech, the term *Self* usually refers to something less unapproachable than the term *Ego*, which, in everyday usage, tends to indicate a better-than-thou, superior stance toward others. (*Wherever* the term *Self* appears in the rest of this book, the reader would do well to note that it closely approximates to our term *Person* or even its somewhat more literary version *Persona* — which, in ancient Latin, referred to the *masks* of actors presenting the stories found in age-old myths.)

Because of the core concept of Person/Self in the Christian West — or to a lesser degree in Marxist China and in Nepal — it is difficult in the extreme for us to grasp what the Zen texts mean when they speak of purging ourselves of Ego.

Well, Zen Masters are prepared to help others because they have succeeded in purging themselves of Ego *to some considerable extent*. But none of us living, sentient humans can altogether purge ourselves of our Self-hood — of that masking *Person*-hood. To do so would be to commit suicide. Zen Buddhism is not in the least suicidal, but the Zen practitioner who is on the path to Self-purging certainly purges *something*.

If not Self, then what *do* Zen practitioners purge when they purge themselves of Ego, and what part of the Self would be left after they have in large part purged themselves of Self-ishness?

It can be said that, for Zen, Ego is that aspect of Self that is completely Self-absorbed. What only concerns ME is concerned with no one or nothing else.

Still, there exists a dimension of human existence that isolates each of us from anyone else. We've popped out of our mothers' wombs into the noisy light of day. Finally! *Nine* long months of swimming around — sometimes even standing on our heads with our thumb in our mouth as we listen to our mother's guts rumbling — and then we are free!

Here I am!

ME!

At last! Here we are.

Now.

You.

Me.

All of us.

I may only be one of many, but I have to truly be an individual even to be *one* of many. Being a true individual, I exist both as one of many and as

all
by
my
Self.
Me!

IN PERSON!!!

Sure: Ego is that aspect of Self that has no concern for anything beyond ME!, but there *has* to be something in the Self that *is* Self-ish — something whose concern is the Self, and nothing beyond the Self. The most saintly of us cannot be saintly unless we simply are — unless we eat, sleep, and can find a warm place to keep us from freezing. *You* can't eat, sleep, or keep warm for *me*; I've got to do those things for *my* Self — through *my* own efforts!

So there seems to be an essential aspect of Self that is identical to Ego, even Ego at its most Self-ish, most *Personal.* The YOU that is Self-*less* and the YOU that is Egotistical and Self-*ish* must to some extent together make an unbreakable unity.

No wonder we humans are always in trouble! We are living contradictions. Or, in the idiom of Zen,

WE

ARE

LIVING

Koans!

And, make no bones about it;

OUR

ETERNALLY

EGOTISTICAL SELF-ISHNESS

FOREVER

O

M

K

C

S

OUR DEEPEST HUMANITY

FOREVER!

What a Koan! Perhaps this is what Zen Master Ikkyu means when he tells us,

Only one Koan matters
YOU![2]

The pair, Ego-Self, *is* indeed a Koan and it is a *living* Koan!
That pair is truly the only Koan that matters.

BUT . . .

but if, in our enthusiasm for virtue, we break up that pair in order to detach our **ME!**-Self aspect of our Ego without attending to its natural divisions, we simply won't matter. We will have been annihilated.

Sure! The Zen Masters all worked to purge themselves of Ego, but we all have to have Ego if we are going to matter, because we would otherwise cease to exist.

What a mess!
But listen to Ikkyu again:

why is it all so beautiful
this fake dream
this craziness
why?[3]

Or, the remark by Tsái Ken T'an:

Water that is too pure has no fish.[4]

Or, Ikkyu's bit of fun:

That stone Buddha deserves all the bird-shit it gets.
I wave my skinny arms like a tall flower in the wind.[5]

And the very beautiful flower of the lotus has its roots in mud and filth.

Isn't that what Zen Master Hakuin is restating when he says:

Zen practice in the midst of activity is a million
times superior to that pursued within tranquility?

Ego's illusions may be crazy and often just plain nasty, but this is *our* human world, the only world we have, and the embrace of Mahayana Zen Buddhism is sufficiently wide to embrace that beautiful, impossible contradiction that is the living human being. (If you can't handle that, Zen isn't for you.[6])

The alternative?

Well, there's always such things as the mass murders of our Enlightened West during the last centuries, as it sought to separate the perpetrators of injustices to produce:

Stalin's "Ego-free" Socialist Heroes;
Pol Pot's back-to-nature "Ego-free" enthusiasts;
bin Laden's pious "Ego-free" Muslim murderers of the Infidels

Damn our **EGO!**

Sure. It's damnable, all right, but, as Zen demands of *its* practitioners, after you've finished damning it, you must then turn your back on it. After all is said and done, this fake dream that is humanity's birthright is filled with wonders. And never forget:

We are **IN** that (kaef) dream!

So, when we come across the term *Ego* in a Zen context, it might be helpful to think,

Okay; damn my Ego. But then I'll sing Zen Master Ikkyu's song in praise of

OUR IMPOSSIBLY HODGEPODGE **HUMANNESS.**

And remember what the Buddhist poet Issa tells us:

Where there are humans you'll find flies — and Buddhas.[7]

All very well. But how does Zen view the likes of Pol Pot, who orchestrated the murder of one to three million Cambodians (**between a quarter and a third of the country's population**) to produce a society without the follies and injustices of other "advanced" industrial societies?

Well, as the Buddhist saying goes, "Suffering is the consequence of Anger, Greed, and Illusion." That is, when Passionate Kindness sleeps with Belief — itself, the son of Ignorance — their offspring are often Murder and its twin, Mayhem.

Zen Buddhism holds that although the core trees hosting banyans are strangled by their guests, *nothing* can ever strangle our heart-mind,

our deathless core that HOSTS that damned Ego.

So, when Prince Siddhartha chose the Strangler Fig to sit under, perhaps — just *perhaps!* — he was showing us that, no matter *how* terribly strangled by Ego's illusions we living Koans might be, our living core is *never* strangled.

We are thus like the artichoke; if we peel off the thorny, inedible outside, we will come to that wonder of tasty wonders,

its heart.

Okay?

Or, as the Vedic saint Nisargadatta Maharaj has it:

> **Wisdom tells me I am nothing.**
> **Love tells me I am everything.**
> **Between the two my life flows.**

The ultimate Koan! And *perfect* Zen!

Desire

*It's an amazing thing, a phenomenon,
when a person is willing to give themselves over to something else.
That's what real passion is.*

(Matisyahu)[8]

The term *Ego* leads us to the term *desire* because, when I desire something, it is I!, that damnable, indissoluble-as-long-as-I-am-alive I!, that desires it.

Because desire often seems to be treated so negatively in Zen texts, the down-to-Earth reader might find this a good reason not to investigate those texts any further. But, to be fair, we should try to understand what's going on here before we reject all Zen thinking out of hand.

So, to begin with, there is no reason to think that when a Zen Master uses a word that can be accurately translated into English as *desire* he is not referring to exactly the same *emotional* event as we do when we use that word. In the West, however, many of us have been taught to think that the feeling we refer to by the name *desire* is, in reality, the way we have been programmed by Evolution to be aware of certain changes in the biochemistry of our blood. And there are also many of us in the West who view it as a witch's brew whose ingredients include our Christian view of the sinfulness of the flesh, our Darwinian views defining desire and repulsion as survival mechanisms, and our psychiatric theories that view *all* of our emotions as nothing more than different levels of biochemicals in our bloodstream — for example, viewing sexual desire as the presence of certain hormones in our blood, those famous "raging hormones." So what *does* that term mean when we meet with it in Zen texts?

The texts seem to consider desire as objectionable because it leads us to consider "objects of desire" as things that are nothing beyond how they can satisfy *ME!* Desire leads to grabbing, to consuming, and so, when that "object" of desire is a living human being, desire involves a kind of spiritual cannibalism. Thus, when we see this term used in Zen contexts, one way to look at it is,

"what leads us to clutch in order to consume."

(Zen writers would *never* compliment something by saying that it was *desirable*.)

Still, neither the Zen Masters nor their monks were in the least warped from living in monasteries far from the real world. Then why would they reject desire so firmly? After all, if we don't act to follow our desires for this and that, why *do* we act? We might as well be in intensive care being fed intravenously. But the vitality of their actions and their writings shows that Zen practitioners resemble anything but barely comatose individuals who should be hooked up to feeding tubes.

So, once again, why *do* they consider desire as *un*-desirable?

Well, for one thing, what we require simply to perform our work is not really *desired* by us. Carpenters *need* hammers and saws. They don't desire them. Likewise with surgeons and their scalpels. Even when a procedure requires an instrument, surgeons don't desire it; they *want* it — that is, they are aware that they lack it, are aware that what they need to accomplish such and such an undertaking is *such-and-such-and-nothing-else*.

How does this differ from *desiring* the missing instruments?

Well, we need and wish for tools because of what *they* are — designed precisely to complete this or that particular task. They are only *tools*, after all, and we choose them because they are what they are *designed* to do, not because they are this and that to ME!, but because *this* job requires them if it is to be completed.

So, speaking strictly, the carpenter who has to drive in a nail doesn't even *choose*, let alone *desire*, this or that hammer; rather, he *locates* the one that is right for the job, and it, so to speak, says, *"Here I am! Hammer away with me!"* It is the *job* he is doing that tells him to look for this or that hammer.

The task at hand determines what the worker looks for; not his or her desires.

(Viewed like this, awareness of need is something like an inside-out desire: the thing calls us, so we don't need to grab it — let alone lie to get it to do what we desire it for.)

Several predominantly Buddhist countries are known for their excellence in the arts and crafts, and this is likely to be at least in part the result of their respect for the use of their tools. It is not for nothing that Korean and Japanese automobiles are ranked among the best. And many American and European woodworkers buy expensive Japanese saws because of their excellent design and the quality of their steel. Professional craftspersons *respect* their tools, and treat them as essential elements in the performance of their professional activities.

On its part, however, what is desirable to us is an *object* to us; the desirable becomes the object of our activity or thought. To the extent we desire anything, we are preoccupied by it to the exclusion of any other concern. Where desire is concerned, it is not a matter of what the desired thing *is* that matters; it's what about it that makes it satisfy *us*.

Furthermore, when our desire prevents us from attending to anything else over a period of time, we say that we are *consumed* by desire. When what we desire consumes us, we become possessed by our non-possession —

BY WHAT WE DO *NOT* POSSESS!

"Now, just one minute, if you please!" you might be saying. "How can anyone be possessed by *non*-possession?"

Well, now that you mention it, no one can.

"Okay. Then what *is* happening when we desire something?"

Okay; if we can't be possessed by what we *don't* possess, then what we desire must be something we *do* possess —

but don't know it!

Doesn't this, in turn, lead us to suspect that we living, desiring individuals are born already possessing whatever it is we ever *will* or *could* feel desire for?

If this is the case, then isn't the day-to-day world we experience the very world we are born possessing, but that presents itself to us in the (desirable!) guise of what we *don't* possess?

Of course, many — and perhaps most — of the objects of our desire are creations of our fantasy that we *mis*-take for real things. In such instances, our feeling of desire boils down to the impulse to bark up the wrong tree. Since we are not hunting dogs, we were not born to bark up any trees — right *or* wrong! But many of us grow up to be something like emotional hounds, forever barking up one tree or another. When we view things as being what *they* are, rather than what we feel *we* want, then we see them clearly: with eyes wide open.

For Zen, to see something as an object of desire is to see it by squinting at it. Awakening — Buddhist Enlightenment — primarily involves our putting an end to our squinting at the world.

AH!
Now *I see!*[9]

To the extent that the Zen texts are on target when they say we desire this or that because we have forgotten what we were born possessing, then when people kill one another to obtain things they desire,

they commit murder out of forgetfulness.

How sad! No wonder Zen has such a negative view of desire.

So, when we come across the term *desire* in a Zen context, it might be useful to think something like,

**our response to something we have,
but that we have forgotten that we have.**

And the cure?

REMEMBERING!

And remembering what we have forgotten we were born with is one of the main goals of Zen Sitting, *Zazen*.

Zazen is very good at helping us to *forget* whatever it is that keeps us from remembering. It's as what Zen Master Ryokan says:

> *Watching the moon,*
> *I spend the whole night mumbling poems;*
> *lost in blossoms,*
> *I never come home.*[10]

(*He* knows what's memorable and what is not — the secret of overcoming desire.)

Sentience & Objects

Zen Master Huang Po tells us:

A perception, sudden as blinking,
that subjects and objects are one,
will lead to a deep mysterious wordless understanding;
and by this understanding
will you awake to the truth of Zen.[11]

Well . . . maybe. But when I look out my window, don't I see trees, crows, clouds, and countless other things — *out there*? How can we possibly accept the *otherness* of what sentience presents to us — all those things *out there* — and, in the next moment, follow Huang Po in actually *denying* the distinction between subject and object? I'm not a crow. We are different, and what I see flying around out there is distinct from me. I am the sentient subject and the crow is an object I experience through my power of sentience. Otherwise, I am badly deceived by what I grasp through my power of sentience.

(Is my power of sentience nothing but Descartes' "evil Spirit" who possesses an unlimited power to deceive us? If so, then sentience would seem to be a curse; why would the Buddha wish to save all *sentient* beings?)

Another reason why the Western reader is likely to be put off by Zen's rejection of that subject-object dualism involves one of the most distinctive characteristics of the Western mind-set: namely,

the three major religions of the West all distinguish between
the Creator of this world we experience,
and us, the creatures who experience it!

In the account of Genesis — one of the West's most commonly accepted accounts of Creation — we humans were even created on a "*day*" different from the rest of Creation. Furthermore, so we were taught, human beings and *only* human beings were created by the *hand* of the Creator, and our very breath of life was breathed into us by our Creator — something that Genesis did not say of any of the other living creations.

The account continues to relate that humans then distanced themselves even *farther* from their Creator by disobeying one of His commands. As a result of this disobedience, the account continues, we were cast — *as punishment!!!* — into a world containing all of the other creatures.

THIS is the world that we presently live in:
A PUNISHMENT![12]

The difference between "Me" and "Them" is thus ingrained very deeply in Westerners.

The three great religions of the West teach us that we humans live in a world where everything *non*-human is quite distinct from us.[13] (Indeed, as the "holy" wars of the last thousand years show, even the three major religions of the West are at odds with one another and, from time to time, their adherents have attempted to kill as many of "Them" as possible.)

What is more, to the Western ear, the expression *sentient beings* refers to that sort of being who more or less consciously detects and responds to any change "out there," that is, in the environment.[14] For us in the West, *sentience* and *conscious awareness* are usually taken as synonyms — and *conscious awareness* means to us "conscious awareness of," namely, of *objects*

OUT THERE!!!

Buddhism holds that being sentient — if it isn't obscured by the intervention of ideas about and opinions concerning — is identical to Awakening-Enlightenment: identical, that is, to embracing all of reality with what the Masters refer to as "a never-despising heart." And for Zen, in particular, to say *yes* to this and *no* to that is a consequence of not really being sentient; being truly sentient is only possible to one who has succeeded in cultivating a non-despising heart. Such an individual is a Buddha, and Zen holds that only Buddhas truly enjoy the fruits of sentience — *and* that we are all *born* as Buddhas!

"But . . . Don't play with rattlesnakes! Doesn't that mean you have to say NO! to handling them? What's this n*on-despising heart* supposed to tell us in such cases as snake handling?"

Simple: when you know what a cobra's venom does to humans, you see, without thinking, that handling cobras is like the smell of a rotten egg and an omelet.

They don't go together
because
each
is
what
it
is;
NOT **because we have to think about it**
and choose whether or not to eat the rotten eggs.

(Even babies pull their hands away from hot objects without thinking about it.)

Furthermore, the Zen texts are clear about their view that sentience does not present "objects" *out there*. Not *those* crows; not *those* trees; not even *those* clouds. And, what is likely to be most unsettling to us in the West, they speak as if they think that when we conceive of something as existing *out there*, we make the same mistake as when we conceive of something as being desirable, to be ignored, or to be avoided: "Things *out there* are nothing to me beyond what I can make of them or how they can be useful to me or hurt me. And this includes you and you and you and me." Zen teaches that we are also just as mistaken when we conceive of ourselves as NOT of a scene that exhibits those birds, clouds, trees, people we love, hate, nurture, murder. . . . For Zen, we sentient beings are

also
OUT THERE!

along with all those things we perceive as being

OUT THERE!

But all these things are *really* together

in that here-out-there.

For Zen, we each *are* in our personal space *out there* with our children, our lovers, and with rattlesnakes, bin Laden, Hitler, Stalin . . . the list is endless.

In short, Zen Buddhist texts seem to say that

*THERE **IS** NO TRUE OUTSIDE-OF-INSIDE,*

and this includes your body, your body, my body . . . *all* our "bodies"—
including those birds, clouds, etc.[15]

"So . . . ? If things being *out there* is a creation of fantasy, what should we
make of those things we take for granted *are* out there or what our sentience
leads us to perceive as *out there?*"

They sure

L OO K

as if they are out there.

So, why do we automatically presume that they are outside, distinct from
us, from the people who perceive them as outside?

Well . . . the Zen texts seem to say that we should take seriously the idea
that our powers of sentience present the world to us similarly to the way
a child is present to its mother and its mother to the child. That is, after
the child has been born, and when it is mature enough to conceive of its
mother as being its mother, then, when the two of them face each other, the
conceived conceives what conceived it — and what conceived the child is
then conceived *by* the child.

Or perhaps we might consider it as a trick of perspective, like the one
that makes us see ourselves in a mirror *as if* we were as far *into* the mirror
when we are really *in front of* that mirror. (Many of us have experienced a
clever dog or cat looking *behind* a mirror to find its own image *in* it. The
animal hasn't forgotten!)

At any rate, isn't this world present to us through *our* sentience — through
your sentience and through *my* sentience — present to us because of *us* no less
than because of *it*? This world is *our* world, the world **WITHIN *in which*** we
were born. We weren't born first and *then* deposited into this world;

A birth certificate is **NOT** A DEPOSIT SLIP.

(It is likely that one of the most difficult obstacles that any Western reader of
Zen texts faces in grasping what they mean is precisely that we are dead sure we
were deposited into this hostile environment; our never-ending mantra is,

WHY ME!!??)

Furthermore, although we may think that the things we perceive are *out there*, those very perceptions are not themselves *out there:*

those perceptions are right here, inside, along with ME, WHEREVER I am when I am perceiving them.

In other words, we do not perceive **our SELVES** as being *out there* while we are perceiving crows and the like as being *out there*. (But the guy standing next to you does, watching *you* watch those crows.) It's an optical illusion, or, as the Zen texts seem to consider it, the root of *all* our illusions.

So when the reader comes across the terms *sentience* and *object* in Zen texts, it might be helpful to think:

**My illusion of
"Things out there"
is only one manifestation
of
the World giving itself to itself —
that is,
to ME,
who perceives them.**

Or, how about this?

**Sentience, like the presence of our newly born children,
reveals our origin giving itself back to itself,**

*WITHOUT **EVER** LEAVING ITSELF.*

The baby "appears" out there. Sure; but, whenever I look "into" a mirror, I "see" myself *clearly* as being "inside" that mirror!

Aren't they both optical illusions?

See why Hakuin says we are bowled over and have to hold our sides to keep from splitting open from laughter?

THE TRUTH CONCERNING OUR

"PERCEPTION"

CAN ONLY BE GRASPED ACCURATELY

WHEN WE REALIZE THAT WHAT IT PRESENTS IS

Both Here and There

and

Neither Here nor There!

TOGETHER!

A

GLORIOUSLY

SLY

KOAN!!!

This is all well and good, but our sensible reader is likely not to be amused by this, and he might be expected to respond, "Yeah, yeah; but again, how about poisonous snakes and bin Ladens? We distinguish between them and what is healthy, don't we? And aren't those unhealthy things rejected as not being *permitted* in our world? We destroy poisonous snakes and, when we can, we neutralize the bin Ladens, don't we? They are all part of that world. No?"

Not altogether; it is precisely because we are what *we* are and they are what *they* are that we see — *without having to figure it out* — that they are properly to be neutralized to permit them to exist in our common world — or better, to *re-locate* them within our common world.

In other words, Zen Buddhism permits isolation by means of prisons and zoos, but it does *not* condone

CAPITAL PUNISHMENT.

(If bin Laden and his gang could be instantaneously transported to some planet, only individuals who are as hateful as they are would still demand their deaths.)

"So, Buddhism is just another squishy Liberal, no-capital-punishment teaching? Who needs more of that?"

Not at all! There is nothing squishy about Buddhism in general, and Zen in particular. Many, and perhaps most, of the pro-death-penalty folk feel that life spent in climate-controlled subsidized housing, with all utilities paid for by Mr. and Ms. hard-working, law-abiding, taxpayer, is, *just perhaps*, not a proper response to heinous crimes. As we read in papers covering trials of those who have committed heinous crimes, the victim's survivors often say, "Death is too good for those guys." Maybe they are on to something, and maybe lives spent in hard labor with the merest of life supports — lives open to the gaze of the public, who learn from such punishments what the commission of certain crimes can lead to — might be appropriate alternatives to capital punishment. This way, some good will even be found flowing from heinous crimes.[16]

"Well . . . maybe; but what if someone is trying to kill me so that he can rape my wife; can't I kill him?"

You certainly can do whatever you can, with *whatever* you have at hand, to prevent the criminal from succeeding — but this doesn't give anyone a license to act as a public executioner.[17] If defending your home and loved ones happens to result in the death of the criminal, that happens. But all the Zen practitioner who is not an ordained monk or nun is warranted to do, according to Zen, is maximally defend you and yours from the criminal's desire to do harm. And laws cannot be crafted with an eye to the most heinous of crimes. Every wise and prudent legislator knows that

EXTREME CASES MAKE BAD LAW.

"That's a cop-out."

No, but think of it this way: Spoiled food makes you sick and can even kill you, and not even the best cookbooks include directions for handling spoiled food. Recipes only deal with food that is edible and prepared *in certain ways*. Isn't that what a good cookbook is — a guide for eating and living well? And don't good books of law contain directions for preparing people to live well?

"Nonsense! Sometimes we have to do battle, not just with everyday 'bad guys,' but with armies of individuals who wish to destroy us."

True. The necessity of waging war is one of the great sorrows of our human existence. But read *The Art of War* by the great Sun Tzu, who lived around the time of the Buddha.[18] That book teaches that we should face an enemy as a surgeon might face a gangrenous leg that must be amputated to save the patient's life; he ponders how to remove as little as is safe to do so. He does not cut off anything that doesn't absolutely need to be cut off for the sake of health.

After all, the father of medicine, Hippocrates, enjoined physicians to do no harm — but that very medical practice often requires physicians to cut and burn to save the patient.

That's just the way things are:

REALLY MESSY!

No?

Meditation[19]

Emperor Wu of Liang asked Bodhidharma, "What is the first principle of the holy teachings?"
Bodhidharma said, "Emptiness, no holiness."[20]

The term *meditation* tends to be used in our everyday conversation in several ways. In one, it simply means planning, as in pre-meditated murder, a murder planned before being committed. In general, the term refers to concentration on weighing alternative solutions to problems.

But since the introduction of Buddhist texts to the West after WWII, the term has been widely understood in another way, a way that is similar to but importantly different from the way it was used in Zen Buddhist texts. In everyday speech we refer primarily to a method of clearing the mind from any thoughts that lead to stressful emotions such as anger or resentment. As such, it is a sort of Self-improvement, stress-reduction technique.

Zen meditation is intended to help its practitioners' day-to-day responses to the world about them, and this certainly involves clearing the mind. But as a therapeutic procedure it is aimed at changing our stress-producing responses to the everyday world we inhabit. It becomes a way to make us more comfortable in our world and our world more comfortable about us being in it. In Zen, however, the term for meditation, *Zazen*, is used in a way that is somewhat similar to, but often richer than, the West's pill-free health-enhancing, stress-reducing, Self-improvement techniques.

To judge from the writings of the Zen Masters, that Self referred to by the expression, *Self-improvement*, is precisely what nourishes *folly*. Self, according to Zen, most certainly should not be improved by *any* techniques. Zen practice aims at Self-*dis*integration, not at its improvement. To the contrary, that part of Zen practice that involves *Zazen* aims at an *emptying-out* of Self. It is not Self-improvement because what we in the West most often experience as Self is actually our illusion of Self. (What could it mean to *improve* an illusion!? An illusion is an illusion is an illusion.)

When, years ago, I asked,

"Why do I hide behind myself?"

I caught a glimpse of a Self that was profoundly obscure and difficult for me to see clearly. What I had previously taken to be my real Self was somehow or other pushed aside for a moment. I then glimpsed what appeared to be a different Self, a *version* of my previous Self that I now consider as my authentic "root" Self.

It may seem impossible at first, but Zen encourages us to make use of that illusory, *counterfeit* Self to reveal the always-present, but almost always hidden, Self that Buddhism refers to as our original, root Self.

Zen meditation is not primarily concerned with how you or I react to the world around us. It aims to help us gain a clearer picture of what we really are, which permits us to see the world clearly as it is.

But . . . how *could* that counterfeit Self — the Self so many of us, East, West, North, and South, have come to view as our *real* Self — succeed in concealing our authentic Self? How could it even *suspect* the existence of another distinct "authentic" Self? And why did the counterfeit hide the authentic in the first place?

What possible benefit could it derive from doing so?

The answer seems to be that the counterfeit Self simultaneously hides and reveals the genuine Self by imitating what it was hiding. (Any successful imitation does that.) Zen meditation seems to facilitate the counterfeit's "melting into" what it counterfeits. That is, the texts suggest that meditation/ Zazen aims at getting the imitation to re-call the real Self into itself. That recalling is a making-present of the real Self that was never really absent — just unobserved because of the various impersonations it assumes in the course of living past childhood.

Zen "realization" involves nothing but our seeing what we have always been.

And when our practice has matured sufficiently we can see clearly what it was that the counterfeit counterfeited.

In other words, Zen meditation *real*-izes — literally *makes real* — the counterfeit merely by revealing the real Self. (Only the original can make sense of its images.)

Zen meditation thus requires that we wholeheartedly concentrate on the counterfeit version of our real Self — a task that, because it tends to make us embarrassingly self-conscious, is *very* hard to maintain through the end. It requires strength and courage to knowingly exploit the essential illusoriness of that counterfeit Self — that we have grown *soooooo* attached to over the years — by making an effort to appreciate fully both its power to hide our real Self as well as its close similarity to our real Self. When we have succeeded, then it is possible for us to expose that real Self.[21]

In short, Zazen helps us to recognize that our counterfeit Self is nothing but a version of our real Self (a *misleading* counterfeit); but it succeeds in this only to the extent that it has helped us to be perfectly clear concerning that counterfeit's enormous power.[22]

It's as if we had spent years only chatting with echoes of our own voice and one day heard the original. Indeed, that counterfeit Self is only a sort of *echo* of the Self it counterfeits. Zen practice requires that we *argue* with that echo — even to the extent that we sometimes *contradict* the echo! It's like what this charming haiku describes:

> *hazy moon —*
> *a nightingale in the canyon*
> *competes with its echo*

Zen aims at helping us realize clearly that our counterfeit Self gains its power from being an echo of what it is not — namely, our authentic root Self. (The only duality here is that of a voice and its echo.) But, once we have seen clearly that the bogus Self is merely an echo of the real thing, the voice and its echo in a sense become one. Zen practitioners sometimes laugh out loud during Zazen. They play with their echoes to make fun of them. Koans often make us do this. It's funny in just the way that a good mimic is funny.

The haiku above was written by Tomislav Maretic Vrapche of Croatia. We find another example of the voice engaged with its echo in the Twelfth Case of the thirteenth-century Koan collection *The Gateless Barrier*.[23] It goes as follows:

> Every day Master Zuigan Shigen used to call out to himself, "Oh, Master!" and would answer himself, "Yes?" "Are you awake?" he would ask, and would answer, "Yes, I am." "Never be deceived by others, any day, any time." "No, I will not."

So, a possibly useful way of referring to Zen meditation is:

Practice for playing both the ventriloquist and his dummy,

or, perhaps,

Practice as a way of learning how to disagree with yourself.

But, you know? That tuneful nightingale is really quite silly: he doesn't even recognize his own voice! And the above Zen Koan is only laughable because Zen Master Zuigan doesn't seem to know whom he's talking to — because he's talking *to himself!*

He does, of course, know whom he's talking to, and that is one of the points of the story, namely, that Zazen helps us to distinguish between our authentic speaker — who we truly are — and that flock of nightingale-like speakers in our heads, singing and twittering words that are only echoes of words we once heard spoken by others — or even earlier, by ourselves.

What was Zuigan up to?

Wasn't he revealing that he is his own *master?* If so, then the Zen stories about students slapping their Masters upon their Awakening is intended to show us that,

To be Awakened is nothing but becoming
YOUR
OWN
MASTER.

(See? Zen really *isn't* a religion![24])

(I have several American friends who find Zen very attractive, but are too put off by the concept of "Zen Masters" to practice it. They don't understand that for Soto and Rinzai Zen, the term *Master* has absolutely *no* meaning except in the context of *Self-mastery!* Just think: those of us who have perfected our skill in any craft have thereby become Masters of it, and thus are no longer in need of a Master; Master musicians don't need to attend Master classes; they *give* them *because they have **been mastered by** their crafts.*)

So, when the reader meets with the terms such as *meditation, sitting, concentration* or *Zazen,* it might be of help to think,

a practice leading to ourselves as authentic speakers —
that is,

**a practice
leading to
mastering
OURSELVES.**

Above all else, the practices of Zen Buddhism aim at

SELF-RELEASE
FROM
OUR
SELF-ENSLAVEMENT.

And when that practice succeeds, we can also hear the words of

**the love letters sent by the wind and rain,
the snow and moon,**

the most beautiful of words, the words lovers freely whisper to one another.

Only true lovers will wish to undertake the arduous search for the treasures of Zen. And it is as Ikkyu's *true* lovers — rather than as barnyard roosters — that Zen practitioners seek freedom from *any and all* slavery.

Finally, just as true lovers never have to search for words to communicate their thoughts to one another, likewise, after many, many practice sessions, we find that no thoughts or words are present in our Zen concentration. Instead, our silence is filled by the sound of the one hand clapping, and the echoes of that silence rise to its surface like champagne bubbles —

**in the exact same way the paintings of a master painter
rise to the surface of his or her bare canvas;
in the exact same way the poems of a true poet
raise out of the poet's silence.**

When we are able to hear those echoes of emptiness and silence, then our world is filled with

**love letters sent by the wind and rain,
the snow and moon.**

And, as we read,

By the Sung dynasty in China (960–1279 CE), the Zen arts of painting and poetry reached their highest stage of development, with the emergence of a novel phenomenon: painter-priests and poet-priests who produced art that broke with all forms of religious and secular art. The only purpose of this art was to point to the nature of reality.[25]

Whoever produces art that points to the nature of the *artist's* reality can also hear those love letters Ikkyu tells us to listen for.

Zen & Koans

The thatched roof [of a Japanese tea house] suggests
perishability; the slender pillars the fragility of life;
the bamboo supports suggest lightness; the use of ordinary
materials testifies to non-attachment. "Abode of the
A-Symmetrical" is also basically Zen, which is the
philosophy of Becoming — a dynamic, endless process.
Symmetry suggests completeness and the "aping of an
*abstract and artificial perfection." In the tea room (*sukiya)
or in the Japanese house, the decorations are always off-center,
the balance occult; sets come in threes and fives; one never
finds the artistic representation of a man on display.[26]

There are many of us who have heard enough about Zen Buddhism to think
we have a more or less definite idea of what it is, and that, although it is
some sort of self-help health program, it is rather different from other self-
help programs. We also tend to look at Zen as somewhat of a members-only
club whose associates, rather than using peculiar handshakes and the like,
talk in such a way as to sound more than a little strange when they come
out with such expressions and questions as, *"What is the sound of one hand
clapping?"* or *"The water buffalo's horns, head, body, and legs got in through
the window, but not his tail; why?"* As if this were not enough, the Zen
practitioners say that their odd questions — they call them *Koans* — have
no particular answers!

Nor do the written records of the Zen Masters shed all that much light
on what Zen is. The Masters were famous for their responses to beginners
who asked, *"What exactly is Zen?"* They sometimes answered with a simple
smack on the beginner's face for asking this obvious, innocent question; at
other times, the beginner was answered with wisecracks such as, *"When you
have finished eating, go wash your bowl."* Such answers will likely teach the

person who asked not to ask again, but neither answer is likely to be the least bit enlightening *or* Enlightening.

On the other hand, there *does* exist a simple answer to that question, an answer anyone would give to someone who asked, "What exactly *is* violin playing?" That answer is:

"Practice and find out."

Zen, like violin playing, is a *practice*, an *activity*, **NOT** a *thing*. And, like violin playing, Zen requires a well-tuned instrument with suitably taut strings stretched over a sturdy sounding board; something like a bow; and, finally, something that can respond to the vibration of the strings when they are bowed on.

In particular, dissatisfaction with your life "stresses" you and this tightens up the strings of your attention; Zen practice, ideally under the guidance of a Master who is an accomplished "violinist," provides the bow to animate those taut strings. What is perhaps the strangest thing about all this is that the Zen practitioner must sooner or later take that bow and "fiddle" with his own unbearably stressed dissatisfaction until he has reached the stage where he can resonate to his *own* fiddling. When he reaches that stage, he has become an instrument playing its own music, music that no one but members of Zen orchestras will likely recognize.

This self-playing is a possibly useful way of referring to what is referred to by the terms *Satori, Realization, Awakening,* or *Kensho*.

So, a useful working definition of the term *Zen* might be:

"tuning-up for serious playing-around."

But what is the sensible "show me!" reader to make of the following example of Zen playing around? It involves the Koan known as the **MU!** Koan. It goes like this.

> A monk who was practicing under the great Zen Master Joshu had been told by Joshu that **all** sentient creatures have Buddha-nature, that is, they are **all** capable of a clear and unobstructed vision of reality. How noble! How exalted! But, the **MU!** Koan goes on to relate, when this monk approached his honored Master and asked him

whether the dogs have Buddha-nature, Joshu shouted, **"MU!"** at him in answer.[27]

MU! means "Naah! Nope! Not at *all!*" But the monk had heard Joshu say, time and time again, that *all* sentient beings have Buddha-nature.

Sounds nice and "religious"; but *dogs?* Although dogs wag their tails at people they know and bark at strangers, they are *dirty* and sniff under each other's tail by way of greeting!

Buddha-nature?
Dogs!?

This was too much for the monk.

"Dogs, *too?*"

Zen Master Joshu shouted, **"MU!"**

Dogs are certainly sentient beings, but Joshu is flat-out denying what Buddhism taught concerning the Buddha-nature belonging to *all* sentient beings: what the Master is saying is that dogs, *who are certainly sentient beings*, don't have Buddha-nature!

Was Zen Master Joshu lying? Contradicting himself? Or was he pointing to what Mahayana Buddhism teaches — whose teachings no dog can, and many monks do not, take seriously.

The account of this episode came to be known as

"The FIRST among Koans."

This Koan — which certainly strikes our ears as being pretty silly! — how can we take it seriously enough to tempt us to enter upon Zen Koan practice?

Well, to begin to answer this perfectly respectable question, let's remember that Koan practice these days is most often associated with the Rinzai branch of Zen, and that it does not presently figure as importantly in the Soto branch. They are both Zen schools, but certain features of their practice differ. However, their goal is the same: achieving Awakening, which opens the gate to a life of helping others end the pain they suffer as a consequence of laboring under delusions. But these answerless questions of Koan Zen strike many sober readers as being a put-on, and the individuals who practice using them seem to look different from the uninitiated.

They suspect that the charm of such practice comes from its characterizing membership in a very exclusive club — a club that charges no admission fees and offers a food menu that is dismal when compared to that of other exclusive clubs.

So why undertake this practice if there are alternatives to it?

Good question!

To look for a possible answer, let's go back to the **MU!** Koan.

One answer is that, when we Sit and **MU!** *(active verb!)* each and every thought that wanders into our consciousness — or, after much practice, even when we are not sitting, but also when we are walking along, eating, etc. — we discover sooner or later that we have finally **MU!**-ed *everything* — even

UNDER-THE-TAIL-SNIFFING DOGS!

"Ah! How about we who are **MU!**-ing this and this and this? When we have **MU!**-ed everything else, how about *us*?"

You must **MU!** you, too. *Especially* you!

"Then . . . Then *who* was that who was doing all that **MU!**-ing?"

"*Whoever* it was, **MU!** it too!"

"Me **MU!** *Me?* **MU!** *on that!"*

So, Friend, when you hear the term **MU!** in a Zen context, remember:

> Q: "What do we seek?"
>
> A: "Who or whatever it is; *MU!* it. *MU! everything!"*
>
> Q: "But, then . . . *what* is it that the one who seeks is *looking* for?"
>
> A: "When you come across it, *MU!* it, too."

Then what you were searching for will turn out to be nothing other than everything you have been **MU!**-ing. What you then see you will see in the light of your **MU!** And, friend, don't forget to include yourself.

(**MU!** appears to be an eraser that ends up erasing itself! Now *there's* a Koan for you!)

The Rinzai Zen Masters tell us to try it. They say that it may take a long time, but you'll sooner or later see why they say "try it." And, so they tell us, when we do see it, it will make us want to sing and dance! Then, when we have finally **MU!**-ed ourselves, we will be as understated as the light of the new moon — and just so full of promise.

In short, that **MU!** exercise has been found to be a very effective way to tighten our Zen strings. If **MU!**-ing everything isn't able to stress you out of your Self, it is hard to imagine anything that can.

That is what the term **MU!** refers to in Zen texts. But once again, **MU!** is to be treated as an *active* verb, and **MU!**-ing, no less than Zen itself, is entirely an *activity*. That is,

ATTITUDE!

AN

NOT

IS

ZEN

What, then, *do* the Zen texts refer to when they use the term *Zen?*

Well, it seems to refer to a practice whose aim is to stress us out of our objecting to this or that. This prepares us to enter into an unreservedly accepting state in which, as Zen Master Ryokan describes it, we possess

"the never-despising heart of the Buddha."

So, it might be helpful, when you come across the term (Koan) *Zen*, to think something like,

An objecting process designed to stress us out of our habit of objecting-to.

When we **MU!** something as soon as it pops into our mind, it leads nowhere: it has been **MU!**-ed, and this leaves its results to the great law of the universe — and us

FREE!

Well . . . once again: what *is* Zen?

Nothing fancy. It's all about us being in a jail. We're standing at the heavily barred window looking out and wishing we weren't inside the jail, and Zen says, "Turn around. That's right. Now, go over to the door. . . .

Yeah; over here. *That's* right. Now. Stand right in front of it and, voilà! There isn't any door! Out you go."

All the Zen Masters are ex-cons.

(AND THIS INCLUDES PRINCE SIDDHARTHA!)

But, none of this quite gets to the heart of Zen. Both infinitely free and infinitely disciplined, there is nothing quite like it in the West. Our doctrine of the essentially flawed character of human nature (or, if we are Darwinians, our doctrines of the dog-eat-dog path to humanness) makes it hard for us to consider seriously the possibility that individuals can become free through practice, rather than through either divine dispensation or through the workings of divine dispensation's current morphs, such as acting in accordance with the teachings of evolutionary biology, submitting to psychiatric makeovers, or adhering to the pop-tart etiquette prescribed by social engineering. But since the time of Bodhidharma's arrival in China around 526 CE, millions of individuals have gained their freedom from the practice he introduced to the East.

And what, again, did that practice involve?

The Zen practice as introduced and interpreted by Bodhidharma was based on his understanding that rituals and "sacred writings" can very easily cloud the vision of the Buddhist practitioner *no less than can addiction to fame or pleasure.* The task he faced was this:

*How to treat the rituals and "sacred writings" of Buddhism with the respect due them as the product of great human beings, while never forgetting that they were the artifacts of human beings who did **not** derive their wisdom and insight from any "higher" source.*

In what follows, the term *Zen* will almost always refer to this version of Zen:

Bodhidharma

Zen.

Well ... okay. But if these texts are nothing but the artifacts of human beings, and not from some *higher* power, what *is* their source?

Bodhidharma's answer is ⌣ , that is:

The human Mind/Heart is merely human
and,
at the same time,

"Unborn and Undying":
THE GLORIOUS SCANDAL
AT THE HEART OF
BODHIDHARMA
ZEN BUDDHISM.

(Zen Master Hakuin)[28]

(Hakuin has drawn Bodhidharma's robe to make the character ⌣)

So, it might be useful for readers who come across the term *Zen* in **any** context, to think,

Human Beings:

MORTAL **Immortality.**

(Now *that's* a Koan!)

"Yeah, yeah; but what about that dog: *does* it have Buddha-nature or not?!"

Answer,

"Discover your *own* Buddha-nature, and *then* you can begin to worry about dogs' Buddha-nature!"

As for the sound of one hand clapping, *all* sounds worth listening to are

**whatever the heart responds to that strikes it as real;
a Silence that speaks volumes.**

And Zen? All the words of the Buddha, the Patriarchs, and Masters do nothing but help us learn the way of silence.

"What!?"

Patience; Zazen's greatest gift, perhaps, is the realization that *if* we learn to be truly silent, then any and all questions answer themselves in that silence.

Examples of Zen silence:

**the blank canvas: to the painter,
the blank paper: on which the poet writes the poem.
Hearing the question. Then, being quiet.
Listening as the question answers itself.**

This is not any strange Eastern jibber-jabber. Try it! It seems to work.
Really!

"Well ... once again, in what way should we practice to get to that kind of silence?"

The Sufi Master Rumi answers,

The Way of melting snow as it washes itself.[29]

(The heart's ardor begins the melting; Zazen practice only helps us to disperse our fantasy clouds that obscure ʻ\ʼ .)

Okay?

"Well," the "show me!" reader might say, "whatever. But, before we leave Koans, why *did* the Bodhidharma come from the West? There were already many Buddhists in China when he arrived. Why did he think that a *new* teaching was needed? He had to *walk* all the way from India — or, if he was really blue-eyed with a red beard! — all the way from *Afghanistan* to get to China. But, even if he sailed, sailing was dangerous. So, *why?* He wasn't just sightseeing, was he?"

Probably not. But look what he told the Chinese Buddhists. Something like,

*You must treat the rituals and "sacred writings" of Buddhism with the respect due them as the product of great human beings, while never forgetting that they were the artifacts of human beings who did **not** derive their wisdom and insight from any "higher" source, but from*

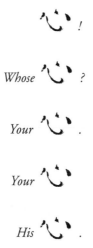

Whose   *?*

Your   *.*

Your

His   *.*

"But ... but *that* means Bodhidharma came from ... from *wherever* to bring himself *to* himself."

BINGO!

That's what Zen Buddhism is all about. *Nothing* else.

WHAT
A
STITCH!

He set out from wherever it was in order to get to wherever he set out from. He left without ever leaving!

What a trip!
  NO! NO! Not "*What* **A** *trip!*"

THE **ONLY** TRIP!

(Zen again ...)

A concluding word about meditation, Zen, and Koans in different branches of Buddhism:

A vast number of Buddhists are Zen — that is, they meditate as a way of Ego purging. This has proven to be a quite useful practice. But, the reader must be advised, another vast number of Buddhists do *not* practice either Koan or silent meditation as their way of Ego purging, and a great many of them have achieved Awakening — without practicing Zen meditation.

But, practices aimed at Ego purging are central to *all* branches of Zen Buddhism. All branches!

"What's going on here? It would seem only reasonable to think that Buddhists' Ego purging practices must involve at least *some* core practice; after all, they all start at the same Egotistical place and work toward a state in which they have largely purged themselves of Ego."

Good question. How to answer it?

Well, look at it this way.

> You are driving down a country lane late at night. It is broiling hot and every night bug — big or small — is out and is attracted by your car's headlights.

Result?

> Your windshield is splattered with bug bits and, after a while, you can't see what's in front of you even though your high beams are on.

What to do?

> Why, you try turning on the windshield wipers and pushing the window wash button.

Result?

> A smear of bug-bit soup so thick that you seem to be looking at a back-lighted screen.

So?

So you get out of the car, get your squeegee, and carefully clear off the mess.

That squeegee can be:

Koan Zazen

Silent Zazen

Chanting

Counting beans.

.

.

.

.

WHATEVER!!!!!

All you are after is a clean windshield you can see through!

And that's **ALL** *it's about.*

Okay?

"But, look; what is it I *see* when I've cleaned my Ego's bug-splattered windshield? Of course, I can see the road, but that's not the point of the example, is it?"

As usual, yes *and* no. A blind windshield, and the Way is hidden, and that Way is the Way we live our lives — but more. When our Ego purging is advanced enough, then we can see the dance of those bugs. It's as if we stopped the car, turned on the parking lights, and watched darkness crowd toward light.

But, the Zen following Bodhidharma insists, when we have succeeded in seeing those things clearly, we have then only truly *begun* our journey on the Great Way. These sights lead us to wonder, and our wonder leads us to silent reflection; and our silent reflection can lead to our Awakening, to what Zen Master Hakuin calls "the Voice of the Dharma," to what the Greek astronomer-mystics called "the Music of the Spheres" which they insisted was superior to *any* audible music. And when we dance to *that* music, we are in the company of Ikkyu, because we can *then* hear the enchanting songs whose words are taken from

the love letters sent by the wind and rain,
the snow and moon.

And *that's* what Zen's "sitting like a bump on a log" is all about!

A final word about Zen:

In the course of just about every month, I hear or read several instances of English speakers who use the term *Zen* in exactly the way the great Zen Masters use it.

How does this happen?

I don't know, but my hunch is that the power at the center of Zen's practices derives from a true part of the human fabric — part of our spiritual-intellectual "hard wiring." It's everywhere, but it is mainly Buddhists who have stressed its power and undertaken to set it free from whatever diminishes that power.

For instance, reading Bill Buford's recent book, *Heat*, I came across a passage concerning his (oh-so-*un*-Buddhist) experience of learning how to use his butcher knife from a master butcher known far and wide as Maestro — which is, of course, Italian for "Master." The Master describes the ideal position of the knife, held *"so that it can discover the lines of the meat."* When a chef uses the proper technique, it is as if *"hand has disappeared into the knife."*[30]

And here is the Shakuhachi Master Fuyo Hisamatsu's take on learning to play the shakuhachi:[31]

A good player of shakuhachi is one who makes
the bamboo shaft alive. A master naturally and

effortlessly brings forth something inconceivable. However, without study it is impossible to enter the boundaries of mastery. You become the bamboo. The bamboo becomes you.[32]

"The bamboo becomes you." Or, as the Italian master butcher says, "Your hand has disappeared into the knife."

No?

Finally, like any other human institution, Zen can only be known by what it produces.

Zen Master and master poet Ryokan is a deep well whose waters are cool and infinitely refreshing.

Zen Master Hakuin is a great mountain of granite, on whose steep flanks are to be found berry-bearing bushes, some that are lethal to pseudo-Zen and others that are endlessly nourishing to those of us who seek encouragement to continue on our journey up the steep path leading to the heights from where we can see the Great Way as it leads to the Capital.

Zen Master Ikkyu is what he named himself: *Crazycloud*; now he is a fluffy cloud, wandering its way through an early spring sky; now he is a raging tornado, destroying the temple-refuges of those for whom Zen is only free rice; now he is an erotic lightning bolt, illuminating our unborn heart's longing for union with its ever-dying body.

So perhaps Zen's embrace is best depicted by the all-inclusive Enso, ⭕ .

(Strictly speaking, that Enso manifests the *living* truth of the person who paints it.)[33]

Zen Buddhism

The Great Way leads through the Capital.
(Zen Master Joshu)[34]

The term *Mahayana* ("the Greater Vehicle") has not entered into our vocabulary in the way terms such as *Karma* and *Dharma* have. But since what many Westerners know as Zen Buddhism is *Mahayana* Zen Buddhism, it might be helpful to have some idea what it means when we meet with it in Zen texts.

Yet to explain it is not so simple. (For instance, there are Buddhists who have denied the authenticity of Mahayana because it did not exist for the first seven or so centuries after the Buddha's passing. But the Zen practitioner whose words this book is concerned with is not in the least involved with those disagreements.) It's enough for us to remark that the branch of Mahayana Zen Buddhism (of Bodhidharma's line) that concerns us views its practitioners' Awakening/Enlightenment as marking the true *beginning* of their work. It holds that only *after* the practitioner has been largely purged of Ego and Self — and this is what Awakening is to *all* branches of Buddhism — can he or she continue and begin to follow the example of Prince Siddhartha. This involves the Mahayana Zen Buddhist helping anyone who is able and willing to work to achieve that Awakening. The *Zen* form of practice to prepare the individual to be a Friend of Prince Siddhartha involves Zazen — and in the case of *Rinzai* Zen, Koans are often used in Zazen practice.

Speaking generally, the Zen of Bodhidharma's line can be accurately thought of as something like *the public branch of Buddhism* or even as *the activist branch*. Once again, as Master Joshu tells us, "The [Zen Buddhists'] Way goes through the Capital."

This view of Buddhism seems to be firmly rooted in accounts of the historical Buddha's life. He was born a prince, and his great realization was that *every* sentient human was born a Buddha, whose life's work (Karma) is to become a shepherd to all who can benefit by the shepherd's help — precisely as he did upon his Awakening.

Here in the West, the practitioners (Sanghas) participating in the meetings of many Buddhist groups proceed under the belief that being mindful of and compassionate to others is the goal of true Buddhist practice, and Zen doesn't deny that. But that branch of Zen introduced by Bodhidharma is, or should be, distinguished from several other branches of Buddhism by its insistence that practitioners purge themselves of Ego and Self *before* they can be truly compassionate and mindful in their dealings with others. It insists, furthermore, that the best way to achieve that purgation is through Zazen practice, preferably under the guidance of a Master, and *not* through reading Sutras or chanting or the performance of good deeds to acquire "merit."

In short, the central characteristic of *Mahayana* Zen Buddhism might fairly be described as follows:

**HELPING OTHERS DEMANDS THAT
YOU,
YOURSELF,
HAVE ALREADY PURGED YOURSELF
OF
YOUR OWN SELF-CENTERED ABSORPTION
THROUGH YOUR PRACTICE OF ZAZEN.**

Then, all that is left of you is the All-Embracing, the no-one-in-particular, whose symbol is the Zen circle:

The individual has become an Enlightened/Awakened Friend of Prince Siddhartha when he or she is prepared to act as a Friend of Prince Siddhartha, as a *Shepherd*.

Such a person is most certainly not a divinity, but merely a human who, *after* being purged through Zen practice, lives his or her life as a shepherd and Friend of Prince Siddhartha. It follows, then, that these Zen Buddhists are not philanthropists in the way that most Western philanthropies are philanthropic. Likewise, Zen's view of what it is to be a fully realized human being differs from most Western philanthropies in certain crucial respects, and their sense of what they can and should contribute to the welfare of others is different. That is, Bodhidharma's contribution to Buddhism includes elements that are not often found in our Western philanthropic organizations whose defining goal is largely to help make it possible for our fellow humans to lead more comfortable and materially productive lives, and requires nothing on the part of its members beyond really wanting to help and having at least one of the skill sets needed to do so. Therefore "Zen Buddhism" refers to Bodhidharma's line of Zen Buddhism, which begins with an unwavering preoccupation with our blindness to the vitality of the world we experience as sentient humans.

Buddhism's practice in general can fairly be termed "therapeutic" because it involves a sort of "ophthalmology" designed to heal those of us who are blinded by our prejudices and our learned behavior patterns. These prejudices and behavior patterns not only make us uncaring of anyone else, they make us largely unaware that anyone else even exists. That is to say, all too many of us are so self-centered that we tend to imagine that no one else can either act or think except by slavishly following what *they* learned from *their* ethnic, religious, and educational backgrounds. Such fantasies — which are almost always merely echoes of what *we ourselves* have learned from *our own* ethnic, religious, and educational backgrounds — hide the really-present world behind a screen onto which we project our own off-the-shelf worlds created for us by unknown producers. (It is almost as if we have television screen cataracts, and what we see on our monitors is written and produced in largely unknown, unnamed production studios.)

Buddhism's version of ophthalmology provides something that might be described as a sort of "cataract surgery" to remove those screens. Then, what we see are meaningful individuals, or *Tathata*. Buddhism's ophthalmologic procedures require daily Zen practice and can sometimes take years — and those procedures are performed without any anesthesia! But, when they are over and done with, the world is truly a sight for sore eyes; it is then full of meaning-filled things neither more nor less fetching than any other — including ourselves.

What is perhaps most striking about Zen's Awakening/Kensho is this: what we see when our eyes are wide open and our vision is not obstructed by our "personal" opinions, is

what it really means to be human:
namely,
a Friend of Prince Siddhartha:

A Shepherd.

Prince Siddhartha was both born a prince and with the soul of a true prince. This does not mean that he was naturally inclined to enjoy all the pleasures an Oriental court could provide him with; such inclinations define the soul of a royal pig, not of a truly royal human being. Rather, this prince came to realize that truly *seeing* who we are will lead us to act as Shepherds — or, as we in the West say, as *pastors* — to each and every human being whose sight can be improved through Buddhism's ophthalmological procedures.

But this is not merely a case of Western altruism being gift-wrapped in layers of intricately patterned Oriental paper to make it more appealing. The West's view of helping others is in certain respects quite different from Zen's. The Christian view of "fallen mankind" can lead us to view altruism as being obedient to a divine command; if we are Darwinians, we will likely view it as the result of our hardwiring compelling us to act in a way which insures that our genetic material will find a receptacle — and this can even lead us to sacrifice our own lives to preserve the life of someone else.

Judging from the texts, Zen views what we in the West tend to view as *altruism* as being what leads us to *selfishly* practice dissolving self. That selfish dissolution of self bleaches out our lifelong habits and learned responses to the world around us, and ends in our becoming *un*-born — which is altogether different from being "born again." But, if we search Zen Buddhism for a version of what we term *altruism*, the closest we can come is something like,

spontaneously trusting our heart's imperative
to purge ourselves of our Ego,
and then helping others to do the same.

So the expression *the Zen of Bodhidharma's line*, refers to an *activity* of a living individual; that is, to the way certain individuals *actively* live their lives as Friends of Prince Siddhartha — and *not* to a set of rules and rituals. The name *Mahayana Zen* tags neither the individual who lives it nor a collection of rules but, rather, it refers to

a certain way of actively living one's life with others.

Because a Zen "Bodhisattva" is nothing but a living human being who lives his or her life in a certain human way — as a Shepherd — the term refers to nothing that is not dynamic and lively; just as *red* only makes any real sense when it applies to something that is *colored* in a certain way, the term, *Zen Bodhisattva* only makes real sense when it is applies to someone who *lives* in a certain way.

Think of stage productions. In these creations, a number of actors say and do things that make no sense to the spectators unless the performance is perceived as a simple whole involving more or less numerous active individuals. That is to say, the players and the props are just up there on the stage: *these* don't make the scene; the *spectator* creates the scene — that, like *A Midsummer Night's Dream*, exists *nowhere*. "Theater" is not what's "up there" on stage; theater is what the *spectator* sees when he or she views what's "up there" on stage. (That "suspension of disbelief" that our literature gurus tell us is the precondition for enjoying a mere "play," is, in *reality*, nothing of the kind. To *realize* what is going on "up there on the stage" — to really *see* it — the spectator must actually *become* a cast member, with or without lines; it all depends on the play.)

And, *that* is likely to be why we value the *ME!* so highly: we fail to think of ourselves as no more and no less *really* real than the spectacle we *the spectators* create as we look at what's going on "up there."

Spectators forget **WHERE** they are!

One way to view Zen practice is:

A way leading us to see clearly that
WE
Create that scene
As being
OUT
THERE
With us in it!!

Following this image, it might be helpful to think of the Zen Bodhisattva — that is, the Buddhist "actor" — as nothing but an ordinary individual who, while being a compassionate spectator of the performances played out on the stage of human life, is also one of its compassionate actors.

And so, when the reader meets the term *Zen Buddhism*, it might be useful to think of a staged play in which several of its bit-part actors are also sub-directors of the production that involves an infinitely twisted plot — whose unknown author is constantly editing the script!

ZEN
IS
A
HOOT!!!

Broadway never, *ever*, came up with *anything* that can even touch it!

Compassion

A Klein bottle is a two-dimensional object with one surface and no edges ... a surface ... with no distinction between the "inside" and "outside"...[35]

Many of us act compassionately toward those who need some help. When we do this, we put ourselves in their shoes to some extent, and this leads us to acts that extend our sense of Self to include others. This requires that we learn to look *into* others, and not just *at* them.

But, given our Western sense of the immeasurable worth of *our own* selves, how can we value the needs of others as being comparable to ours? The whole of the European West's "Enlightenment" is squarely based on the individual's sense of the absolute value of his or her own existence, and "altruism" is quite often viewed as nothing more than a hidden form of manipulation either by our genes or by our fellow humans, whose help we might need some day: "One good deed deserves another." Many of us have been taught from our earliest days that our inherited human characteristics aim at maximizing our chance to win the battle for survival. It's a dog-eat-dog world, and compassion is no part of it!

But compassion can, and often does, in fact, lead us to rate someone else's need as the same as our own, and thus to appraise someone else's essential worth at the same rate as ours.

"Maybe; but why isn't any compassion, Buddhist or not, merely sentimentality? A guilty conscience for having more than others? Or maybe a sort of bribe to make 'Heaven' smile down on our undertakings?"

Well, still, there are certainly large numbers of kind and generous individuals in the West who certainly *appear* to act generously and selflessly toward those who are less fortunate than they. When we describe their acts as *compassionate*, what we mean echoes what the Zen texts refer to as compassionate behavior.

That said, there is still an aspect of Zen Buddhism's view of compassion that is uniquely Zen: its *forcefulness*. For many of us in the West, compassion tends to be viewed as characteristically sweet and gentle. But this is by no means always the case in Zen. Shouts and blows on the part of the Master toward his students are often characterized as manifesting signs of the Zen Master's "grandmotherly care" — or "compassion" — for his students.

This is not to suggest that Western Zen practitioners should necessarily seek out such severe Masters. However, if we do not take careful note of this characteristic of Zen Buddhism, we will be ignoring an important aspect of it.

There seem to be two related reasons for this severe dimension of compassion in the Zen Masters' treatment of their students. If we don't take these into account, it is almost certain that we cannot really appreciate what Zen means by the term.

One of these is that the self-purging of the practitioner must be carried out vigorously; no years-long psychoanalysis. The hair roots of our Ego's crabgrass are numerous, and many lifetimes would hardly be long enough to root them out one by one. So Zen takes a backhoe, as it were, to this clotted mess and, with a single-minded and often brutal intensity, undertakes to help us purge ourselves of our self-centeredness. Indeed, to judge from the texts, the more the Master gives any sign of recognition to a student's sense of his or her self-esteem, the more that self-esteem flourishes; even the *least* recognition of the existence of the student's self-esteem nourishes it. Thus, the Master attacks *any* manifestation of it with blows and shouts.

Just as would-be professional football players and aspiring ballet dancers *willingly* submit themselves to the often brutal demands of their coaches without knowing if they will make the cut, so do Zen students give themselves to their Masters. Furthermore, the more promising the student, the harsher the demands of the (truly compassionate!) coach or dancing instructor are likely to be. (Pity is true compassion's evil twin; the least hint of pity will destroy true and vigorous compassion.)

It is only the most dedicated of students who can profit from that severity. The willingness — even eagerness — of students to undergo the harsh demands of their coach or Master transforms what would otherwise be cruelty into what Zen considers compassion. Ballet instructors, professional sports coaches, and Special Forces drill instructors would understand this aspect of Zen compassion entirely — even if they wouldn't want to admit their behavior was "compassionate." That very same compassion can be found wherever Masters — be they Zen Masters, ballet masters, football coaches, or Special Forces drill instructors — undertake to whip their *willing* charges into shape.

The Zen Master's compassion, then, is characterized by its uncompromising rejection of the student's self-esteem — something most of us would rather die for than live without.

So if Zen practice makes them feel better, they are probably doing it wrong. Those who have stayed the course *do* feel better, but they didn't drink just any soothing soup to get that way; *Zen* soup is burning hot and spicy — but, oh!, how nourishing! And it is the Master's ardent *compassion* that provides both the fires needed to cook that soup and the spices to flavor it.

So when we meet the term Compassion in a Zen context, think of something like:

What prompts Zen Masters,
grandmotherly pro football coaches,
and
ballet masters
(as well as those Special Forces drill instructors)
when they bear down on their charges.

In short, Zen's compassion is quite similar to what we in the West know as

tough
LOVE.

But, once again, unless we have learned to look *into* others — rather than just look *at* them — we will only see what more or less suits us. Buddhist compassion requires Awakening, and only Awakening permits us to look *into* things, rather than *at* them. One of *the* great Zen insights is that true Compassion requires true *in*-sight, and true *in*-sight/looking-into, is nothing but true Buddhist Awakening.

(As stated earlier, the Zen meaning of the term *compassion* is particularly difficult for us in the West to grasp accurately. For, when Christianity's tide succumbed to the irresistible pull of the Enlightenment's full moon so that it receded almost out of sight of the European West's shore, we were left a vast assortment of shells of once-living creatures on the exposed beaches. These shells are vestiges of the various forms of Christian piety — pre-eminent among those vestiges being Marxism and runaway sentimentality dressed in the public persona of a certain variety of political liberalism. Westerners, especially those who are college-educated, may be powerfully tempted to understand Zen's use of this word in terms of its meaning in Western post-Christian social science.)

To sum up: the Zen Master's Compassionate beatings are smart; they "teach" nothing, but force the student to ask, "What am I doing wrong?" That way, the student is led to master himself or herself.

This is Zen Mastery: *Self*-Mastery.

Suffering

"But, why ME?"

The first of the so-called "noble truths of Buddhism" is: "There is suffering (*Dukkha*)"; the second is, "There is an end to suffering."[36]

There certainly is suffering. And in the West, the sometimes immense malpractice awards for "pain and suffering" are designed, it seems, to stress the second noble truth, "There is an end to suffering." That is, sums of money are given to the sufferers to compensate them for suffering and, presumably, to *end* it; after all, if getting money doesn't *stop* the suffering, why award it?

In general, we in the West feel that there is a solution to every problem, and suffering is one of those problems we attack with remedies such as pills, support groups, and treatment programs. When any of those methods work, it's all well and good. But if we have figured out legal and medical ways of eliminating suffering, why bother with the teachings of Buddhism? Or, alternatively, perhaps we can look at the various branches of Buddhism as being non-Western support groups that don't encourage lawsuits or the use of pills.

Why not? Just trim off a lot of the Eastern mumbo jumbo that, our anthropologists are likely to tell us, is nothing but the vestiges of bygone cultures and, *Presto Change-o!*, a number of brands of Zen-Lite will, like mushrooms after a downpour, appear in the Empowerment sections of alternative-health markets in the morning.

As you like. But since there are readers who, for whatever unfathomable reasons, seem to think that Zen Buddhism might more suitably address their suffering than our Western approaches, here is what Zen Buddhism says about the subject.

First, in Zen Buddhism, our suffering, if not pain, is viewed as one of the principal effects of what we might term "our genetic disposition toward" anger, greed, and Self-delusion. Only our purging of these can reach down to the roots of our suffering and get rid of them. Endless suffering might not be necessary, but refusing to self-purge makes it likely that we will continue to suffer. According to Zen Buddhism, freedom from suffering — if not from pain and sorrow — is ours to achieve.

But, it can be objected, if our suffering is essentially a consequence of our *inborn* ignorance, greed, and self-delusion, how can we set about uprooting what was born with us? Wouldn't that destroy us? Not only that, but how can *one* thing that is inborn purge us of *another* thing that is inborn? Isn't our impulse to *uproot* inborn ignorance, greed, and self-delusion *also* inborn? We naturally just don't *like* to suffer. Are suffering and its antidote *both* inborn?

What an interesting idea!

Yes; interesting indeed, but we humans are strange beasts and, to judge from the Zen texts, we have an inborn impulse that, if followed, helps us dig up those *other* inborn roots of suffering. That is, our Zen practice is designed to help us reach what is known in Zen as Awakening (Satori or Kensho) — that is, Awakening to our true Self that knows no suffering. We might continue to experience "physical" pain and "spiritual" sorrow, but we won't suffer because of them.

Still, if the roots of our suffering are born in us, how can *Self*-realization rid us of those roots? Our self seems to be the problem, not the solution!

Zen's answer seems to be that there is a self that most of us mature into as we grow from newborns to mature adults, and a Self that is unborn — that unborn Self being what the sixth Chinese Buddhist Patriarch, Hui-neng, refers to as *"our aspect before our parents were born."*

But isn't this just another form of our Western distinction between "nature" and "nurture," with our aspect before we were born being identified as our nature, and which is afterward profoundly modified by — nurtured by — our experiences as we grow into adulthood?

Not in Zen Buddhism's view, which holds that our "prehistoric" nature cannot be nurtured in order to be modified:

it needs *neither* nurture *nor* modification.

For Zen, the West's notion of a nurture that modifies our inborn nature is replaced by a notion that nurture *obscures* that inborn nature and thereby provides fertile soil in which our follies take root and flourish.

Furthermore — and this is likely to be a central reason we find it difficult to understand Buddhism's take on *suffering* — our Western scientific view is that we cannot return to our "natural" state that has been irretrievably lost through evolutionary history's makeovers; if we are Christians, it is forever lost through Original Sin. (The death and subsequent resurrection of Jesus Christ are viewed as offering salvation *to those who are chosen by Heaven to receive it*,[37] and salvation cannot be earned through our acts or deeds. Moreover, Christian salvation points in the direction of the *after*life, and thus does not promise an end to suffering in *this* life.)

But is Hui-neng's idea of "*our aspect before our parents were born*" nothing but a more poetic expression of rational statements about suffering? After all, outside churches and courtrooms, we hear almost nothing about suffering, only about what "bends us out of shape," namely,

Since this issue is important both to East and West, why not look more closely at Zen's view of suffering as being the result of a sort of strife between our "pre-historic" nature and our nurtured nature that overlays it?

Okay; but how should we begin?

Well, Hui-neng suggests that some of us do, in fact, occasionally experience shame and sorrow at things we have done. There is something in us that makes us blush to remember those things and to wish, a thousand times over, that we had not done them. How many men and women have broken off marriages and lived to regret it until their dying day? How many of us have broken off old and dear friendships in a moment of ill humor, and then regretted it endlessly? If not all of us, certainly many of us. And we were hardly suffering from schizophrenia when we experienced the grief and sorrow that was caused

BY OUR *OWN* MIS-BEHAVIOR!

Those experiences certainly seem to point in the direction of some sort of internal strife. Choosing to do something, *and then later regretting it*, does not point in the direction of a single source; rather, it strongly suggests that there are two selves, one of which is a self that views us as historical, living beings — as the children of our parents — and another, unborn Self that is not the child of our parents or history, namely,

"our aspect before our parents were born."

That latter self is what we have been calling our "pre-historic" Self, the Self that, for instance, bids the man who was an abused child to remember that his pain-filled childhood was merely a bad dream and that humans, *as* humans, were originally born into a world where the contours of the heart's ardor are those of the mind's architecture.[38] That man's healing of the damaged child he once was could only have been the work of something that had not been rendered inoperative by that abuse —

because it *could* not be rendered inoperative by it.

However puzzling this may seem, it is the way things are, and it provides an example of what Zen refers to when it talks about suffering and Self-purging. To deny the existence of this "pre-historic" Self flies in the face of human experience. To give an example, when a Lutheran pastor in a Nazi death camp volunteered to starve to save the life of a Jew, he did so because he was moved by the same power in him that originally led him to be a pastor. His Christian practice had purged him to the extent that he saw clearly that his true Self — *his pastor's Self* — knew no suffering, and thus, that the death he had chosen was no more than agonizingly stupefying illusions.

The dreadful beauty of one of Zen Master Dogen's most famous poems captures the reality of this human world and its stupefying illusions as few other poets have succeeded in doing:

> *The world? Moonlit*
> *Drops shaken*
> *From a crane's bill.*[39]

When he ends that splendidly gentle, wise poem with "Shaken from a *crane's* bill," Dogen locates us in the world whose loveliness cannot be denied even by the existence in it of the horrors of the last hundred years — that are *also "reflected in dewdrops shaken from a crane's bill."*[40]

Still, why, according to Zen, are we *born* into suffering? The Buddhist tradition includes no story of any primal disobedience of a first woman and man, a deed that our Western tradition teaches us led to the human condition, which is full of hard labor, pain, and death.

So...?

So, even if one of the noble truths of Buddhism states that there is an end to suffering, why is there even a *beginning* to it? If we can't bring ourselves to challenge Zen to answer this question — and keep at it until we receive an acceptable response! — then Zen appears to be just another faddish, crypto-Christian support group whose primary charm lies in its strangeness.

Well, Zen's response seems to be that an essential part of our life's great work involves

our return to "our condition before our parents were born."

In the condition where there *is* no suffering.

It seems that for Zen, suffering can be characterized as something akin to our *longing* to return to that condition. After all, is longing anything other than forgetfulness fermenting into memory? (We do great violence to our souls when we mistake the ardor of that fermenting for the heat generated by desire's chafing. The ardor of longing fires the *Refiner's* crucible.)

We can only long for what we have somehow possessed; otherwise, how could we even *think* that we don't posses it *now*?[41]

If this is on target, then the Zen term *suffering* is the same as our human longing to remember what it is to be truly human.

So, when we come across that term, *suffering*, in a Zen context, it might be useful for us to think something like:

WHAT REMINDS US NOT TO FORGET TO REMEMBER.

But, if and when someone succeeds in remembering, this by no means promises an end to sorrow — only to suffering. One great Zen Master after another speaks of bathing the sleeves of his robe in tears as he views the human condition. Further, Prince Siddhartha gathered his Friends around him at his Great Awakening. He could have just said, "*Whew! I'm glad that's over and done with!*" But he didn't. His Great Awakening was not the end; it was the true beginning.

Suffering is loud and raucous; sorrow involves us in a silence so deep that we can hear the voice of the true Dharma in it — what the ancient Greek philosopher-mystics referred to as "the music of the Heavenly Spheres." In the music of the Middle East — presumably influenced by Sufism — we often hear splendidly joyful melodies played in the deep minor keys associated with sadness. The effect is very much that produced by Zen practice:

sorrowfully *joyful*
&
joyfully sorrowful.

Our Awakening to the truth of Zen is a realization that we must simply refuse to turn our backs on our often-despicable humanity. This we must do, *as* ordinary humans!, if we are to be of service to our fellow humans. *That* is what the texts refer to when they tunefully invite us to bear the sorrow of walking the Great Way as it leads through the Capital — the Way that is filled with all manner of marvels of loveliness and horror.

Only when we clearly see that our very *Being* as humans points us in the direction of a *gateless!* barrier, then through it and onto that Great Way, can we know the terrible burden of our human forgetfulness of our original nature.

But how superior is the sound of sorrow to that caterwauling that is the incessant racket made by the sufferers!

Listen to some of the sounds of sorrow:

this world
is a dewdrop world
yes . . .
but . . .

and,

The world of dew
is the world of dew,
And yet . . .
And yet . . .

or:

Even though I'm in Kyoto,
when the cuckoo cries,
I long for Kyoto.

(Issa)

Or, as Zen Master Ryokan tells us,

Though I think
NOT
To think about it,
I
DO
think about it
And shed tears thinking about it.

So when we come across the term *suffering* in a Zen context, it might be useful to think,

"Life is hard, and then you die. ... "

NO!

NO!!

NO!!!

Life *is* hard. Sure. So ... ? So, *sing* yourself toward your death! If you don't know a good tune, let yourself hum along and clap in time with Zen Master Ikkyu as he sings,

Pain and bliss, love and hate, are like a body and its shadow;
Cold and warm, joy and anger, you and your condition.
Delight in singing verses is a road to Hell,
but at Hell's gate — peach blossoms, plum blossoms.[42]

YES!

YES!!

YES!!!

When Ikkyu wrote that, Japan was in the midst of a terrible civil war that utterly destroyed the city of Kyoto. When he was eighty, the beloved temple he had practiced in years before was burned to the ground, and he spent his last eight years, often very ill, collecting funds for rebuilding and being its overseer. He knew, firsthand, what Hell's gate looked like, and on the path to it, he saw

"PEACH BLOSSOMS, PLUM BLOSSOMS."

Truly such song-filled sorrowing souls are even more splendid than the dream-scattering trumpet-blasts announcing the rising of the sun, even more splendid than those anguished silences to whose music the full moons of autumn dance their serious joy across the night's star-studded floor.

The key to the gate into Zen Buddhism is

JOY,
not
suffering.

And that *Zen* joy? What is it?

Zen joy is, above all else,
SENSIBLE *Joy,*
the endlessly playful child
of that happiest of unions,

W   n   e

o   d   r

&

Sentience.

The Buddha's claim that there is an end to suffering should be understood to outrank his observation that there is suffering.

Suffering leads to anger;
It *does* not *lead to Zen*

and the ferry boat on which suffering humanity finds itself afloat is an ocean of joy, *not* despair. Buddhist compassion is *not* nurtured by suffering, but by joy.

So ...?

So ... so when things get too stormy,

J

  U

   M

   P

   S

  H

   I

P

That's all.

"But ... but won't I *drown*!?"

No!

UP!

YOU

BUOYS

JOY

To which our ever-vigilant SHOW ME! critic might properly be expected to answer,

"**NO!** All this talk about joy and blossoms at the gate of Hell ignores *why* we suffer:

WE-ARE-AFRAID-OF-DYING!!,

and we know that all the medical advances in the world can, at best, only gain us a few years. *At best!* If Zen can tell us how to escape death, then and *only* then, can we soberly agree that Buddhist teachings, or any other teaching for that matter, soberly answer our greatest fear,

DEATH!

"Get it? So ... How does Zen answer *that*!?"

Well, Friend, the texts seem to imply that if we practice sufficiently and behave ourselves, we will come to where we view death *not* as the ultimate root of our suffering. This is especially difficult for us to consider seriously; our Western teachings about death are a very great obstacle for those of us who wish to consider the Way of Zen seriously.

"Oh? And just how *does* Zen practice lead us from *that* root of suffering?"

Zen practice claims that it leads us to a state of

AN ENDLESS WONDER,

as what is unborn and undying in us contemplates our removal from that *undying* world that gave both itself and ourselves to us in our birth.

No?

"**NO!** The prospect of my death is not wonderful to me. My feeling about it is located somewhere between abject terror and wavering hope. What in the world could Zen mean when it claims that death is a wonder to us? Not to *me*!"

Ah! Well said. But look. Here we are — you and I and him and her. ... When we are not sleeping, eating, relieving ourselves, or washing up, we are pursuing our dreams, praying to our gods, killing one another to realize our hopes or to dispel our fears, weeping over the loss of our parents, writing books that, if we are fortunate, will survive us for a while.

ALL DURING THE SAME LIFE!
*AND **THEN** WE TURN UP OUR TOES AND DIE!*

That's what's so wonderful!

WHAT A TRIP!!!

So, when the Zen texts speak of "the Great Matter of Life and Death," they point to the splendid mystery of our immortal vitality that departs at our passing in death. The phrase, *the Great Matter of Life and Death*, helps us to consider that we are

LIVING

KOANS!

LIFE

&

DEATH

ALL

SCHMUSHED TOGETHER!

Now, that's wonderful (in a hair-raising sort of way)!

And, you know? Possibly the single biggest obstacle we in the West must overcome to grasp Zen's view of death is this: We have been taught for nearly two thousand years that

DEATH **IS A** PUNISHMENT

Visited on us because of a sin committed

L O O O O O O O O O O O O O O O NG

BEFORE WE WERE BORN!

Once we have overcome *that* obstacle, then — just as the morning sun peeps over the eastern horizon, chases away dreams, and beckons them back as it disappears over the western horizon in the evening — so are we *beckoned into* this world of light and darkness, and so we are *beckoned back into* that incomprehensible realm that we were summoned out of at our birth — back into that realm that Zen Master Lin-chi tells us is not understandable while we live! However, none of this is punishment. NONE of it.

Furthermore (if this account of Zen is accurate, as Zen has no doctrine, any conclusions about it — these as well as those of the Masters — are tentative), the picture we get is of ourselves outsourced by our Source. As the Outsourced, we are obligated — *by what we really and truly are* — to repeat that outsourcing in our helpfulness to others and in our return to our Source through that clear and unhindered sentience that we access in our Awakening.

Zen Zazen helps us in our search for a clear-sighted openness to that very world that gave us our birth and our sentience to grasp it during our life; when we have reached that clear-sightedness, the openness to that world, we are one with it — with those moons that rose long before our birth and will do so long after our passing.

But

WE ARE **ONE** WITH THAT WORLD.

So,

THERE'S NO PLACE ELSE TO PASS ON TO!!!

Or, better, remember what the Zen poet-translator Paul Reps tells us of death:

> *Sound of flute*
> *Has returned*
> *To bamboo*
> *Forest.*
> *An echo returning to its source. Nothing more; nothing less.*[43]

Dharma

(If you wish to hear the voice of the Dharma,)
Only listen to the voice of pines and cedars when no wind stirs.[44]

When we readers of Buddhist texts come across the term *Dharma* — sometimes also given with lowercase "d" as *dharma* — we might well be puzzled.

Sometimes, when it is used to name the teachings of the Buddha, it seems to mean something like what we mean when we speak of Scripture, the Word of God, or Law, divine *or* human; then, in other contexts, it seems to mean "the way something ordinarily is, the way we can fairly expect it to be." In short, *Dharma/dharma* is used both as the transmitted teachings of the Buddha and as a generalized term for the *way* a thing exists, its way of being, or even the rules and regulations according to which things do what they *customarily* do.

Since, strictly speaking, the Zen branch of Bodhidharma's line doesn't recognize anything as Holy Scripture, there is, except for its meaning as "Law," no true "capital-D" Dharma in Zen texts — no divinely inspired texts to guide the Masters who act as guides to their students — only those *spontaneously* arising by Expedient Means (*Upaya*) to help practitioners purge themselves. For Zen, it almost always refers to pointers and not to any divinely revealed eternal truths.

With respect to the lowercase occurrence of the term *dharma*, it is not so easy to locate a translation in our day-to-day Western vocabulary suitable to what Zen means by *dharma* — something like, "The *ordinariness* of what appears to us as sentient, living human beings."[46] The ordinary is the *present*, the *now* in all its kaleidoscope of ever-changing immediacy.

Still, an approach to finding an acceptable equivalent for the term *dharma* might be something akin to

"the way the ordinary occurs,"

for instance,

"The sun rises in the East and sets in the West."

In this example, the term centers on the way things are without anyone adding to or subtracting from them. What is ordinary is more or less predictable and, to that extent, *dependable*. (It is the accuracy and dependability of the collection of texts claimed to transmit the Buddha's sayings and teachings that led to their being termed a Dharma — with a capital "D." Strictly speaking, however, that capitalization can be considered "off-center Zen.")

This poses a problem for those of us who are interested in Zen practice: namely,

we Westerners pride ourselves on being

that is, we are disposed to view the ordinary, the *status quo*, as being nearly always in need of fixing.[45] This leads us to devalue the ordinary; the expression *the status quo* is quite often used in the West to express our contempt for the way things are, and so we are poorly prepared to understand the simplicity of Zen's concept of *the status quo*. We in the West are a restless people who often take drugs such as Prozac to calm down as we wait for the next fix of real or perceived inadequacies in the *status quo* to take hold. Also, we "throw the rascals out!" who were responsible for the *presently* insufferable *status quo*, and feel that, after the next election, things will improve.

So, is Zen just another fix, merely a replacement for some over-the-counter version of Prozac?

Not really. The texts make it clear that we who need fixing can only be fixed by ourselves.

When the moon of your mind
becomes clouded over by confusion
you are searching for the light outside.

(Hozoin)[46]

There *are* no Zen pills. Zen only offers guidance to those of us who, for whatever unfathomable reason, are willing to entertain the possibility that we who need fixing are the fix. Zen's guidance only involves our self-examination leading to our self-purging. It holds that *only* we can fix ourselves because it was *only* we who broke ourselves. And when we have fixed ourselves, then we are to go about doing whatever we are able to, to help others fix both themselves and live in the Dharma-world they were born into.

But *"only we broke ourselves"* sounds cruel. There is, after all, a nurture/nature conflict. Even the pope wasn't born Catholic and criminals weren't born criminals. As Zen Master Ikkyu reminds us,

Buddhas are made, not born.[47]

Our social engineering theorists would wholeheartedly agree. ...

So, was Prince Siddhartha a forerunner of our social engineers, and is Buddhism merely a form of (*Self-referential*) social engineering?

As is usual with Zen, the answer is both yes *and* no. That is, when the way a group of people is nurtured in society severely corrupts and defiles them, then Buddhists, especially Zen Buddhists, aim to help wake up the individuals who contribute to the institutions that are responsible for that spiritual warping. Zen Master Hakuin heaps scorn and contempt on those monks whose practice fails to prepare them to counsel rulers and their magistrates on public issues.

(There is a story of a newly minted Zen Master who, when given the task of officiating at an event involving dignitaries, sweated and trembled; he was sent back into the daily practice of the monks and remained there until he felt absolutely comfortable in the company of the rich and powerful. That took him *three* years!)

Here is a painting by Zen Master Hakuin. Its central, outstanding element is the character for *middle*.

The calligraphy says, "Zen practice in the midst of activity is a million times superior to that pursued within tranquility."[48]

Hakuin added: "Those who practice only in silence/tranquility, cannot establish their [internal] freedom when entering into activity. When they [that is, those who have practiced only in silence — tranquility] engage into worldly activities, their usual Satori (enlightenment) will eventually disappear without any trace."

At the center of Zen thought, then, is a concern with the world in which people live, meditate, and interrelate. Zen is strongly set against public teachings that glorify greed or angry responses to real or imagined slights. Such teachings delude, divide, and confuse people, and this makes it all the more difficult for them to realize who they really are and who their fellow humans really are. Soul-scorching teachings give rise to destructive Dharma, that is, to

bad CIVIL law,
or, more accurately,
to
UN-*CIVIL LAW.*

(Remember: the Buddha of this age was a prince. Remember, too, that Zen Master Changsha Zhaoxian said, "The whole world of ten directions is reflected in this monk's eye." This monk's eye is the eye of "that monk Gautama. ..."[49])

Doesn't this seem to lead us to conclude that, behind all civil Dharmas, there is the Dharma of the All — of "the whole world of ten directions"? But, be clear about this: that Dharma is not our "natural law," because our "natural law" knows *nothing* of Prince Siddhartha's compassion. "Natural law" is to Zen's Dharma what a heartless computerized robot is to a living, loving, wondering human.

To continue, "the Great Way" of Prince Siddhartha, of "that monk Gautama," is a way that leads through the Capital. There, in the Capital, we will find that well from which the people draw Dharma. So, if the leaders lose their way, the people will be lost, too. That Great Way is *The Dharma Way* or, better, perhaps, The Great Way is *The Great Way of the Dharma.* And the Friends of Prince Siddhartha live all along that Great Way to the Capital.

In short, we find a teaching about the Dharma at the heart of Zen Buddhism.

For Zen, the realm of the sentient human being is precious; it is there that Buddha-mind — nothing more than *ordinary* mind purged of its attachment to Ego! — manifests itself to living beings in their essential ordinariness, and hence

in their effortless interconnectedness within the Dharma.[50]

The very *ordinariness* of that ordinary mind points in the direction of Prince Siddhartha's injunction for each of us ordinary folk — that is, folk who are not stupefied by all manner of theories and prejudices — to make a supreme effort to purge our fellow humans of their *extra*-ordinary minds that create such monstrosities as $E=mc^2$ and mustard gas.

In place of those scientifically produced instruments of mass murder, the infinitely ordinary folk of Prince Siddhartha's Zen create Zen architecture, poetry, calligraphy, painting ... and Buddhism, whose Masters are sometimes referred to in the texts as "Dharma-kings."[50]

So, when we meet with the term *Dharma* in Zen texts, it might be helpful to think something like:

That thirst-slaking water to be found in the Capital.

All well and good. But the last seventy or so years have revealed horrors that really and truly happened. These events, including concentration camps, 9/11, hurricanes, and earthquakes, do much to shake our confidence in our world being governed by principles sustaining the ordinary and trustworthy. Such talk sounds all too full of sweetness and light to reflect the "real" world that leaps out at us from the TV and the daily newspapers. How does Zen defend itself from the accusation of being designed for the inhabitants of some Never Never Land inhabited by the likes of Peter Pan and Tinkerbell rather than the likes of bin Laden's suicide bombers or "natural(!)" catastrophes such as tsunamis and hurricanes? (Isn't what happens "naturally" also included in the Dharma?) Do the Zen texts even *imply* an answer?

Good question.

To begin to answer it starting from what is written in the Zen texts, we would do well to remember that during the twenty-five hundred years that Buddhism has flourished, the Far East has often been wracked by earthquakes, volcanoes, wars, and slaughters, and sometimes the brutal suppression of Buddhism. It was during this period that the Zen of Bodhidharma's line appeared and continued to flourish.

So where was that Dharma — that *also* embraces the life of sentient human beings! — when all those destructive events took place? Were the Masters and Patriarchs simply mad? Didn't they *see* what was going on around them?

They were neither mad nor blind. But — and this might be one of the more original and powerful characteristics of Zen Buddhism — the Masters who lived during and through those times of universal war, pestilence, and natural cataclysms were filled with sorrow and compassion for the victims, but they didn't *suffer* because of them. In the midst of those terrible upheavals, they experienced the rock-solid, although profoundly sorrowful, calm that is the gift of Awakening. As Zen Master Ikkyu is quoted as saying,

> *"Joy in the midst of suffering is the mark of Ikkyu's school."*[51]

The *image* of that beautiful full moon on the lake is, to be sure, broken up and scattered by a wind; but winds always die down. And the *reflected* moon isn't shattered by the winds of Earth, even if its images are — at least temporarily.

So, the Masters knew that despite the Hell around them, they were not to be spiritually scorched by its fires: sorrowful and compassionate, yes, but not blistered. They are known in Buddhism as Dharma Kings: they neither deny nor fall under the yoke of cosmic *or* political catastrophes; as the Zen texts say, "They observe them." The reflection of the moon on wind-ruffled water is broken and, if the wind is strong enough, only bits and pieces of it can be detected of the water's surface. ...

But the moon remains whole and serene.

Still, when all is said and done, Christian Westerners consider that the universe revolves around human beings, that Jesus Christ died for *human* salvation. Precisely that teaching has led the West to a blinding optimism toward each and every scheme we draw up; we invent, deploy, and use weapons of such terrible power that a nuclear winter is not such a remote possibility. But, in our Peter Pan optimism that things will somehow turn out all right — an optimism not in the least shared by Buddhism! — we shrug off all such probabilities and consider anyone who does not as being an alarmist, a paranoid basket-case.

Well, even if there *is* a nuclear winter, there will somewhere or other still be moons that shine. The Dharma will still regulate things in their strange and terrible ambiguity. But still, we humans, although we are most certainly *not* the center of the universe, are really quite amazing! We laugh and sing and build, as well as cry out, weep, and destroy. And it is that *same* dharma-drama that reveals peach blossoms and plum blossoms as we approach a spinning, moonlit, blood-drenched, flower-covered mud ball.

So? If worst comes to worst, what good will Zen or any other Way do us? We will all be doomed anyhow! Eh ... ?

Well, as the old saying goes:

You must die *before* you die,
OR
you'll die *when* you die.

Zen practice is designed to lead us to one of the truly delightful song-and-laughter-filled ways of dying *before* we die. *That* way, whenever or however we die, we've *already* died. So, let life enjoy you. As Ikkyu reminds us, the *score* for the music of those songs and dances is to be found in the

love letters sent by the wind and rain,
the snow and moon.

One last remark. The texts all say that the Zen Masters have never said anything detailed about what they achieved after their Awakening. Likewise, Plato's account of the limits of human knowledge, which we find in his cosmological *Timaeus*, begins with Socrates' question, "One, two, three, but where is the fourth . . . ?"[52] (That fourth is the Deity beyond all humanly recognized Deities — "one, two and three" apparently referring to the planetary manifestation of the Greek sidereal deities, Ares [Mars], Zeus [Jupiter], and Ouranos [Saturn]. Somewhat echoing a thought we find in Lin-chi, Plato remarks on the inaccessibility of the ultimate Source "where things arise and disappear.")

Whatever doubts the practitioner seeking Awakening might have, foremost among these should be doubts concerning that ultimate Source *"where things arise and disappear."* But, as Zen Master Nishimura points out, it is only through great doubt that the practitioner will arrive at great trust. The Great Trust is the fulfillment of The Great Doubt. In other words, The Search requires inhumanly great courage and stamina. Unless this fact is perceived and admitted by practitioner-seekers, they will likely be tempted to give up in despair.

But, if we are tempted to give up the search, we should try to remember Ikkyu's injunction that we first

Read the love letters sent by the wind and rain,
the snow and moon.

Try. Or, as they say, "Have a ‿ !" Hang in there!

God

*And Moses said unto God: "Behold, when I come
unto the children of Israel, and shall say unto them:
The God of your fathers hath sent me unto you;
and they shall say to me: What is His name?
What shall I say unto them?"
And God said unto Moses: "I AM THAT I AM";
and He said: "Thus shalt thou say unto the children of Israel:
I AM hath sent me unto you."*[53]

Many readers are likely to be puzzled by the near-absence in Zen texts of allusions to and discussions of God, YHWH, or Allah. But, the Zen texts most certainly do not seem to have been written by atheists. Atheists' arguments concerning the non-existence of any "Higher Power" sometimes seem to have been generated by a computer-like logic machine trying to crank out non-existence proofs (even though elementary logic classes teach that logic cannot prove the non-existence of anything, only that such-and-such is *il*-logical, that is, can't be proven logically!).

Still, we read that several of the greatest of the Zen Masters have told their students,

"If you meet the Buddha, kill the Buddha."

Now really! Do *sane* people talk like that? And why would anyone who *is* sane want to read about, let alone follow the practices of, people who *do* talk like that?

Well, large numbers of sane people have talked like that who are not in the least crazy.

So . . .? So, why *don't* the Zen Masters talk about God or whatever the term might be in the oriental languages? And why do they make such wild-sounding statements as that one about killing the Buddha? What *is* going on here?

To begin answering these questions that anyone really interested in understanding Zen should ask, let's remind ourselves how we in the West have been brought up to think about these matters. Until we are more or less clear about this, Zen's view will be hidden behind our own ways of looking at the question.

Many Westerners have been taught for millennia that our Deity — God, Allah, YHWH — who is also our Creator, is hidden, and that He only reveals Himself to us when He wishes to do so; no creature, so we have been taught, can approach the Creator unless the path for that approach has been especially prepared by that self-same Creator. In other words:

He is *essentially* apart from His creation.[54]

The Christian teaching of the Incarnation of the Word (Logos) of the Creator in the "person" of Jesus Christ, presents that event of God-Become-Man as taking place in the Creator's own good time — and certainly not in response to something done or said by any creatures.

Martin Luther's Protestantism — which, along with Calvin's teachings, can be said to provide the basis of present-day American Evangelical teachings — is summed up by Luther when he attributed Divinity's choice of whom to save or not to the unsearchable will of God alone (Romans 11:33), together with Luther's illustration in *De Servo Arbitrio* that every person is like a beast of burden who is ridden either by God or the devil.

Christianity's view of this matter is much more complex on the surface, but, as St. Paul and Martin Luther point out, even God the Father (who Christians believe was sent to redeem His creation) is ultimately known only through Self-revelation.

In short, that is to say, our Source, who is also our law giver, is absolutely different *in kind* from what It creates and regulates; It tells us directly of Itself that

I AM THAT I AM,

together with how we creatures are to behave ourselves to assure our continued life in the world created for us.[55]

Zen certainly has its list of do's and don'ts, and these are not all that different from the Old Testament's Ten Commandments or the pre-Sinai injunctions known as the Seven Laws of Noah.

These seven laws of Noah, or variants on them, are embedded in the laws of most of mankind's civic institutions.

So? Why *isn't* Zen Buddhism just another religion? It has priests, temples, beautiful vestments, chants, sutras; all that.

What are all those for, if not to worship some Deity or other?

Indeed; what *are* they for?

Well, as we have remarked earlier, in Zen's view,

ZEN PRACTITIONERS ARE WHAT THEY SEEK,

and all the "window dressing" of temples, priests, chanting, and the like are ways to help beginners enter the Way leading to, of *all* things,

THEMSELVES!!!

(What a hoot!)

The clear vision of those who achieve Awakening is a clear vision of what they always *have been* but hadn't realized, along with a clear vision of the life they must live in order to be *actively* what they are. (The judge who takes bribes is no true judge; he is a fake judge. Likewise, the abusive father, husband, lover, wife . . .)

In this view, the activity of being human appears to involve a sort of pilgrimage whose goal is, well, is

to return to the *starting point* of our pilgrimage!
To become what we have always been.

Nothing more.

Or less.

To the extent that this is on target, the goal of Zen practitioners can be fairly described as involving a *returning to/recovery*, and thus as a *redeeming/ restoring* of the Unity of that *singular* living Mystery that, according to Zen, is the Source of everything — including Zen practitioners.

In this view, we could, following Zen Master Lin-chi, be said to be

ECHOES,
returning the original to itself.

(Isn't that precisely what any echo does?)

This is different from the Judeo-Christian view of the Deity as the *one-way* Source of everything — from Creator to His Creation. But these views — Judeo-Christian and Zen, East and West — are still sufficiently similar in terms of certain shared features that the confusion of the two views is all but inevitable. Still, it is a con-fusion — a fusing of two viewpoints that, whatever their similarities, are very different in many important ways. Such points of similarity tempt many of us who are interested in Zen to ignore the major differences between these two views of our Source; but, when we do that, we end up with a compromise candidate for the position — faithful to neither. On the other hand, there have always been practitioners of Judaism, Christianity, and Islam who have followed the Zen Way leading to themselves, and have found that it was what they recognized as being their Source. So the belief systems are not mutually exclusive.

The distinct ways in which Buddhist and Western traditions pursue the goal of uniting with the Source are central to the difference between the practice of Zen Buddhism and the practices of the three major Western religions. For Zen, that Source is to be found in that of which it *is* the source. It takes most Zen practitioners many years of Self-discipline to realize this clearly through their success in *re*-uniting with it.

But, the Way to the Source is not, Zen insists, through rituals, good deeds, or chanting sutras; nor does it opt, according to Zen, to reveal itself clearly to this or that person for *its* own good reasons and in *its* own good time. Rather, for the Zen practitioner, finding the (Gateless!) Way to his or her Source only requires the seeker's Self-purging during every waking moment. Nothing more; only requiring helpful Shepherds, the Friends of Prince Siddhartha, to point out the way.

(For Zen, the Gateway we must pass through to find our freedom to be what we are is located somewhere in the wall of that all-but-impenetrable prison that is our Ego. *Our* work is to find the Gateway — that the Zen Masters assure us *has* no gate! So, once we have found it ... why then, we can just sashay on through it and from there out onto the Great Way, whose scenery manifests the vitality of its Source to the Friends.)

The *Way* to our Source, according to Zen, is obscure to us because we seek it *outside* ourselves. The Zen texts speak as if our Source as sentient beings is obscured by that very world given to us through our sentience.[56] This is yet another reason why it is so difficult to grasp Zen's views on what we in the West consider to be the Source of all things. (As we have remarked above, our confusion here is a matter of not noticing that Outside and Inside are optical illusions.)

Our Orthodox Western religions are *revealed religions*; as such, they teach us that our Source is "up there" and that nothing except our Source can bridge the gap between Itself and us. It is a bedrock of our Western view of the world, and a principal reason why the texts of Zen Buddhism, especially those concerning our Source, are likely to appear so strange to our ears.

But even worse, Zen Master Lin-chi, the founder of the Rinzai branch of Mahayana Buddhism, says, concerning our Source, that the closest we can come to comprehending that Source is to realize that

> *"the place where things appear and disappear is*
> ***unattainable***,*"*

and, he continues,

> *". . . so that you are like an echo answering the Void,*
> *unconcerned wherever you are."*[57]

As strange as this might sound, doesn't just *being* a sentient being identify any individual as a "place where things arise and disappear"? What *else* except

> **Now a bird cheeping**
> **while a dog barks**
> **then a horn beeping**
> **interrupting this memory**
> **then that thought**
> **· · · · · · · · · · · · · · · · ·**

is being constantly experienced by *any* sentient being who is not sleeping dreamlessly?

So, each of us, as well as what is present to each of us through our sentience, are all "children" of our common Source and, having the same Mother, we are all alive with the same life. (It's like me and my children; we certainly have the same *life* — even if not the same *lives*!)

Zen in effect tells us to just look into a mirror; there we will not even see the Mystery, only its *echo*! The Zen texts speak as if

we humans: an echo of Mystery.

But, even so, we are in a world *ringing* with echoes of Mystery — with echoes of our *inaccessible* Source.

Lin-chi was a Chinese Zen Buddhist, but the Japanese Shinto religion and its teachings concerning what they call *Kami* resonate with his thought.[58]

An Internet search for *Kami* resulted in the following definition: "A Kami could loosely be termed the 'spirit' of virtually any aspect of existence possessing its own discrete identity and vital force (*tama*)."

In Zen's view, similar to Shinto's view of the Kami, our world is not only alive, but it is also *Self*-revealing to those of us who really look at it; to those of us who look *into it* rather than merely *at* it — that is, it only reveals itself

TO THOSE OF US WHO ARE FULLY AWAKE.

Still, as different as this seems to be from our Western view of these things, there is a sense in which even those of us in the West who become SHOW-ME's when they are adults, started out life in a world chock-full of Kami.

For instance, when my children were small, I read them *Goodnight Moon* at bedtime, and they always ended the story with their calling out in unison, "*Goodnight, Moon!*" They knew that no one would say *goodnight* to the Moon unless they thought that the Moon could somehow hear them and understand what they were saying to it.

They knew they were not talking to themselves.

Their

"Goodnight, Moon!"

was their contribution to a conversation involving them and the Moon. And,

"Moonshine!"

was Moon's greeting — a *real* exchange between *real* children and the *real* Moon's *real* moonshine.

As children, we all, *East and West alike*, live in a world filled with Kami, with things that both possess their own discrete identity and vital force as well as reveal it. But, in revealing their own discrete identity, they are thus

their own DISCRETE identity!

Until it *out-sources* itself, any source is just *there*; even to *be* a source, it must be a *source-of*, and this means it must breach the definition of its limits. Any source is essentially both *here* and *there*.

Kami are not secretive and they are not miserly; still, the Moon-Kami (if we may speak of it so) demands something akin to a "*Goodnight, Moon!*" from us down here as a response for its glorious Self-revealing up-there-ness in the sky.

Moonshine!
is the Moon's "voice";
"GOODNIGHT MOON!"
is the children's voice.

And, make no bones about it, if we don't greet it appropriately, then that Moon up there won't even shine the same way to us.

Thus, for instance, a futures trader in, say, hog bellies, walking to his car and thinking about his last bid, might answer a secretary who works in his office who says, "Mr. Jones! Look at that moon!" with, "Yeah. Nice. Be sure you finish that typing tomorrow. . . ." *He didn't even really* see *that Moon!* He was preoccupied with hog bellies, and this left no room for **moonshine**.

In short, when they are properly acknowledged, Kami are "conversational" and thus call forth a response by means of their Self-revelation — if only an *Ahhh!*

That world of Kami is a world in which things' insides are not hidden by their outsides, or, to the extent that they are, one might be tempted to say that the inside of the true Individual — as opposed to a fantasy individual — is *outside* its inside. (Aren't fantasies fraudulent because they have an outside *without* any inside? Aren't they all "show," with nothing to show?)

The world of Kami is a world of real, *self*-overflowing individuals.

Indeed, we might do well to think of "the Source" — as Zen refers to it, or, as "the Creator" as we in the West refer to it — as a Generous Unity that overflows the bounds of its Unity and thus "transgresses" those very bounds. (In one of his poems, the great Sufi mystical poet Rumi speaks of Creation very much like this.)

And, make no bones about it!, such an overflowing results *both* in sentient beings *and* what is present to them *as* sentient beings. That is,

**The sentience of sentient beings
represents an instance of their**

Source

O

U

T

S

O

U

R

C

I

N

G

itself.

But then, isn't something like this what a woman does when she gives birth to a child —

especially to a *FEMALE* child?

The Zen texts sometimes seem to speak as if being truly human, doing the true work of humans, involves laboring to return to, and thus to "redeem," that absolutely *primal* transgression of outsourcing by returning what was outsourced to its Source. It is as if we are meant to live in and through our *working-to-return* — something we can attempt to do by undertaking to re-establish the oneness of that Unity by returning to it.

In short:

- as the painter can be said to redeem the (inviting!) white expanse of his or her canvas or paper in manifesting something of what that empty expanse encloses — in the act of returning something to it;

- or, as the poet's words can be said to redeem the (inviting!) silence of the unspoken by his or her words which that silence encloses — in the act of returning something to it;

so we humans seek to redeem our Source by our return to it through what Zen knows as Enlightenment or Awakening. That is, we seek to Awaken to that world that is our Source, as it actively *out*-sources itself: birds cheeping; dogs barking, and so on. (But Zen tells us never to forget that what labors to return is a living human who sleeps, eats, helps, hinders, and all the rest of what it is to be a human.)

Buddhist Awakening is something like this and, when all is said and done, that Awakening is merely the ultimate refinement of sentience.

See that Moon?

Yes!

"GOODNIGHT MOON!"
"Goodnight, Children!"

But, re-entering, "recapturing" as it were, this world of Kami — and this requires us to recapture our power of sentience! — is not so easy for us adults. Indeed, the Indian writer Gita Mehta reminds us, at the end of her book *Karma Cola*,[59] how difficult it is even for Asian adults, *even if they are Buddhists!*, to see our world as alive and Self-revealing. She says:

A Buddhist priest in Japan, revered as a National Treasure for his wisdom, explained the hazards of being a Teacher to one of his disciples, a friend of mine. The Zen master had brooded over the Buddha's dilemma.

The Buddha had said, "God is Nothing!" and been elevated to divinity.

The more the Buddha explained the Void, the faster his disciples rushed to fill the Void with the Buddha. Groupies hate a vacuum. In the end the Buddha survived. He died. But even at the moment of his death, his disciples were busy planning his monument. How did the Enlightened One wish to be buried? The Enlightened One picked up two empty alms bowls and placed one over the other. This gesture was promptly immortalized into the monumental Buddhist stupas, which are, to this day, a must for the discerning tourists. The Buddha's point with the alms bowls was simple, he was covering emptiness with emptiness, but the devout wouldn't have it.

An empty alms bowl . . .

How clearly it manifests itself to anyone not blinded by greed, anger, or "BIG IDEAS" (as in the expression, *What's the big idea!?*"). How lively it is in calling forth a response! The person who places food in it responds to the emptiness of the bowl, *not* to the beggar — whose presence only serves to identify it as an *alms* bowl. To place food in the alms bowl is to respond to its essence as a self-manifesting here-ness. And, remember:

NO GIFT EVER LEAVES THE HAND OF ITS GIVER!

To grasp this, we must clearly grasp the *active Emptiness* of that bowl: we must "hear with our eyes."

To hear the voice of the beggar's bowl (or the upturned empty hand) amid the clamor of our fantasies yapping for our undivided attention, each of us must try to become still. *Very* still. When we have succeeded, then the silence between us and the beggar's bowl "re-presents" the Source of all speech.[60] Then,

Silence out-sources itself in that echo.

So, given all this, how might we say that Zen thinks of what we in the West term "God"?

Well, how about something like,

> *What announces its presence*
> *in the silence of*
> *the beggar's bowl*

That sort of thing. Nothing complicated. It's like what Ryokan says:

> *In my begging-bowl*
> *Violets and dandelions*
> *Jumbled together*

Or, how about this, by John Tierney, printed in the *New York Times*, August 28, 2007: "That simple gesture, the upturned palm, is one of the oldest and most widely understood signals in the world. It's activated by neural circuits inherited from ancient reptiles that abased themselves before larger animals."

(Reptiles *abasing* themselves . . . ? Such a good start! What a silly conclusion!)

Void

The way of Zen is the way of the spontaneous;
a spontaneous up-rising from the depths of the Truth Body.
Because that is the way of all things:
Wooden Lambs are leaping out of the Void.
(Zen Master Dogen)

That is, for Zen Buddhism, the term,

E

M

P

T

Y

does not refer to any particular

STATE

Rather, it seems that Zen understands *Empty* as something like,

THE

ARDOR

OF

BE-ING,

that guarantees the perpetual appearance and disappearance of whatever is. For Zen, the world is, above all else,

FILLED WITH THE ARDOR OF ITS SOURCE.

We in the West tend to think of the terms *void*, *nothing*, or *empty* — each of which is used as a translation of the Sanskrit term *Shunyata* — in several ways. Those of us who consider these words in non-scientific ways will sometimes associate them with Genesis, the Jewish and Christian biblical account of Creation, and are likely to take *Void* to refer to something other than space for this or that. Rather, it is just *there*; the biblical Void need never have been filled except that the Creator decided to create things that He placed in it. Nothing spontaneous takes place in it. It is not an *emptiness for* anything, nor is it a Nothing in the sense of *negation*; that is, it didn't occur as a consequence of being actively emptied of something. According to the account in the Jewish and Christian Bibles, it was "*In the beginning*"; it was

BEFORE ALL BEFORES.[61]

To sum up, in the Jewish and Christian teachings, the terms *void*, *emptiness*, and *nothing* do not refer to something that anticipates something further; consequently, what the biblical Void *does* refer to is not alive in any sense of that word. It is *lifeless*, and only a totally foreign cause entirely distinct from it can alter its lack of features by placing anything *into* it. The biblical Void neither anticipates anything, nor has it been created by being emptied of anything.

(Surprisingly, considering that the West's sciences tend to consider themselves above all such "superstitions" as we find in Genesis, the scientific Western world of the European Enlightenment is similar to that biblical view — it largely views these terms as referring to an inherently inert, featureless field, in which effects faithfully follow their causes precisely *because* there is nothing to modify the effects of causes. Nothing "just happens" in it; everything in it is an exact, faithful effect of something prior that took place in it.[62])

But many of us humans, East *and* West, who live and breathe in that supposedly dead, infertile field have a quite different take on these matters. We experience *spontaneous*, that is, *self*-generated, *un*-caused, *un*-anticipated, acts of generosity and affection; we see young boys and girls *spontaneously* break out laughing in their delight at their being beautiful and young. Yet we are in no way prepared to be filled with the wonder we experience at the splendor of blazing sunsets, or at the silence-shattering beauty of August's rising full moon. Nor can we explain or even *anticipate* the generosity of those hard-working families who take unwanted children, abandoned by their birth parents, into their homes and share what little they have with them. That unanticipated nowhere "out of the blue!" from which these things sprang forth was certainly not our biblical Void as implied in the account of Creation to be found in Genesis:

That Void is colorless.

"Okay. So, to what *do* those terms refer in the Zen texts?"

Well, sometimes the texts speak as if Zen views the terms *Void*, *Emptiness*, and *Nothing* merely as words that are useful for helping the Zen practitioner *not* to view the world as one that can be grasped as simply defined by laws of cause and effect. But, some texts also seem to suggest that they refer to the "original home" of the uncaused, of the unanticipated, and thus of the spontaneous that *does* have a sort of "home" even if it has no cause.

"Well, perhaps. ... But then, where does whatever is spontaneous come *from*?"

Zen's answer is, "From the Empty, the Void — that is,

from NOTHING."

For instance, Zen Master Ryokan's poem:

> *"Where did you come from,*
> *following dream paths through the night to reach me,*
> *these deep mountains still heaped high with snow?"*[63]

None of this refers to a negation, but to a something that is grasped without any effort on our part, as when, for instance, we really look at and listen to a master musician's flute when it is being played; if even *one* note got stuck inside the shaft of the flute in the middle of a tune,

what
a
RACKET!

Wouldn't it be accurate to say that the music doesn't come from the flute, but from its *silence*? Is it stretching it too far to claim that the player reveals what is hidden in the *silence* of the flute?

Well, it sounds strange, but still, this is not "just another one of those Eastern word puzzles."

For instance, echoing this thought, our contemporary tough-as-nails American literary critic Camille Paglia says:

> My advice to the reader approaching a poem is to make the mind still and blank. Let the poem speak. This charged quiet mimics the blank space ringing the printed poem, the nothing out of which something takes shape.[64]

(Paglia's "charged quiet" is a fine way of naming what Zen refers to by terms such as *Void*.)

Only true Nothing speaks, because only true Nothing "has" anything to say. Everything else is an echo of what has been said over and over and over. For Zen, that Nothing is its own infinitely fertile womb, and the world in which sentient human beings live is alive with the same life as those sentient human beings who live in and experience it. And, as for our *experience* of our world, isn't our Sentience a sort of "daughter" of the Source from which we obtained our Sentience,

at

our

birth?

Everything present to us through our sentience belongs to precisely that world that *gave* us our sentience *at our birth as human beings*!

In this, Zen offers us a way of reminding ourselves that, even faced as we are with the terrible *anti*-life impulses that seem to drive us in this blood-drenched age, our world is still alive with itself. That is, the world entered into through our Zen practice is a world that, although wracked with mass murder and pain, is still fragrant with eternally spontaneous wonder, generosity, delight, and laughter. It is the world in which Jakushitsu, Zen Master and splendid poet, reminds us,

wind whistles through bamboo,
playing a previous dream.[65]

Anyone who hears the playing of a previous dream hears the music of that Nothing, the music of

BEING,
ACTIVELY
BE-*ING*
ITSELF.

So, when readers come across any of the terms *Void, Nothing, or Empty* in a Zen context, it might be useful for them to think something like,

the silence whose echo is life, and . . .

". . . what *are* you talking about?"
NO!
    YES!
        NO!
          YES!
            NO!
              YES!
                NO!
                  YES!
                    Um . . . *maybe?*
                    No?
                    Aw, come on!

Okay; how about,
    "Nothing" seems to be its right name . . . but, no; that's wrong too. Names are shaped hot air,

and
even hot air is SOMETHING!

"Hey! This Nothing is beginning to look like *Whatever!!*"
Well, Whatever *is* **something**. (*And so is everything else.*)
So, to finish the thought that was interrupted above, when readers encounter any of those terms in a Zen context, it might be useful to think . . .
"Excuse me for interrupting, but those terms all mean . . . ***whatever???***"
Exactly!
"***Exactly*** Whatever?"
Yes. For example:

- What's on the paper of a poet? *Whatever* he or she writes? (Exactly!)

- What's on the canvas of a painter? *Whatever* he or she paints? (Exactly!)

- What's on the composition paper of a composer? Whatever he or she composes? (Exactly!)

As the contemporary Japanese Zen Master calligrapher and swordsman Tanchu Terayama describes the moment before the calligrapher puts his inked brush to the clean paper:

> Raise the brush as high as you can just as you finish drawing in breath ... Enter the state of *konton-kaki*, the primordial void that exists before creation. In Zen, the state of vital repose contains everything. Out of the chaos of images and thought in *konton*, a vivid image will emerge. Just as that image begins to manifest, your brush should start its journey. [He describes the motion of the brush and finishes as follows.] Keep your spirit in the stroke even after the brush leaves the paper. The movement continues on and on, returning to the primordial void from which it emerged.[66]

In the case of Zen practitioners, they might, with hard work, reach the state where they *actually* become that blank paper — a sort of living mirror. When this happens, what might otherwise be experienced as utter emptiness, loss, and despair, is experienced as

a state of vital repose

as Terayama calls it. Or, perhaps it is what Buson had in mind when he wrote of

a butterfly sleeping on the temple bell.

(How could anyone *not* love Zen!?)

Source

The vast inconceivable source
Can't be faced or turned away from.
(Zen Master Shitou Xiqian)[67]

There are several Zen words that are particularly difficult to import into the West in a way that makes clear-cut sense to us. *Source* is one of these. Our Western ear is prepared to hear the term either in the context of the activity of an all-powerful, all-knowing Being who created the universe and gave laws to us humans, or in the context of physical events ruled by laws of Nature whose source is worthy to be listed alongside the most spine-tingling of the most Hollywoodesque of brainstorms:

The BIIIIIIIIG BANG!

As a consequence, most of us think of the term *Source* as referring to something "out there," something that is both essentially *foreign* to us as well as entirely *responsible* for our existence.

Essentially foreign to us as well as entirely responsible for our existence.

What a pair *that* is! (And tough-minded SHOW ME! readers think *Zen Koans* are strange!)

At any rate, the three great religions of the West are all *revealed* religions. According to them, the Source, for Its own reasons and in Its own good time, "reveals" Itself to us. On the other hand, the sciences tell us that "natural" post–Big Bang processes such as evolution *caused* humans to have the ability to become cosmologists and evolutionary theorists who have evolved sufficient brain power to ask questions concerning the source of the brain power of cosmologists and evolutionary theorists. (Another Koan that would tax the capabilities of all but the greatest Zen Masters to cook up.)

Zen begins the other way around. Siddhartha, whose practice made it possible for him to become a man whose sight was unobstructed by egotistical self-absorption — and something like this is what the term *Buddha* means to all Buddhists — was born a prince. His past was thought to determine his future. When he rejected that past by giving up his claim to his father's kingdom, he also gave up his future for quite a different one:

that Prince became the Buddha when he lost one past and realized another to replace it.

He thereafter lived only in **his** *Now*. For Zen Buddhism, the *Source* of each and every future is an immensely vital *Now* — and not any *Then*.

But, if our source is not "out there," what could it mean to say that it is immediately, that is, *un-mediatedly*, present? Are we to think that, for Zen Buddhism, we *exist* in our source?

That thought, strange as it seems to us Westerners at first sight, has been recently echoed by an American theoretical physicist who was quoted as remarking that any Universe presently being described by theoretical physicists is not *intelligent* enough to have produced theoretical physicists. But it is not a *logical* impossibility to think that sometime in the more or less distant future a theoretical physicist might appear who *could* conceive of a Universe that *was* intelligent enough to produce theoretical physicists such as himself. In that case, the subject/object, cause/caused, Universe/ theoretical-physicist distinction would not apply to the mind of the physicist who conceived of the Universe that was intelligent enough to produce him. A particular theoretical physicist *who was the source of a theory that included himself* would therefore *be* the source of what his theory explained. That is to say:

He conceived the universe that conceived him!

There is the Zen Koan derived from an incident in the life of the sixth Zen patriarch, Hui-neng, that points in the direction of, or at least echoes somewhat, this conclusion. It goes as follows:

The wind was flapping a temple flag, and two monks were arguing about it. One said the flag was moving; the other said the wind was moving. Arguing back and forth they could come to no agreement. The Sixth Patriarch said, "It is neither the wind nor the flag that is moving. It is your mind that is moving." The two monks were struck with awe.[68]

(As well they might be.)

"It is neither the wind nor the flag that is moving. It is your mind that is moving."

What could that mean? The monks' minds didn't blow. And that flapping flag, what does *it* have to do with the monks' minds? Their minds didn't flap. Minds neither blow nor flap. Nor, for that matter, move. Do they? Do the Zen texts mean to claim that this dynamic world present to us as sentient beings is "all in the mind"?

That's *crazy!*

Well, Hui-neng pretty much clearly states that only mind moves — but, remember that in the Buddhist texts, *mind* is *heart-mind*, 心, and that heart-mind doesn't just think; it always *means*.[69]

For Zen, heart-mind 心 is living and intentional — filled with meaning. Its very activity is *meaning* — not *just* "figuring out"[70] such things as: if X + 2 = 6, then X = 4.

But, what is perhaps most puzzling of all, this Koan seems to be saying that the Sixth Patriarch identifies heart-mind 心 as the *source* of our perceptions of the world around us; he remarks that it was the monks' *heart-mind* that "presented" the sight of the flag flapping in the wind to them!

Well, if a theoretical physicist can even *conceive of* a theoretical physicist who can conceive the world that could conceive him, why can't you and I, ordinary sentient folk, conceive this world that conceives us? Isn't that precisely what happens when a woman is "impregnated"? The child she gives birth to is given to that selfsame world to which she was given in *her* birth.

The very fact that we *are* sentient to begin with suggests that the world conceived *by* us sentient beings in that world is the very same world that conceived us sentient beings. That is:

**isn't the sentience of a living human being a matter of the world
giving itself to itself?
After all,
when we were born, the world gave us to itself**

and,

in and through our

SENTIENCE,
itself to us

(No?)

Being a sentient being is turning out to be a very ambiguous being; likewise, to be the Source of sentient beings is turning out to be a very ambiguous source, namely,

> **a Source that gives Itself *to* Itself.
> ("Out-sourcing" Itself *to* Itself.)**

But, when you think about it,

> **what else *IS* there to give Itself to?**

So, when we hear the term *Source* in a Zen context, it might be well to think:

> **"What do you think it all *means*?"**

How about,

> **"You, and all the rest?"**

(Anything that doesn't *mean* anything, almost surely *isn't* anything.)
In other words, for Zen, the character for heart-mind 〝ᵕ〟 refers to:

> **Source-as-fountain-of-meaning;[71]**

our very sentience reveals our Source meaning Itself to Itself.

It's like when people say:

**"*I* said it
and
I MEAN it!"**

They meant to say it and they meant *what* they said.

I gave it its meaning.

"No! What gives *you*, or *any* one else, for that matter, the power to *mean* something? If *what* you mean doesn't mean anything at all by itself, nothing you can possibly do will make it meaningful. Eh?"

So when I say, "**I** mean this or that," it's the *this* or *that* that does the meaning?

"It has to be that. Doesn't it?"

But ... still, I certainly also *do* mean this or that sometimes. No way around it.

"What a mess! If **it** doesn't mean anything, then **I** can't mean it. But, if it *does* mean anything, it certainly doesn't need *me* to mean it."

Now, now ... don't pout. There is a third way.

And that is ... ?

We mean each other. *That* way ...

Well then, that irritating question, "What's the sound of a tree falling in the forest if there's no one around to hear it?" has a simple answer:

WHO CARES?

Even just *asking* questions like that is an example of trying to give meaning to something that as no meaning of its own. It's like that temple bell; until it is struck, even a butterfly could sleep on it.

But, when heart-Mind ⌣ is "touched" by something, it resonates, like that temple bell; and Zen seems to view that resonating as *meaning*. (The great Zen Master Hakuin tells us that he reached his Great Awakening at the sound of a far-off temple bell, and another master was Awakened by the sound of a pebble hitting a bamboo stalk.)

Thinking

All things born of causes end when causes run out;
*But causes, what are **they** born of?*
*That very first cause — where did **it** come from?*
At this point, words fail me, workings of the mind go dead.
I took these words to the old woman in the house to the east;
The old woman in the house to the east was not pleased.
I questioned the old man in the house to the west;
The old man in the house to the west puckered his brow and
walked away.
I tried writing the question on a biscuit, fed it to the dogs,
But even the dogs refused to bite.

(Zen Master Ryokan)[72]

We readers are puzzled by the Zen texts that, over and over again, tell us that conceptual thinking hides reality from us, and that using what they refer to as *ordinary mind* avoids conceptual thinking. So, what *is* this "ordinary mind"? And why does Zen seem so negative about conceptual thinking?

The texts seem to be in at least superficial agreement with what the great Chung Tzu, author of the *Tao Te Ching*, tells us, "a sage steers by the bright light of confusion and doubt. In doing this, rather than relying on your own distinctions, you dwell in the ordinary. This is called illumination."[73]

To judge from the texts such as these, that ordinary mind seems to be what views all this hubbub down here without even blinking; it seems to see the real world as a vast crowd of Koans — at least, when seen in that "bright light of confusion and doubt."

But exactly how should we readers understand the expression *ordinary mind*? Precisely what does it think about? And *how* does it work when it thinks? Doesn't it follow rules such as if A = B and B = C, then A = C?

The Zen answer seems to be that it's not so much a matter of how ordinary mind thinks, but, *what* it thinks about.

Ordinary mind doesn't think about anything in particular.

"What kind of thinking is *that*?"

Take the Zen story that is to the point here. It relates that although professional swordsmen admired Zen Master Shoju's teachings concerning the importance of concentration in swordsmanship, they scoffed at them when it came to their usefulness in actual sword fighting; it might make the swordsman more alert, but that is all. The Master offered to take several of the professional swordsmen on, using only his fan — which had a metal backing. They leapt at the invitation and he first parried each sword and, to make sure that the swordsmen got his point, slapped each of them on the head with his Zen fan after he had parried their long swords.

This Master Shoju also said:

> *"If your eye is true and your mind unobstructed,*
> *there is nothing you cannot overcome, including a*
> *sword attack."*

For Zen, the question of thinking doesn't concern its rules; rather, it concerns

what is properly considered to be grasped through thinking
and
what not.

As the Sword Masters say over and over, if you think about your sword or opponent for a moment, you will be cut. Think of nothing, and what is to be done will come to you:

When you live in emptiness and work in form.
You become your opponent.

So, it is not that Zen attacks thinking in general; rather, it rejects what we in the West usually view it as being — namely, the *sole* power of the brain/mind that is all we humans have to pursue the answers to questions. Descartes' "I *think*, therefore I *am*," is viewed by Zen as being only part of the story. Aside from balancing the checkbook and making a budget — that sort of thing — thinking is best used, the Zen texts seem to say, when it is employed in distinguishing between two things:

1. what we "have in mind" in our attempts to satisfy our desires to get rid of whatever we thinkers have contributed by means of our fantasies or illusions);

2. what we can know effortlessly because we have minds.

Our intellectual constructions such as hypotheses, mathematical demonstrations, and the like — that is, the fabrications that are the highways along which our thoughts go from one thing to another — are ways of getting to some truth or other. Or, at other times, they provide the tools we use to consider more closely some statement whose truth we are not altogether sure of. But those truths had to be there *before* we formed our hypotheses or proofs; otherwise, we would have to say that we formed the *truths aimed at* by our hypotheses and proofs on the way to *forming* those hypotheses. That is nonsense.

"I'm sorry, but I don't get all that. Please explain it again."

(Explain; explain; explain.)

"Ah . . .

Yes!

NOW I get it!"

And so, when we have arrived at the conclusions of our theories and mathematical theorems, we discard those theories and theorems — that is to say, we then discard what Plato referred to in *The Republic* as "the scaffolding" — constructs that we used to get to our conclusions. (Plato's teacher, Socrates, and his school spoke as if they thought that our day-to-day thinking was helter-skelter and usually built on prejudices we hadn't really considered; the Socratic Method is essentially an organized way of finding out just what our prejudices really *do* imply. "Scientific hypotheses" are essentially the Socratic Method applied to the empirical/experimental foundations with which scientists in a given discipline start.[74])

Most of the trustworthiness of the scientific method is grounded in the fact that it begins with *pre*-rational observation: that is, science begins with our observation of things,

as

they

pre**sent**

themse**lves.**

It is on this basis that science constructs its hypotheses and tests them. (Otherwise, we say that the researcher "cooked" the data.)

But, just as it is hard to perceive fully the architecture of a building before the builders' scaffolding has been taken down, so it is difficult to grasp what thinking leads to if the thoughts leading to thinking's goal obstruct it. Medical students will not become capable physicians until they have fully "absorbed" the lessons they heard in their classes. (Who wants a surgeon who is reading how to do an appendectomy while he's operating on you or a loved one?)

Furthermore, reason, as is true of any tool, can be used for inherently desirable ends or otherwise, and can lead us either to results such as global warming and weapons of mass destruction or to wise, humane institutions that use reason in all modesty and are guided by the most exact scruples.

Reason does not,
because it cannot,
distinguish between
research into cures for cancer

and

WAYS TO USE ATOM BOMBS
TO DESTROY WHOLE CITIES
FILLED WITH
MEN,
WOMEN,
AND CHILDREN.

Reasoning leads us to where we can realize this or that truth.

It only *leads* us to what it is we seek to know.

But, it is only Mind ⌣ that *views* truths to which our thinking has led us.[75] If our prejudices have not been purged *before* we reason, then the "truths" that reason leads us to are partial illusions, and lethal consequences may follow from taking these illusions as complete, accurate pictures of the way things are.

Zen Koans are useful because they lead us to where we are prepared to see that almost all our dearly held eternal truths are merely our long-held prejudices. (Socrates would have delighted in Koans.)

A short aside here illustrating the essentially *auxiliary* role of reason in scientific thinking. "On Gravity, Oreos and a Theory of Everything" by Dennis Overbye in the *New York Times*, November 1, 2005, contains the following statements concerning Harvard physicist Dr. Lisa Randall by colleague Dr. Raman Sundrum:

> Dr. Randall's biggest strength, he said, is a kind of "unworldly" instinct. "She has a great nose," Dr. Sundrum said.
>
> "It's a mystery to those of us — hard to understand, almost to the point of amusement — how she does it without any clear sign of what led her to that path," he continued. "She gives no sign of why she thinks what she thinks."

Dr. Randall, it seems, is *intuitive*; she has an "unworldly" instinct: a great nose.

But how does this help us in the West to grasp *why* Zen says that "conceptual thinking" presents enormous obstacles to our clear, unobstructed vision — to our Awakening to the world, a *living* part of which we became when we were born?

Well, how does *intuitive thinking* differ from what one knows as *conceptual thinking*?

To judge from the Zen texts, what we know as *intuitive thinking* is pretty much what these texts refer to as the activity of Mind-heart ˈᗆˈ. When that ˈᗆˈ is active, we feel what we think and think what we feel: falling in love is both rational and *ir*-rational *together*. As we will discuss later in the Heart section, ˈᗆˈ refers to what is both one and not-one *at the same time*. Think of a twelve-year-old boy: he is both child and man together; likewise, that most unimaginable of Koans, *the living human being*, who is *both* an advanced two-legged life-form that eats, sleeps, and defecates, as well as something that sets fires and puts them out, murders and is remorseful, kills and heals, gives and grabs.

Although it requires that individuals — such as Harvard physicist Dr. Randall — be highly trained in their disciplines, subsequent intuitive thinking, which *presupposes* that discipline, is effortless. It comprises what is often called "horse sense" or "common sense" — which is so-called precisely because it is spontaneous, and requires no intellectual effort. What we refer to as "horse sense" and "common sense" the Zen texts refer to as the operation of *Ordinary Mind*.

It seems that Ordinary Mind is Active Mind, which effortlessly knows the truth *when faced with it*; its work is effortless because ... well, because that's what mind does. Indeed, first-rank athletes say that when they are "in the zone," what they do is effortless; Active Mind is *always* in the zone. When we have re-achieved that ordinary mind with which we were born, all traces of subject-as-thinker and object-as-thought-about disappear. Then, rather than what we think about being grasped by our thinking, instead, what we search for using our thinking comes to us on its own. The saying, "It occurred to me that ..." is only another way of expressing that it came to me on its own.

Thus, for example, merely competent professional musicians have learned to play their instruments without making mistakes; truly *excellent* musicians play the music rather than their instruments. Self-taught Andrés Segovia's musicianship far surpassed that of most conservatory-trained guitar players. He played music, using his guitar to do so; for lesser musicians, musical compositions give them a reason to play their guitars.

The Shakuhachi Zen Master Fuyo Hisamatsu tells us that a good player of the instrument makes its bamboo shaft alive. He continues to say that the player and his or her instrument become one. This requires that the player be infinitely open to the music. He points out that "The Zen practice of living in emptiness and working in form applies to the self and the heart."[76]

In a more recent form, we find this about a theoretical physicist who is viewed with some alarm by his colleagues,

> Like all inspired inventors whose fertile imaginations make them both researchers and artists, Mr. West also still manages to bring a Zen-like focus to his endeavors. "If I'm concerned about what an electron does in an amorphous mass then I become an electron," he allowed. "I try to have that picture in my mind and to behave like an electron, looking at the problem in all its dimensions and scales."[77]

And precisely what does it mean to "behave like an electron"? And why should any of this sort of thing be of interest to the reader of a book concerning the language of Zen? When our physicist behaves like an electron, he stops thinking and speaking. (Electrons don't do either!) They just are, and for electrons — unlike Hollywood stars — "just being" does not depend either on talking or on being talked about!

Zen words point to what we can only realize when we keep quiet and are at rest *in a certain way*. Zazen is designed to teach us to keep quiet and still, *in that certain way*. When we have succeeded in reaching that inward quietness, then we have stopped both talk and thought — and then we are prepared to be *in*-formed by exactly what we sought in our practice of non-seeking, non-thinking, and non-speaking. When that happens, the truth of what is seen is alive with the one who sees; they both share the identical form —

the identical *meaning*!

Isn't that what the term *information* really refers to — *in*-forming? Just like the musician who plays the music rather than the instrument, our here-and-now body becomes the instrument that the music *in*-forms. Indeed, when I am in good form, my fingers *dance* on the strings of my guitar. I watch them do so, and I am amazed.

The music has taken over my hands!!!

Then,

the Music IN-Joys

Me!

(This description is not metaphorical. It happens in just this way.)

To lose personal identity, individuals must first become *un*-(in)formed so that they live in emptiness or formlessness that is then *re*-(in)formed by what they seek in thinking or playing or working or ... or *whatever*. ...

As the Masters insist, we must seek our formless self — that is to say, the self that has no unvarying form and which, therefore, is entirely open to *being (in)formed*. Then we can live in emptiness and work in form —

THE goal of Zazen practice.

Live in

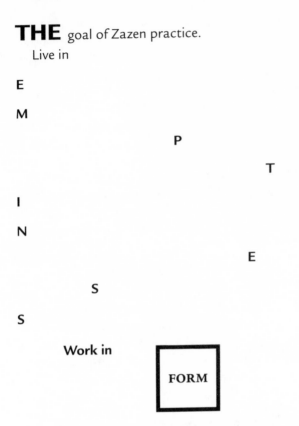

E

M

P

T

I

N

E

S

S

Work in

FORM

But, as the Shakuhachi Master insists, we must prepare ourselves by becoming blank paper to what it is we wish to know. This takes work! It would not be in the least overstating it to remark that the *erasing* required to become open to any field of human work or inquiry is sometimes exhaustingly demanding. But, it is only *after* the erasing that we can truly be open to whatever is to be gained through erasing. As the drill instructors tell us, their harsh discipline is intended to "break us down and build us up as soldiers." Precisely the same thing is involved in the rigorous training of the Zen monk. Likewise to the training of the ballet dancer.

It follows from this that, for Zen, the expressions *objective truth* and *objective love* are **CLAPTRAP**. Where humans are concerned, there is neither truth nor love without the living mind, that is, without ⌣ to animate us. The rest is only stuff we bump into in the dark.

In short, Zen appears to hold that the true activity of what we in the West know as "mind" *always* involves what we often think of as the exclusive activities of the heart. This relates to a central problem touched on in this book: for Zen,

when that "Mind" is acting in accord with its true nature, then the ever-present, never-absent, activity of "Heart" is also present and weighs in its infinitely accurate scales each and every motion of "Mind," every thought.

What we in the modern West know as true mind Zen thinks of as a *counterfeit* of true mind.

(The scientists who constructed the atom bomb didn't really

MEAN

to create a world moving ever-closer to a nuclear Armageddon. Make no bones about it: this cutting apart of the activity of mind and its constant oversight by heart could be said to be both the greatest obstacle that any Western reader interested in Zen thought must overcome, as well as a very grave danger to our world.)

Once again: the activity of mind, *always hand-in-hand with heart*, is what the Zen character ⺖ refers to; its lack in modern times has led to the invention and unleashing of hitherto unimaginable instruments of slaughter.

In short, when mind is stripped of the authoritative oversight that only Heart can provide, the mind's activities degenerate into lethal *cleverness*; but when its activities are carried out under Heart's ever-present supervision, it recovers its native *intelligence.*[78] As Aristotle tells us in his *Metaphysics* — and the Zen texts seem to be in agreement with this — *"Mind's activity is* minding *Mind."*

AND THAT MINDING REQUIRES
HEART'S EMBRACE
OF THINKING.

In the terms of this present thread, the true activity of Mind could be said to involve the never-ceasing minding, the *caring about*, the activities of that Mind; our contrary Western view makes it extremely difficult for us to grasp Zen's views on this matter.

"But do the Zen texts say anything about *why* thinking is even necessary? Sometimes the texts seem to say that we shouldn't think at all! That's crazy!"

Look at it in this way: some of the Zen texts contrast the way a very young child views the world and the way that same child views it when he or she has grown up. Nothing *surprises* the child because it *expects* nothing. It lives in endless *nows* — in emptiness. When it becomes taxed by what it sees, it either cries or goes to sleep. But, by the time we are mature, we have formed vast numbers of opinions concerning everything in our experience. These opinions hide the living **now** world from us.[79] Reasoning helps us to tease out the opinions. Still, however successful we might be in teasing out these opinions, Zen is clear that to some extent, all of us live in a fantasy world of our own making, in an ego world. However friendly and civil we may be, each of us is a living universe existing in a galaxy of living universes. Because we are separate selves — only I can dream my dreams — we are self-centered. That's both the price we pay, as well as the gift we receive, for being born in the first place.[80] No escaping it, except by

DYING.

Then, how can we live in a world of our fictions and also be awake to the world presented to us by our sentience — let alone be Shepherds to others living in our world alongside us?

The Zen texts tell us time and time again that it is very difficult, but not impossible. Indeed, our arts and sciences such as medicine and engineering are based on a real insight of mind as it views the true world around it. Physicians and engineers only need to think when something comes up in the course of their work that their training has not prepared them to meet. But when this happens, their "creative" medicine tends to be quack medicine, and no one would choose to live in a house constructed by someone who was in the process of learning the rules of house building as he went along.

So, excluding the arts and sciences and our personal laboring to clear out our stereotypes, we only need to think when we experience events that are new to us; we then recognize them as such. Our reason searches for ways to identify new experiences as similar to things we have already experienced — or, more rarely, as something truly novel.

In short, our human birth into our human world leads us to think about how to "naturalize" experiences so they fit what we perceive as our needs. Zen helps us be open to the world's meaning; this permits our world to naturalize *us*.

For Zen, Mind is not to be considered as merely alive; it is

ardently alive!
It is ⌣ *!*

And so, when we have been sufficiently *re*-naturalized through that ardor of ⌣ heart-mind, we can then begin the work of answering our life-world's needs by acting as Zen Shepherds — Friends of Prince Siddhartha,

and our sentience becomes a *re*-conceiving of the world within which
we were initially conceived.

When we have *finished* thinking about the score, then and *only* then can we begin to

PLAY MUSIC
rather than
WORK *THE INSTRUMENT!*

And, when we musicians-of-life have succeeded in playing life's music rather than working its instruments, we then *mean* the music and the music *means* us. We musicians and our music *completely* mean each other.

Like two lovers.

(Beyond such things, what is there to think *about*?)

"Well ... whatever. But, when mind *means*, what, **exactly**, does it mean?"

Zen might respond, "What does your wife *mean* when she tells you to *mind* the children?"

If you have to *think* about what she means when she says that, then you probably aren't capable of minding the children!

SEE WHAT I'M SAYING?

Mind & Heart (⌣)

The most fundamental meaning of ⌣
is "bhutatathata (shinnyo),"
that is,
The source of everything.[81]

To say that we love someone with all our heart, or that so-and-so is "heart-less," or that someone "has heart" — meaning courage or generosity — is to cover the Western uses of this term pretty well. As was the case with the term *compassion*, however, the term seems to have several senses in the Zen texts that don't appear to be covered by our uses of the term.

For example, I was once invited to attend a gathering that recognized students of exceptional achievement at my college. After the ceremonies ended and prizes distributed, we faculty were introduced to the parents of the students, and I entered into a conversation with the pleasant-looking middle-aged father of a young woman who had won a prize for her poetry. When I asked him about his profession, he answered that he worked for the army, developing ways to create biological weapons — in particular, aerosol bombs, designed to deliver such agents as anthrax and bubonic plague to populations that were spread out over wide areas. This man, who was sending his daughter to college with funds he earned by figuring out ways to kill large numbers of people — including daughters — using biological agents, was proud of his daughter's success in writing poetry. He had what was generally considered to be a good mind and, to judge from his pride in his daughter's accomplishments, a good heart.

But heart and mind didn't seem to meet in him. He didn't *mind* that, if his work were successful, it could lead to the painful, miserable deaths of large numbers of men, women — and *their* children. It seemed that his heart was, as the saying goes, "not in the right place." Or was he a sort of schizophrenic monster with the loving heart of a father and the mind of a mass murderer? Or was his heart in his work, but not with the same loving heart that he regarded his daughter?

Can a man have *two* hearts? Using this example, it would seem so. For instance, many researchers who carry out painful, disfiguring experiments on living animals have much-loved pets at home; from nine to five Monday through Friday, they subject living animals to terrible pain "in the name of medical research." From five PM to nine AM, and on weekends, they are pet lovers who take their cats and dogs to the veterinarian at the least sign of illness. After working hours, they wouldn't harm a fly.

As noted earlier, the Chinese character ⼼, which is translated as *heart*, is, depending on the context, also translated as *mind*. So it looks like a man *can* be of two heart-minds, one that ponders how to help his much-loved children and pets in their day-to-day life struggles, and another that ponders how to deliver deadly biotoxins to kill people and animals — all depending on the time of day and the day of the week.

What are we to make of this?

Well, even here in the West there are criminal acts that are deemed "heinous." This is a legally acceptable classification, and it is often used to argue that a criminal's crimes warrant the death penalty, or, at the least, life in prison without the option of parole.

Heinous crimes make us draw back and throw up our hands and cry out that such acts are *inhuman*; that rehabilitation is required for individuals who commit them. They are "heartless," and thus "inhuman" — *as if obeying the dictates of our hearts defines our humanity.* On the other hand, the work of such people as Mother Teresa and her fellow Sisters in the slums of Calcutta are beyond the reach of most of us; we call such people saintly, or exceptional, and because of their good deeds we look upon them as superior to the bulk of mankind. Such individuals are often viewed as being somehow *more* than merely human.

Most of us view ourselves as falling somewhere around the middle, somewhere between heinous criminals and the saintly. We generally consider ourselves basically good-hearted and sound-minded, needing only occasional nudges to help us remember that we must not let the stresses and strains imposed on us by unpleasant bosses, bad drivers, or difficult children get to us. Unpleasant, hurtful people are considered (most often, correctly) to be merely unhappy people who seek to lighten their own burden of misery by sharing it with others. We conclude that, if others stress us unintentionally, or even intentionally, it is because they are being thoughtless, and it is our work to learn to respond to their lack of consideration by being considerate, "Mindful," of them — or, in Buddhist terms, we should be "heart-mindful" of them. Being stressed by others is, many Zen practitioners tend to think, *our* problem, no less than the problem of those who cause the stress.

And so it usually is. But the "Mindfulness" toward others as exhibited by the Friends of Prince Siddhartha, the Buddha, is more complex than that. Zen involves a detachment that we usually don't associate with acts of what some of the Masters term "grandmotherly care" toward others. Zen's grandmotherly care is the *compassion* of the Friends of Prince Siddhartha and, as we have mentioned in an earlier section, may even involve severe stress for its practitioners until we are purged of all those Egoistic characteristics that permit us to be stressed to begin with. Zen's grandmotherly care can include slapping someone's face and shouting at them. And when that shouting and slapping succeed in helping the practitioner reach a clear and unobstructed vision of his or her formless core being and the living world — that is, reaching Satori/Awakening/ Kensho — then no trace of any past Ego-driven deed remains, however heinous it might have been.

For Zen, true Awakening wipes away all past deeds. *All of them*. They are thereafter merely illusions of a bygone past, no more real than memories of particularly vivid nightmares remembered long after they were dreamed. No eternal damnation and no Divine dispensation for damnable acts; so therefore, no humans either invoking damnation or getting either rich or powerful by providing indulgences.

There is a Zen story illustrating this. It involves a man who murdered his lord and ran away with the lord's wife. The wife turned out to be so vicious that the man left her. The story relates that he then traveled far away until he came to a mountain village part way up a mountain. The only path around it was very narrow and exceedingly dangerous; year after year, travelers were killed falling over the side of the mountain. So, wishing to make amends for the murder he committed, he began to dig a tunnel through the side of the mountain. After some years, he was well into it when the murdered lord's son caught up with him to kill him. "I deserve to die at your hand," said the man, "but let me finish the tunnel first." The son agreed. After watching the man for weeks, he became bored and began to join in the work. Several years later, the tunnel was completed. The murderer turned to the son and told him he was ready to die. "How can I kill my teacher?" the son replied, weeping as he did so.

Awakening wipes out all past misdeeds. For Buddhism in general and Zen in particular, there is no time-chain linking any previous then-*now* to any future-*now*. How could there be if there is no Creator in a first then-now, Who links together all the subsequent *now*s? Furthermore, Zen speaks of my "unborn heart" ⌣ ; this means that my grandfather's heart is mine too — precisely as that Moon "up there in the heavens" is one with its reflections in the myriad dewdrops.

But getting back to "grandmotherly care," it closely resembles what is in the West often called

"TOUGH *Love*."

Love that is not tough is self-indulgent sentimentality — and sentimentality is one of brutality's masks; toughness that is not loving is mere self-indulgent cruelty. For Zen, Heart-Mind ⟁ is the source of *minding*, as in the expression, "Mind the children for me while I shop," as well as the source of *caring*, as in the expression, "I promise to love and care for you."[82]

The translation of ⟁ as *either* heart *or* mind — depending on the context — is reflected in our two expressions, "*Mind* the children," and "I will love and care for you with all my *heart*."

So, when the reader meets with either of the terms *Heart* or *Mind* in a Zen context, it might be useful to wonder,

What do I have in mind when I say I care about something?

For Zen's Heart-Mind — ⟁ — there are neither reasons nor cares that are not shared *both* by the Heart and Mind.[83]

That union of mind with heart could be characterized as

Zen Buddhism's version of the West's address to
the
MIND-BODY
PROBLEM!

So, when the reader comes across either Mind or Heart in a Zen context, it might be useful to think,

Keep it in Mind
to
NEVER
STOP
CARING!!!

Or, if that sounds too wishy-washy, how about,

"DO YOU CARE THAT I'M OUT OF MY MIND IN LOVE WITH YOU?"

Part II

I'D LIKE TO OFFER SOMETHING TO HELP YOU;
BUT IN THE ZEN SCHOOL, WE DON'T HAVE A SINGLE THING!

(Zen Master Ikkyu)[1]

Some time ago, I met a Japanese Buddhist, the curator of Oriental texts at a major American university, who knew a great deal about the practices and characteristics of different Buddhist sects. After he told me that he was a member of the Pure Land sect of Buddhism, I told him that I followed Rinzai practice; he at once quipped,

> *"Ah! Madcap Zen."*

He certainly knew what he was talking about. Rinzai shows us an array of nimble dance steps, some not so easy to follow, but all of which are intended to be danced to music — and *not* to the dancer's desire to express himself or herself. For an example of Rinzai's madcap ways, consider this stanza of a poem by the Zen Master Ikkyu with the title, "Self-portrait":

> **Wind-crazy crazy person rouses crazy wind,**
> **comes and goes in whorehouses and sake shops.**
> **Who with the eye of a patch-robe monk will give me a try?**
> **Paint South, paint North, paint West, East.**[2]

Now, *that's* madcap Zen!

That's

RINZAI ZEN!

More about that word, *Zen.*

With very few exceptions, when we have used the term *Zen* in this book, we are referring to what the contemporary Zen Master Zenkai Shibayama says concerning the term *Way/Tao* as it is used in Zen. He speaks of

> **the Zen of Bodhidharma's line,** *which stresses the importance of experience and is the most practical in nature of all Buddhist teachings. ... [As it] spread and flourished as a new type of teaching in China, the old traditional term, Tao, with its experiential connotations, began to be used as a Zen term referring to the Truth of Zen. (Emphasis added.)*[3]

That "truth of Zen" is the truth of Prince Siddhartha.
But more.

That "Truth of Zen" was, it seems, largely nowhere to be found in Buddhism until the monk Bodhidharma came from ... (probably Afghanistan, since he is credited with blue eyes and red hair). His teaching implies a worldview that is utterly opposed to some of the West's deepest and most strongly held beliefs about the nature of things. Bodhidharma's teaching pointed to the world given to us humans as sentient beings as

MEANING *ITSELF* TO US.

That is, his teaching was heard by the Zen Masters of his line as saying that it is our *sentience* that links us — those who are born into this world, only to leave it at death — to that world given to us by our sentience.

That is,

The world into which we are born

means

US,

and,

when we have matured in it,

WE

mean

IT!

We who were raised in the non-Muslim West have been raised on the premise

I think. Therefore I am.

This has accustomed us to feel that nothing is authentic except what we have authenticated — "proofed" — by rationally examining it. Anything that is "ir-rational" is subjective and exists only in our fantasies. So, for example, love — which no one would soberly claim is susceptible to rational examination — has been oh-so-rationally dissolved into heightened concentrations of complex macromolecules (hormones) that we evolved to incline us to sexual intercourse, to ensure the survival of our species. (Maybe that defines *lust*, but certainly not *love*.)

Welcome to the world of the West's new-and-improved, entirely rational,

ENLIGHTENED
LOVE!

And welcome to Soviet Russia's scientifically devised, entirely rational Five-Year Plans, policies couched in enlightened proletarian love, that just happened to require the starvation of 10 million or so Russian peasants. Tough! But, as the saying goes, "A man's gotta do what he's gotta do."

For Bodhidharma's world of mind is of a world of Heart-Mind, of 心.

For him, and for the Zen that follows his line of thinking, without 心 there *is* no true mind — only an instrument for overcoming obstacles to whatever it is that our Egos present to us as desirable.

All of which boils down to this: of all the difficulties we in the West face when we try to understand what is being said in the texts of the Zen Masters, none begins to touch the magnitude of the obstacle we face when we attempt to grasp what the Masters in Bodhidharma's line of Zen mean by 心.

Oh! But it's worth the labor to do so — ten thousand times over!

Introduction

All my life false and real, right and wrong tangled.
Playing with the moon, ridiculing wind, listening to birds. ...
Many years wasted seeing the mountain covered with snow.
This winter I suddenly realize snow makes a mountain.[4]

In Part I, we considered a few of those Zen words that are likely to strike the ears of Western readers in particularly misleading ways and we discussed how readers might be misled if they took it for granted that the way we typically heard these words was more or less the way Zen Masters intended them to be heard.

In Part II, we will address terms that readers might care to consider further. This discussion will sometimes be more wide-ranging in scope, so a few words about Zen Buddhism and its distinctive approach to understanding human experience might be useful as an introduction.

To begin with, Buddhism is a jewel with many facets.[5] It has been around for more than 2,500 years, and it has been cut and polished by many different hands whose cutting skills and aesthetic tastes were acquired in many different climates, with different histories and political institutions. As Zen Master Hakuin's successor, Torei, is quoted as saying

> *Shinto is the root,*
> *Confucianism is the trunk,*
> *and*
> *Buddhism is the flowering and sweet fruit.*

This diversity resulted in Buddhist practices that differ from one another in many ways — in some cases, even in their vocabularies.

Some of the differences between the schools of Buddhism are superficial, and some are not. To my mind, the most essential difference concerns the understanding its members have of their practice *after* they have attained release from anger, greed, and blindness — that is, after they have experienced Enlightenment, Awakening (Satori or Kensho). Some schools see Kensho as the final goal of Buddhism; others, including Mahayana Buddhism (the Zen of Bodhidharma's line, which includes both Soto and Rinzai Zen), see it as the *first* step leading to the true work of the Friends of the Buddha. That difference is central to this present book concerning Zen words.

Mahayana Zen views Awakening as precisely the beginning of mature Buddhist practice.

After the death of Prince Siddhartha, the historical Buddha, several schools of Buddhism focused their practice primarily on meditative concentration — Dhyana in Sanskrit, Ch'an in Chinese, Zen in Japanese. Buddhism then split into two major divisions, known later as the Hinayana and the Mahayana branches. The Mahayana holds that every human is capable of Awakening. But, as time passed, many Buddhists came to feel that this was still not The Way that Prince Siddhartha had intended his followers to pursue: Siddhartha was born a prince, and he both acted and spoke as a prince, that is, as a shepherd, or pastor, to all who followed his Path.

The Mahayana branch, which includes Soto and Rinzai Zen schools, have *never* discarded meditative concentration as a *central* part of their daily practice; rather, they saw their meditation practice as an important instrument to help them in their quest for the perfect shepherd's unselfish vision of the world. That branch of Zen could fairly be termed *pastoral Zen* — the Zen of Prince Siddhartha's shepherds.

The guiding principle of pastoral Zen: only an Ego-free, *uncluttered* vision of the world can properly prepare us to live as Prince Siddhartha taught we should — namely, as caring but, above all, as *intelligently unsentimental, compassionate* shepherds to our fellow human beings who could benefit by our care.

(Once again, Mahayana Zen of Bodhidharma's line is presently represented in Japan by two main schools, Soto and Rinzai. Since this book is only about the *language* of Zen, and not a commercial for this or that branch of Buddhism, suffice it to say that an given individual's temperament will determine whether he or she will choose to undertake the practices of the Soto school or those of the Rinzai school. Each can claim an ancient, honorable line that has included many great Shepherds.

The routines characteristic of Rinzai Zen — often involving the use of Koans in its practice — are discussed frequently in this book. Still, pretty much everything important that can be said about Rinzai Zen can be said of Soto Zen; but for the sake of simplicity, our remarks will more often than not be based on Rinzai Zen's practices — but only in the context of its use of Koans.)

Rinzai Zen, a true-blue branch of Buddhism, is not a religion as we in the West usually understand the term.[6] Rather than being considered to be a religion, Rinzai is better viewed as a *Way*, a Path, whose entrance is Ego-free wonder: no miracles for Rinzai; its wonders are just those that we find in this everyday living world around us as our practice helps us to see them.

This by no means should be taken to suggest that Rinzai Zen Buddhists are atheists! Rather, it means that what is commonly considered to be the Deity "up there," somewhere "outside" us, is considered by the Zen Buddhists of Bodhidharma's line to dwell in the unborn, undying heart of *each and every* human being.

To be entirely comfortable with Rinzai Zen, however, one needs to be a word person who is delighted by contradictions rather than put off by them. Such people have a certain *playful* feel for words: as the Zen Master Lin-chi (in Japanese, *Rinzai*) — the founder of the Rinzai branch of Buddhism — said, such individuals are "leaping with life." Unlike that widely accepted view of Buddhism that describes Buddhists as remote, detached, frosty, and other-worldly, Zen practitioners laugh, cry, love, don't love, and then ... And then? Well, when they have had a good laugh, cry, or love session, they go about their business. They simply do not hang on to things — which is essentially what the term "detachment" refers to when it occurs in Zen contexts:

*nee****ext!***

When we are deeply into our Zazen practice, our immediate **MU!** response to all those things that pop up out of nowhere begins to move on to the *nee****ext!*** one until nothing more pops up or something answers "Yes!" *That's* when practitioners sometimes laugh like crazy people.

"Yeah, yeah; but *what's* next after you've finished with the nixing nexts?"

Well, once you get into the knee-jerk habit of nixing *Nexts*, then, when you are doing something, that *next* doesn't nix anything. At the precise moment *this* job is done ... why, the *next* whatever pops up on its own.

"Well, okay, I guess; but I'm bored and don't have anything to do. It's Saturday morning. The news is all bad, the comics are okay, but I've read them all. What next?"

To which Zen is likely to say:

GET
A
LIFE!!

"What . . . ?"

Yeah; just feed a squirrel and look at it until it gets to you. You and that squirrel! If you really look at it until you see it — and nothing else; no anything but that-squirrel-there! — then you and that squirrel, together, will effortlessly create a strange-pair Koan:

THE SQUIRREL-ME WORLD.

There's nothing else then. Just the squirrel-me — *not* a *squirrel- &-me* world.

Really! Try it. If you live on the twenty-fifth floor of a condo, either move or go to the park where squirrels hang out waiting for a handout. Then, after a short while, one of them will see you, come up to you, and demand his peanut! Then you will be in that delightful, never-boring

SQUIRREL-ME WORLD.

(There is a squirrel in my neighborhood who, if I don't see him first, runs up in front of me and makes me stop. Once, when I didn't get the peanut out fast enough to suit him, he put his hind paw on the toe of my shoe to show his impatience with me.)

Alongside the promise of such delightful experiences, I was attracted to the writings of the great Zen Masters because, it seemed to me, they clearly and modestly understood the ambiguity of human life that so anguishes us. Here we are, an incomprehensible hodgepodge of passions and opinions that savagely pull at us in all directions. In spite of the folly and cruelty that so often result from our attempt to avoid our suffering, many of us, in agreement with Zen teachings, opt not to flee from our humanity into those realms of mayhem that teach that we must, *while still living among our fellow human beings*, reject our humanity and live in anticipation of passing from this (admittedly) deplorable state into one of "purification," into *non*-humanity. One of the inhabitants of such a realm, a European humanity-fleeing medieval priest, replied, when he was told that a "heretical" city contained many of the faithful, "Kill them all. God will know His own."[7] Osama bin Laden is only an up-to-date version of that humanity-fleeing crew of ruffians and murderers. No humanity there! And no humility.

The great masters of Zen's "pastoral" branch have pointed out a path they claim will, if we undertake to follow it, toughen us until we are sufficiently hardened to live with the agonizing distress and pain of viewing our fellow humans destroying both themselves and those we love and care for. As any dancing master or football coach knows, true toughening-up is a difficult and painful process. But then, there are no alternatives, are there? At least no *viable* alternatives. For when we reject our humanity, humans killing other humans becomes no more morally objectionable than humans burning trash and garbage, that is, those people who disagree with them. But if we become toughened enough to accept the humanness in ourselves and others, we might well reap such human delights as humane laws, good poetry, delightful play, music, and dance. As we are told in an essay concerning Japanese Buddhism:

> Rinzai Zen had Kyoto as their headquarters, and developed much of what is now seen as the most typically Japanese, namely the Zen gardens, the refined temple architecture, and tea ceremony.[8]

And, how on target the Zen Koans are in this: time and time again, they insist on the necessity of good manners if we wish to approach the living mystery of our sentience's grasp of the world around us! As the Koan says,

> if we speak of it, we offend; if we remain silent, we again cause offense.[9]

Something like an infinite modesty is called for. As the Koan continues,

> to approach it, one must not approach it at all.

"But … but, if we can neither approach nor not approach, what can we do?"

> We can only trust the counsel of our ardent hearts,

Precisely as a lover approaches the one he or she loves.

Zen Master Hakuin tells us that, one night while doing Zazen, he became aware of the quiet sound of softly falling snow, which then triggered his comprehension of the Koan. He says, "a young girl's power of meditation surpasses that of the Buddha's wisest disciple." Shy, and quiet as the sound of softly falling snow, she approaches the Great Mystery prepared only with the strength of her dedication.

The ardor of our ⌣: that's *all* we have that can even begin to measure up to the splendor of what it is we seek. We are moons, luminous reflections of our sun.

The Great Way of Zen is no more than our Moon's orbit.

"What the hell does *that* mean? This talk of being *moons, luminous reflections of our Sun*... all that poetic jibber-jabber is for the birds! I'm both revolted and outraged by the murderous hate all around me that leads young women to blow themselves up in order to kill and maim strangers, and all *you* have to offer is talk about 'moons and shadows of our Sun'?"

Well... that's the voice of your bruised heart speaking. As the great Zen Master Dogen points out,

> All Buddhas' compassion and sympathy for sentient beings are neither for their own sake nor for others. It is just the nature of Buddha-Dharma.[10]

> Isn't it apparent that insects and animals nurture their offspring, exhausting themselves with painful labors, yet in the end have no reward when their offspring are grown? In this way, the compassion of small creatures for their offspring naturally resembles the thought of all Buddhas for sentient beings.[11]

In other words,

We humans are just *built* to be repulsed by seeing cruelty.

Nothing fancy. Fish swim; birds fly. Why? It's just the way fish are. It's just the way birds are.

Bin Laden and the suicide bombers? *They* are birds who have been rendered flightless because they have been soaked in the oil slick of the hate-filled, heretical sermons of insane preachers. *They* are the beached fish flopping around in a medium that cannot support life. But, when all is said and done, it's just that they haven't the *courage* required for trust in their ⌣.

And *that* isn't any "poetic jibber-jabber"!

So... on to Part II, where we will expand somewhat on a few of the words addressed in Part I. Our remarks will be particularly addressed to the SHOW ME! sensible people who are interested in the world and what it has to offer, but who are by no means an easy sell. The Rinzai texts will often strike them as strange in ways that even other Eastern offerings are not likely to. Indeed, the great Zen Masters of both Soto and Rinzai point out, time and time again, that their interpretation of the Buddhist canonical works, the Sutras, is often very different from that of other branches of Buddhism. For example, in one place, we find Lin-chi (or Rinzai) taking a phrase that names one of the great misdeeds of Buddhism — "killing your father"[12] — and re-interpreting it in a way that makes it one of the great virtues of *Zen* thought!

The simple fact that pastoral Zen is a *Mahayana* school of Bodhidharma's line immediately distances it from other schools that are not.

One more time:

JUST WHAT IS THAT "PASTORAL" MAHAYANA SCHOOL OF ZEN?

It's the school where Buddhist Masters use Buddha-frogs to show us how silly we look if we just sit there, never doing anything except making like a frog.

Just sitting there,
GRINNING
&
MEDITATING.

(like a Buddha-frog)

But enough of this! On to the dessert cart!

Bon Appétit!

Words (Living and Dead)

When I am talking like this, many people are listening.
Quickly! Look at the one who is listening to this talk.
Who is he who is listening right now

(Zen Master Bassui)[13]

The great Zen Master Bassui insists that we must never forget the distinction between "dead words" and "living words." There seems to be no such distinction in the West, and this may tempt the reader to dismiss Bassui's advice. But since it is crucial to Zen thought, a few words concerning this distinction are in order.

In Arthur Braverman's splendid translations of talks in Bassui's *Mud and Water*, we find a long section treating of the difference between dead and living words. Here is a passage that *clearly* introduces the problematic character of words in the Zen tradition. It is a conversation between Zen Master Bassui and the monks in his temple, who are the "questioners."

> *Questioner:* "It has been said that what has not appeared in any of the texts since ancient times is no subject for discussion by wise men. If it has never appeared in the sayings of the Buddhas and Patriarchs, who would believe it unquestionably?"

> *Bassui:* "There are no words for the Way. That's why it is independent of the sayings of the Buddhas and Patriarchs. Though it is innate to all people, words are used to express it. ... "

> . . . .

> *Questioner:* "An ancient said. 'If your understanding is based on living words, you will never forget. If your understanding is based on dead words, you will not be able to save yourself.' What does this mean?"

> *Bassui:* "In understanding based on dead words,
> function does not exist apart from the context. If
> your understanding is based on living words, it is
> because you have exhausted the way of thinking."[14]

. . . .

Our ears are, of course, *our* ears, because we hear words and phrases in the *context* of our language. As Zen Master Bassui insists, if we continue to hear words as we have always heard them, then, as Bassui says, *"In understanding based on dead words, function does not exist apart from the context."* But, Bassui assures, *"If you understand how to treat it, even a dead serpent will come to life again."* (To judge from the Zen texts, this seems to mean that, if the hearer keeps his or her mouth shut and really hears the *meaning* of the words spoken, those words can be resuscitated even though they seem to non-listeners to be dead when spoken.)

This is exactly what this book is designed to do: alert us to try to re-animate dead Zen words so that we treat them as if they were alive to us, that is, to "re-hear" them as if we heard them for the very first time — as when we say, "Ah! So *that's* what you mean!!"

Bassui seems to be saying something like,

> Living words are words that are alive in the unity
> of the intention of their speaker and their meaning
> to their hearer; they have no past and no future.
> They are only alive in the NOW of their utterance
> and the simultaneous reception by the listener,
> whose comprehension is identical to the meaning
> of the speaker in speaking them.

The dictionary's definitions of such words is beside the point; what matters is the speaker's *meaning* in speaking them and the hearer's *receptivity* to them. What may appear as jibber-jabber to those who do not know how to listen can be music to those who disregard the way in which the words were spoken or written.

A few more observations concerning living and dead words. Zen (especially *Rinzai* Zen) is known for its strange use of words. Sober, no-nonsense readers are often puzzled and somewhat put off by it. When I related Hakuin's *"Listen to the sound of one hand clapping"* Koan to an old friend of mine, a professor of English literature, he was simply puzzled. He made it clear to me that, in his educated opinion, this was an improper use of words, and since we were very old, close friends, he was distressed to think that I took such verbal craziness at all seriously. I dropped the subject and didn't bring it up again. After all, years before this, he had kindly alerted me to the difference between a sentence and a paragraph. But, I did *not* stop my Koan practice, a practice that led me to an appreciation of words that was far beyond anything I had experienced before.

"Okay; but if we are willing to play along and concentrate on Hakuin's Koan, 'hear the sound of one hand clapping,' what could we possibly hear?"

Obviously, *nothing!* (One hand needs *another* to clap. . . .)

"Oh! *That's* me! *I'm the other hand.* You and I. *Two* hands . . . ! Living words. . . ."

But, look at your *other* hand; isn't it the mirror image? A hand and its mirror image; how many hands is that?

Possibly, but "hearing *nothing*" requires most of us to work hard at concentrating. We begin by learning to stop ourselves from responding, "It's illogical! You can't hear *nothing*." (Bad grammar. Worse Zen.)

But, if we reach that stage, we will have learned how to be silent.

And, when we have learned to be silent, then we have learned to listen to ourselves listening — to distinguish between the sound of spoken words, which anyone with ears can hear, and what they mean to *us* who hear them. "You haven't heard a *single* word I've said, have you?" is not a question about the hearing capacity of an individual. "Ah! *Now* I hear what you are saying" is not a statement about my ability to hear the sounds of words spoken to me.

When we have learned to listen to ourselves listening, we will have succeeded in grasping what Bassui terms, "*What is it that hears.*"

Zen Master Bassui's distinction between dead words and living words is as old as Buddhism itself. As recounted in an earlier section of this book, when the Buddha of our period, Prince Siddhartha, realized that his end was near and that he had to appoint another man to be Shepherd in his place, he stood in front of a large gathering of his followers with a flower in his hand and, *without speaking a word*, slowly twirled the flower between his thumbs and fingers. Only one man, Mahakashyapa, responded — with a smile. It was he who was chosen to be the new Shepherd to the Friends of Prince Siddhartha: he had listened to, *and heard*, the Awakened One's silence.

Nearly two millennia later, the great Zen Master Hakuin came to a Zen that was dying because it could no longer distinguish between living and dead words. In his book *Zen Words for the Heart* (also known as *Poison Pills for the Heart*), he breathed new life into Zen's corpse by uttering wonderfully inventive blasphemies and telling tall tales that only a drunk would buy into.

That woke Zen up from its deathbed, and to this day, centuries later, Zen practitioners look to Hakuin as a very great Shepherd — as a sort of magus who could resuscitate the nearly dead — as a sort of Asian Dr. Frankenstein!

Living words are words Zen Masters use to help anyone they meet who *can* be helped by the words that particular Master utters in that particular set of circumstances —

*in **this** or **that** now.*

Conversely, words given without regard to their appropriateness in each case become dead words.

Ego-trips *for the speaker;*
"Blah," "Blah," "Blah" *to the hearer.*

In short, living words are words uttered in response to the *receptivity* of their hearer. This is probably what Prince Siddhartha meant when he claimed that he never uttered a word during all the years he was teaching: in other words, he never spoke just because he felt like "expressing himself." The only necessity for speaking he recognized was the *receptivity* of the hearer. (Great teachers can speak to large crowds in such a way that each member of the audience hears the teacher's words as if the words had been addressed directly to him or her.)

Those sounds coming from Prince Siddhartha's mouth were not "his" words; they were the *listener's* words — that is, words the listeners *would* have uttered *had* they known what they needed to say to themselves.

And, when all is said and done, aren't living words just those words that we forget immediately on hearing, because their meaning so completely absorbs us?

The **meaning** of living words, and *only* of living words, *deafens us to the sounds of those living words.* Another possible reason that Prince Siddhartha might claim he had never spoken a single word during his long years of preaching: the *meaning* of Prince Siddhartha's words had deafened their hearers to the *audible sound* of his words.

("What did George say?" "Well . . . I can't remember his *exact* words; but the general idea was . . .")

Well . . . maybe. But that SHOW ME! reader who is, after all, nobody's fool, will have problems with this approach to living and dead words, and might conclude, with considerable justification, that Zen seems too unrealistic, too emotional and idealistic. He'll remind us that the scientists who discovered ways to create instruments of mass killing were certainly using *some* sort of words to do so, and it's not likely that so-called "dead" words could be effective enough for the job. He'll argue that all this talk about living words makes it sound as if only nice, gentle, and compassionate people know how to use language effectively; but that those words used to create terrible agents for destroying large numbers of humans or to persuade young men (and young women!) to blow themselves up in order to throw their enemies off balance, are certainly words of power, aren't they?

JUST

L O O K!

AT
THEIR

C

O

N

S E

Q U E

NCES!

Dead snakes don't bite, and dead words can't persuade anyone, young *or* old, to annihilate themselves for a cause that they have been told, *using words!*, needs them to do so.

Can they?

After all, what *are* words anyhow, except useful conveniences? If they turn out to be useful for something, they are alive; if not, then they can be considered dead and useless. Aren't "useless" words what Zen has been referring to as "dead words"? Those scientists in white coats busy making WMDs, they use words that are *very* useful, *very* effective; what they make with those words bites like a *live* rattlesnake.

No?

Good! *Very* good!

It isn't as if Zen means that dead words cannot poison and kill; they certainly can. When Bassui spoke of *dead* words, it is likely that he meant more than that they just lie there. They can poison the mind, lifeless as they are.

FOOD POISONING CAN KILL.
WORD POISONING CAN KILL, TOO.

But, before continuing, let's first remark that this way of looking at living words as *now* words poses yet another serious problem for many of us. Namely, we in the West have been brought up in traditions where the words of our holy books have *futures*; they are by no means *now* words. That is, the three religions of the West — Judaism, Christianity, and Islam — are all "of the book," and, in the West's three holy books, "The Lord said" becomes "what is to be." Consequently, the concept of living words as being *now* words is not an easy one for us to grasp.

The Jewish holy book contains the recounting of a promise — made long ago! — by the Creator to Abraham and his children. The text sets forth a history of something said — the Creator's covenant with Abraham — and the *future consequences* of that covenant on the descendants of that man. But no less centrally, perhaps, the Jewish Bible also includes a collection of prophecies uttered by individuals who were listened to as being living, historical mouthpieces of the Eternal Deity speaking concerning what *was* to be before it *came* to be. In both cases, we find words at the heart of the holy books that define Judaism —

WORDS THAT WERE SPOKEN TO BE FULFILLED:
Anticipations.

Again, in the holy book of Christians, the claim that Jesus was the messiah to Judah, the remnant of "Israel," was squarely based on the person, deeds, and words of Jesus as comprising the *fulfillment* of the words of the prophets of Israel. Jesus was identified to his believers as being "The Awaited One," that is, as the one who appeared

as told by the prophets.

And so with Islam and its holy book, the Koran, on the basis of which the prophet Muhammad was seen to be

the seal of the prophets,

Muhammad was seen to be the *final* fulfillment of the words of the Creator to Abraham and of the prophets of Israel.

In none of those three cases were the Buddha's words

existences without self-nature,

that is,

merely useful conventions.

Finally, it would not be inaccurate to say that, for Zen Buddhism,

silence,

and not

SP O KEN

words,

is supreme.

Since the very beginning of the branch of Zen that was established by Bodhidharma in China, there have been *no* holy books, *no* sacred words. The Buddha-Dharma refers to words and teaching that may help practitioners in their labors aimed at Awakening. They are respected as being trustworthy *guideposts, but not as holy scripture!*

Indeed, the Zen Master Hakuin says that the canonical books of Buddhism, Sutras, are only useful for wiping up dirt and filth — *except* insofar as they can be used by individuals as measures of progress on the Way. *Then* they are valued highly again, *only* as tools for practitioners to use in measuring progress. Some of the Zen texts illustrating this point are likely to offend the sensibilities of Westerners who consider the words of their holy books to be a true part of Creation, not just useful — another reason why Rinzai is so difficult for us in the West to consider seriously.

The only thing in the Zen Buddhist assessment of the value of words that is comparable to the constancy and solidity of the words in the holy books of Judaism, Christianity, and Islam are the individual Buddhist's vows — first and foremost among which is the vow to work to save all sentient beings from that folly that is a consequence of ignorance, greed, and anger. But such Buddhist vow takers are seen as nothing more than human beings whose original, uncaused ardor somehow shines through the mists of beginningless anger, ignorance, and greed, and it is *only* the fire of that *inborn!* original nature that illuminates the Way of the Shepherd.

That vow of the would-be Shepherd is not a prophesy and it is not a promise; it is the statement of the *ever-present, animating* ⟡ that supplies *its* (eternal) imperatives to the practitioner who took those vows. And all other spoken or written words of the Zen Masters are, *one and all*, valued at the same rate as a floating log to which one clings in order to cross a river; on the other side, that log is valueless — although, as Hakuin points out, we are all "always on that other side."

(*Zen, again!*)

In cases where the statements of Zen Masters appear wildly irrational and bizarre, they are most often, *but not always!*, no more than reminders to the listener of the merely useful character of those statements. They sometimes appear wildly irrational and bizarre because . . . well, because what they are talking about is so unnoticed by us. But the recorded words of Zen Masters sparring with other Zen Masters are sometimes simply incomprehensible.

So? How *do* these dead words poison the mind?

Well, living words *don't* poison the mind. Ever. Their meanings can always be referred back to the *living*, ardent Heart-Mind ⌣ of their speaker;

*and those meanings "speak" only to the **living**, ardent Heart-Mind*

⌣

of the listener.

But they have no particular sound associated with them. Indeed, the no-sound of live words is the sound of *all* sounds — that is to say, the sound of living words is *the sound of no sound in particular*. As we have seen Camille Paglia say:

> My advice to the reader approaching a poem is to make the mind still and blank. Let the poem speak. This charged quiet mimics the blank space ringing the printed poem, the nothing out of which something takes shape.

That "blank space ringing the printed poem" is an example of the sound of no sound — the unwritten poem that is each and every poem.

"This charged quiet"

is the "blank paper" for all words; and ardor, pen, paper, and meaning all merge into "This charged quiet," whose symbol[15] in Zen is

Living words silence us as they deafen us; indeed, the true living words of which Bassui speaks were audible when first spoken, but their meaning immediately deafens us. They are spoken to the need of the person to and for whom they are spoken, and not to their ears. Like the water buffalo in the Koan, the sound of living words is, as it were, stuck halfway down into a person's ears; it can't make it all the way into this or that person who needs what the words mean. Living words deafen the "hearer." In this sense, at the very least, the living words of Zen are sounds that don't make "sense": they are only vehicles of meaning.

Take, for example, this Zen Koan:

> What if you are hanging by your teeth from a tree on a one-thousand-foot cliff, with no place for your hands to hold on to or your feet to step on? Suddenly, someone asks you the meaning of the Ancestor coming from India. If you respond, you will lose your life. If you don't respond, you do not do justice to the question. At just such a moment, what would you do?[16]

Well, when the Masters create or use such Koans, they only have its *listeners* in mind. Living words are only *half* alive — namely, *half* their vitality is that of the Master who utters it to his student; the *other half* is provided by the mind of the listener. As the Masters insist,

you must become one with the Koan,

and unless the (*alive!*) hearer does just this, that Koan is just a noise, a (**DEAD**) word.

What is more, the living word, considered by itself, is not *completely* living: it is only *half*-alive — like the sound of that poor, lonely tree falling in the forest with no one to hear the noise it makes when it hits the ground.

But, those dead words scientists use to create such monstrosities as atom bombs, biological agents of mass destruction, and the like, those words are not at all alive; they kill, and the people they kill become **DEAD** people, and the scientists' dead words that created WMD cannot *re*-animate the people they kill. Nor were they ever intended by the scientists to do so. They are, at best, like eggs in a barnyard without any roosters; hens can sit on their eggs forever; all that will happen is that those eggs will become rotten and stinking.

Dead words cannot deafen people;
but they can certainly **stupefy** *them*
or
lead to what can **kill** *them.*

Living words, although audible as mere noises, make no sense to anyone except the person to whom they are directed, that is, to the person *for whom* they are spoken. They are, above all, ***one-of-a-kind*** in a life-realm including both the *giver* of the words and their *hearers*.

In short, it makes sense to say that living words are both heard and *not* heard — precisely as it makes sense to say that semen, taken by itself, is only *half*-alive; and it is not unlikely that it was this to which the Buddha was referring when he claimed never to have spoken a word in his fifty years of preaching. His words were, at best, only *half*-heard words. Only the person to whom they are addressed really "hears" them — as in the interchange,

"You're not listening!"
"Don't worry; I get what you're saying."

In short, the sound of live words is a sort of

Initially

NOISY,

then

MEANING-FILLED,

silence.

"Hear what I'm saying?"
One last reminder.
In the holy books of the West, the Creator created everything by means of words.

"What language did our ancestors who lived in Babel speak before the dispersion of languages?"
"Why, the same language the Creator spoke in creating the world!"

Our sciences have reshaped this teaching by claiming that there exists a "natural" language of Nature:

THE LANGUAGE OF MATHEMATICAL PHYSICS.

Of course we in the West are puzzled by Zen's claim that *all* living language is a human creation that does no more than point to what is contained in silence.

Ego/Self

"Irrigators guide water;
Fletchers shape arrows;
Carpenters fashion wood;
Sages tame themselves."
(The Buddha)[17]

Before further discussing the terms *Ego/Self* we meet with in Zen texts, it should be remarked that the Zen writers were perfectly well aware that each and every living human being is a Self. The Buddha was what he was and it was he, and no one else, who spoke the words that are the foundations of the Buddhism of this historical period.

There is an aspect of Buddhism that could — and has — led many people, East or West, to consider it a sort of Nihilism, a teaching leading to the rejection of everything we sentient human beings experience *as* sentient human beings. However, this teaching most certainly is *not* the teaching of the Bodhidharma line of Zen, that is, of Rinzai or Soto Zen. Rather, the great Zen Masters were powerful individuals whose teachings suited large numbers of students, but did *not suit* other large numbers of students — and several of the great Masters never had more than one or two students! Furthermore, when any given student had achieved a clear Awakening, his Master sent him to *other* Masters to solidify the experience of Awakening:

Different Masters are different!

Readers of Zen texts who are put off by their sense that Zen practice leads to a sort of death-in-life — to a sort of entire denial of humanness — will properly throw down the texts in disgust. But they will be making a grave mistake.

The Way of Zen is
Above all else,
LIVELY,
JOYFUL
&
ARDENT!!!

It most surely does involve extremely painful self-purging, but anyone who has not undergone that self-purging will likely be filled with that rage whose results we read about in the newspapers.

But sure: we all must purge ourselves. But there is a self and there is a Self.

The goal of Zen practice involves, whatever else, purging the individual of certain aspects of his or her *selfishness* — of that strangely dynamic entity that leads us to believe the world revolves around us.

When that purging has been completed, what is left is what the texts sometimes refer to as "the formless Self." In this present discussion of Ego/Self, that formless Self will be referred to as such; otherwise, *self* will refer to the egotistical self-centered dynamic individual.

Almost all of us — whether we are one of those poor souls who agonized through one or more years of algebra in middle school, or one of those happy few who sailed through it — are likely to be confused by Zen's view of Ego for a rather unexpected reason:

> Ego turns every single thing into a sort of algebraic X that has no meaning except either as a part of the solution to a problem **I** wish to solve or as an instrument for overcoming some obstacle that stands between **me** and what **I** want.

When put that way, algebra sounds more than merely intimidating; it sounds downright egotistical:

algebra *reveals itself*
as
a thinly disguised version
of
precisely *what Zen attacks about Ego!*

"Ah, come on!"

Well . . . take the following: **"If X + 2 = 6, then X = 4."** But this does not mean that X is a symbol for something that is the number 4 — except in cases where X = 4 is the answer. But **if X + 2 = 8, then X ≠ 4**. In this problem, **X = 6**.

In short, the symbol X stands for

A N Y T H I N G ,

ABOVE THE EARTH,

On the Earth,

or

Under the Earth,

that can be used to solve the problem in which it occurs.

That's X for you!

And this is *exactly* what Ego does to the world around us; everything becomes MINE! to use as it suits *MY* present purposes. Thus, for example, although a painter might wish to "capture" a sunny landscape on his canvas to cheer up his rainy days, a developer sees that very same landscape as something to "develop" — completely "transform" — for money to buy a condo and a yacht to cheer up his rainy days.

For those in the West who are truly Enlightened and progressive,

THE WHOLE WORLD

IS NOTHING BUT

AN

E N D L E S S

SERIES

OF

ALGEBRAIC

X'S.

That algebra takes the world into which we were born and re-creates it into a new universe of real or potential *solutions* to what we recognize as our problems — or simply to be ignored as being of no account.

But that X, that "Ego number," if we may term it so, is not what the ordinary man in the street, the non-mathematician, usually thinks of as a number — for example, a number of apples, a number of oranges, a number of children, etc.; rather, the algebraic Ego number does not refer to any *definite* this or that; it is only an element in a machine designed to overcome obstacles that prevent us from attaining some goal or other. As such, algebra works hand in glove with the operations of Ego.[18]

In short, our inborn Ego-centric treatment of the world around us is strongly suggestive of the way we were taught to solve problems using algebra. The two support each other and, given the importance of algebra to the progress of science and industry, we industrious, science-soaked Westerners might be expected to be particularly puzzled by Zen's view of Ego/Self.

"And what *is* Zen's view concerning that 'Ego/Self'?"

Well, for one thing, we can't live without it.

"So, are we damned by it? If so . . . well, we have all manner of teachings here in the West about ourselves being damned no matter what. . . . We don't need Zen for *that*. Many of our churches are full of such preaching."

True, true. We don't need Zen for that because Zen doesn't offer any such view of self.

"So . . . ? What view of self *does* Zen offer?"

Well, as my own Zen roshi (coach) directed me:

**You should annihilate everything you meet with
until you meet with your *formless* Self.**

When that happens, our once-born, ever-dying self meets our unborn, undying Self and the two embrace! The undying and the ever-dying become friends. They become a glorious Koan!

"'Formless' Self? What's *that*? Some sort of Hollywood-created ghost-fog? Some sort of ectoplasm?"

The formless Self refers to that in us which,

like a perfect mirror,

doesn't grab hold of anything to the exclusion of any other thing.

The Zen Masters clearly say that our Ego/Self must be emptied of each and every thing that can prevent any *other* things from presenting themselves to it. The nearer we come to achieving that state, the more nearly our "original Self" can function as what embraces the living world — in *that* world's generosity.

That living world is *our* living world. Zen Buddhism doesn't view us as inserted into an essentially hostile, strange environment, into an environment that must be endlessly *subdued* in order for us to live in it; rather, it seems to view the world as something we humans are to endlessly *shape* and *cultivate* in order both to reveal its beauty and to be in-joyed by it.

"But, don't we have to *subdue* the likes of bin Laden and his cohorts? They are certainly in *this* world."

Of course! But the imperative to neutralize him and his variety of human being is no different from the one that tells us that we must work to overcome anything we find *within ourselves* that takes us out of our true life-world: the world of

life,

love,

law,

L I G H T .

The Zen texts tell us that these and their like define the elements of the original world into which we were all born, and it is the work of the Friends of Prince Siddhartha to guide our fellow sentient humans back to where their original sentience will function as fully as it can.

"But doesn't that work demand an active *rejection* of bin Laden's world?"

Yes. But, once again, that rejection is merely a form of annihilation of whatever obscures the real world. That annihilation involves no more than a

WAKING UP!!!

This, in turn, is no more than a man telling a friend that the road he is driving on leads to a washed-out bridge, so he should take such and such a detour. When the friend listens and acts accordingly, he doesn't really reject anything; he has only chosen the right way to get where he is going. When we neutralize bin Laden and his kind, we have, in effect, awakened from that nightmare world he occupied alongside us. We do what we need to in order to replace the nightmare-fantasy world *containing* him with a waking world *lacking* him. (There is, of course, an endless procession of bin Ladens waiting to appear on the scene; waking up and staying awake is an endless task.)

So, when the reader comes across the terms *self* or *Ego* in a Zen context, it might be useful to think:

self's the problem, and

F

o

r

m

I

e

s

s

Self is the cure.

"Cure? There *isn't* any cure. My kids have to go through the same things my parents and their parents and so forth had to go through. Parents don't get along, and the children get twisted out of shape. And then they twist *their* children out of shape, along with *their* spouses. What's all this about cures? There aren't any, are there? If so, where? We, the readers, would like to go there and get some of them."

Yeah, Zen; where *ARE* all these cures?

Well, now . . . Buddhism only promises an end to *suffering*, not to *sorrow*. And what is suffering? Our illusion that we have lost something that is rightfully ours. Something like that. And Zen's view of what's yours and what's not yours is simple:

*Nothing that truly belongs to you **can** be taken away.*
Including your life.

"Huh?"

What is yours was present at your birth, so it can't be taken away. Brutality can sometimes hide it from you, but only that; nothing can take what's yours from you.

"And when we die . . . ?"

Find out what is really yours while you are alive, and *only then* ask that question again. Not until. As the old saying has it:

"You have to die *before* you die,

or

you'll die *when* you die."

To judge from the Zen texts, that famous self — as in self-respect, self-help, etc. — is a sort of blank slate onto which we write our lives. Only *after* we've erased all the badly smudged scribbling of our family, history, biology, and the like, can be we "free and clear," as the expression has it.[19] If we don't succeed in that erasing — and that erasing is what Zazen aims at accomplishing — then that self is merely a marked-up piece of scrap paper with a great deal of illegible scrawling defacing it.

"Hmm."

Furthermore, Zen holds that it is Ego/self that gave us the idea in the first place that everything we can see or imagine is in some sense rightfully ours to avoid or grab hold of and hang on to.

"So that teaching leads us out of suffering. But it doesn't make everything sweetness and light. The Friends of Prince Siddhartha may spend their lives actively preparing us to live joyfully with their sorrow; but, since they have no teaching about the Original Sin of our ancestors, why should there even *be* any sorrow in the first place?"

Ah! But that question presupposes that sorrow is something *imposed* on us from an outside source. But Zen says that it is the Ego/self that we were born with that nourishes the idea of outside sources that burden us with sorrow.

"And . . . ? The alternative . . . ?"

The alternative? There isn't any. It's just the way things are. We are not *caused* to be sentient beings; we are not *caused* to laugh with delight in our own youth and beauty; we are not *caused* to adopt abandoned children; so, why must we think we are *caused* to be sorrowful when we see our fellow human beings — or ourselves! — wandering around bumping into things that we could easily avoid if our eyes were wide open?

Can't sorrow simply be our entirely human response as we view the trance-like daze in which everyone around us seems to linger? To realize that this is a result of our self-centeredness and that it is causing totally unnecessary grief as we trip over what is entirely obvious to those who are wide awake? (To judge from the music of their poetry — for instance, the Middle East's Sufi poetry and singing — the sorrow of those who are wide awake is a different hue of sorrow. Not in the least gray; a kind of reddish purple shade of sorrow?)

So, when readers come across the terms Ego/self in Zen texts, it might be useful to think:

Blindfolds

Take them off!

WAKE UP!!!

Just think how wonderful it would be to see the world just *full* of wide-awake human beings enjoying the wide world around them!

Desire/Love

The true Lover finds the Light only if,
like the candle, he is his own fuel, consuming himself.
(Sufi Master Attar)

When we read Zen texts that say that our suffering is the consequence of our attachment to things — by our desire and/or love for them — some of us might be tempted to think that this is just another loveless no-smoking, no-drinking, no-dancing, no-enjoyment teaching. The message we expect to find accompanying this sort of teaching is that human life is a test: its attractions are nothing but disguised obstacles to virtue and, ultimately, obstacles to our redemption from an eternity of damnation.

We don't need any *Zen* version of that teaching. We have our own home-grown versions of that sort of message. No need for any Asian imports.

To begin, Zen's view of the danger posed by desire and love is absolutely pragmatic and not at all merely disapproving. After all, *any* undertaking that demands both mental and physical skill also requires that practitioners live close to the bone — careful diet, no smoking, only occasional carousing, etc. Ballerinas, professional football players, physicians, professional soldiers — all of these must undergo more or less painful discipline and practice if they are going to, first, master the details of their professions, and then go on to practice them. On top of all that, Zen practitioners have to face the obstacles of their own self-absorption. "No pain, no gain," is not inaccurate when applied to Zen practice; true gain in Zen practice involves pain because, if for no other reason, it involves purging ourselves of everything that is rooted in and nourished by our self-esteem — and what could be more painful than the *Self*-induced loss of our treasured self-esteem?

Furthermore, when we desire something, it becomes desirable to *us*; that is how we view it, as an "object" of *our* feelings and, in pursuing it, we view that object as being "subjected to" *our* feelings. When we view an "object of desire" in this way, then the thing that at one time was there — just as we found it to be initially, *before* we desired it — no longer exists. It is now an *answer*, namely,

*an answer to **MY** desire.*

But nothing was put on the face of this broad green Earth just waiting for one or another of us to come along and claim it as being the answer to some desire of ours. ("We were made for each other" is a very dangerous thought and, when it turns out we were *not* made for each other, we all too often react to this blow to our infallible judgment by brutalizing that former object of our affections.)

So, if, after long and arduous Zen practice, you and I no longer view the things around us as having been made for our exclusive use and enjoyment, then they are conceived of as being what they always were. Then, *and only then*, can we *meet with* our world, the world into which we were born. Then, and *only then*, are those "objects of desire" seen as creations of fantasy which, when we really see them, present themselves as real things

*that can mean **themselves** to us,*

something only *real* things can do!

In short, the emotion of desire is almost always loaded down with ME!, and our desires are usually only an extension of how we feel about things. Desire then becomes what is basically the feeling that such and such *exists for me* — again, the reason why so many "lovers" brutalize their "estranged" love *objects*.

Estranged. What a description of living human beings — as if they were no longer *really* real! She must have been strange until you came to desire her, but then, when you "lost" her, she changed back to being strange again?

Zen practice leads us to see that it's properly the other way around: it's **never** the *pre-ME! she* who is strange; it is the *desired she* who is strange — who has been "stranged." Desire changes the thing desired into something different from what I originally met with that I found desirable. (Think of a developer looking at a beautiful meadow; he only sees building plots: *precisely* what desire does to us.)

But this means that I never really desired *her*! Not the *real* her. The objects of my desire turn out to be constructs of my fantasy superimposed upon some real person, place, or thing. Their (desirable) essence is defined by the fact that they only truly exist in a world where my Ego, my self, is the center. If we look at it this way, desire appears as the first step toward spiritual cannibalism.

If this seems too harsh, consider the February 2008 Reuters article that reported:

> SYDNEY (Reuters) - Want someone killed in Australia? The average price for a "hit" is $12,700, but you can get it as cheap as $380.
>
> A study of contract killings in Australia has found most are not ordered by criminals, but by angry spouses and jilted lovers.
>
> "The most common motive or reason for hiring the services of a hit man was in relation to the dissolution of an intimate relationship."

Seen in this light, desire — the way we feel about the world when we selfishly view it as nothing but a collection of individuals who are potentially of use to us — appears as the great transformer of true individuals. All those things "out there" are either to be ignored or used to scratch some itch — however insistent the itch, however violent its scratching. The bounty of the Earth is considered to be there to be "subdued" for our individual human satisfaction — as one of the West's foundational holy books teaches us (and sometimes "subduing" it requires that we *destroy* it).

This may be on target where desire is concerned; but what about love? Even if some people are heartless, there are others who really do love one another. And we can't love without desire, can we?

Well, the great Persian mystical love-poet Rumi says, concerning love:

> *If they ask what Love is,*
> *say,*
> *the sacrifice of will.*
> *If you have not left your will behind,*
> *You have no will at all.*[20]

In the West, however, we refer to individuals "who have no will at all," as *zombies*.

This gets us to the kernel of another problem Westerners might have in taking Zen practice seriously: what could it mean to say that the goal of Zen practice is to have no will at all — that is, both not to be *self*-ish but also **not** to become what is in effect a zombie?

Even asking that question presupposes that the only true connection we ever have to anything is one forged by self-interest: "What's in it for me? Look at it. Then ignore it, grab it, or run from it."

On the other hand, consider painters looking at a stalk of bamboo, preparing to paint it. What is that bamboo *to* them?

Zen's answer is that, to the extent we succeed in purging ourselves of our willfulness — of our Egos, our self-centeredness — there is *nothing* between what the painters are and their interests. It is not overstating it to say that, according to Zen,

THE BAMBOO PAINTS ITSELF
USING
THE SKILLED HAND OF THE PAINTER.

Read Eugen Herrigel's *Zen and the Art of Archery* or *The Unfettered Mind* by Zen Master Takuan, or Miyamoto Musashi's *Book of Five Rings*. Or, remember Toshihiko Izutsu's description of what the great Haiku master Basho taught about the art of haiku poetry:

> One can delve deeply into the spirit of a thing only by delving deeply into his own self. And delving deeply into one's own self is to lose one's own self, to become completely egoless, the subject getting completely lost in the object. This spiritual process is often referred to in the East by the expression: "the man becomes the object." The painter who wants to paint a bamboo must first become the bamboo and let the bamboo draw its own inner form on the paper.[21]

Or, listen to what is reported of Frank Okamura, the bonsai master:

> "I have no notes on bonsai," Okamura once said. "I use a kind of sixth sense for knowing the needs of the tree. If you look at the tree every day, the tree will talk to you."[22]

When Zen practice succeeds, we can truly say to the world, "You mean yourself to me" — only another form of Frank Okamura's "*The tree will talk to you.*"

When the world "talks" to you,
And you listen to what it says,

then

ITS
meaning
replaces

OUR
desire.

And love? In this light, love manifests itself in two people sharing one meaning. The lover doesn't *desire* the loved one; the loved one *becomes* what the lover means — or, as Rumi has it,

> the one who is ardent is the one who gives birth to
> ardor in another.[23]

Considered in a Zen context, lovers are a sort of collective individual:

two individuals, one meaning.

Or as the contemporary British novelist Salley Vickers remarked during an interview concerning her book *The Other Side of You*:

> *Seldom, very seldom, do two people unite through*
> *sheer reciprocal joy in the other's being.*

She goes on to point out that, all too often,

> The reasons people end up with each other are to do
> with projection and insecurities. It is rare to actually
> take simple delight in another person's being. Most
> associations come freighted with an implicit demand
> or need.

> But then rather quickly our possessiveness and
> need to control starts to take over, and our need to
> turn the other person into something we want.[24]

Listen to a verse from Rumi as he speaks of preparing to love and be loved:

> Become like melting snow; wash yourself of
> yourself.[25]

In light of all this, it might be useful when coming across either of the terms *love* or *desire* in a Zen context, to think something like:

*Whatever is mine **is** mine because what **I** mean is . . .*

it!

"It" does all the work. All we have to do is let *it* be **IT**, rather than **MINE!**
"I don't get it. Tell me what do you mean?"
See!? I mean that 'it' that you didn't get.
And there's the Zen story about a monk who claimed to a Master that the rock in front of him was in his mind, and the Master responded,

"Your mind must be heavy!"

"What?"
Apparently, he means that we — you, me, each of us, all of us — are, that is, *truly be*, only to the extent that our *meaning* — *not* rocks themselves; only their *meaning!* — is precisely the meaning of what has succeeded in meaning itself to us. (Geologists are really and truly *rock people*.)
This is also what Zen Master Lin-chi seems to be talking about when he says:

> In this lump of red flesh, there's a true person
> without position always going in and out through
> your face. Those who have not experienced this,
> look, look![26]

Isn't that "true person without position, always going in and out through your face," **you**, as you take your meaning from what is in front of you when you

Look!

Look!

Look!

That is, isn't that true person "always going in and out through your face" just you as you are "*real*-ized" by what means *you* as you mean *it*?

If so, to quote the novelist Siri Hustvedt:

> *Descartes was wrong. . . . It's not*
> *"I think therefore I am."*
> *It's*
> *"I am because **you** are."* [27]

No?

"I guess. . . ."

Well, do as Ikkyu tells us we must do,

> Read the love letters sent by the wind and rain,
> the snow and moon.

"Okay. Very nice and cozy. But that love . . . it's very powerful and can tear you apart. That Zen talk sounds like something an old monk might say. I'm not an old monk, and I *really* don't want to become an old monk. You can't tell me that love — I mean, the once-in-a-lifetime love that bowls us over and stomps on us when we are down — that *that* love is just Ego at work; it makes fools of us and humiliates us, and we *feed* on it! That's not Ego. That's *love*; maybe not *Zen's* love, but it sure as hell is love as most of us readers experience. Eh?"

I hear you. And, you know? You're right . . . *and* not-right!

"You're going to try to wriggle out of this one with that 'We humans are all Koans!' song and dance, aren't you?"

Well, yes *and* no. No! Don't sulk. No tricks. I promise.

"Let's see."

Well, look: many poisons work because their chemical structures are so similar to the chemical structure of certain *non*-poisons; the receptor sites in the body can't tell the difference between them and what they imitate.

"Ah! You're talking about counterfeits again!"

Yeah; Miss Jones may be poison for Tom Brown, but he adores her, *not* because of what is poisonous about her!, but because of something in her he detects — most often without *dreaming that he has detected it*! — that is fine and lovely. Only a mad-man would want to embrace what is obviously bad for him.

"Those love letters sent by the wind and rain, the snow and moon . . . ?"

Yes! Most of the time, we read them upside down, and think they are anything *but* love letters; maybe *moon*; but *wind* and *rain*? *They* don't seem to be a sort of love letter. But, according to what Ikkyu seems to be saying, that's only because we *mis*-read them.

"So these 'fatal passions' we actually enjoy hearing about at the operas — both soap and grand — and on screen ... we don't see that they are what happens when we *mis*-read those love letters sent by the reality of the person we are mad about, but who is poison for us?"

Looks like it.

"Ah! And, when that happens, and we *do* read those love letters accurately, then what?"

Then, my ever-loving **SHOW ME!** friend, we are filled with sorrow, *not* fury. Sorrow. That's all. No killing; no beating up; no temper tantrums. Only sorrow, and maybe tears.

"And then?"

And then, longing's sugar will sweeten the all-too-salty suffering of anger and reduce it to sorrow.[28]

Okay?

Heart (͡° ͜ʖ ͡°)

Tell me where is Fancy bred,
Or in the heart or in the head?
How begot, how nourishèd?
(Shakespeare)[29]

When you see forms or hear sounds fully engaging
body-and-mind ͡° ͜ʖ ͡° , you grasp things directly.
(Zen Master Dogen)[30]

As we have seen, the character ͡° ͜ʖ ͡° is used both for Heart and Mind in (pre-Maoist) Chinese and (still) in Japanese. Zen proceeds on the basis of that identification.

This pairing of heart and mind might well be confusing. Many of us, East or West alike, often say that we do things following the dictates of what we consider to be our hearts, which, it seems obvious, are by no means in agreement with conclusions we reach when we consider them rationally, using what we consider to be our minds.

Furthermore, in the Enlightened West, especially since the time of Descartes (who lived from 1596 to 1650), it is widely held that *all* mind does is reason; it solves problems by reasoning that is employed in finding solutions. For us, *mind* and *reason* are pretty well interchangeable terms: mind reasons, *and nothing else*. (*Feeling*, Descartes taught, is mind's *pre-scientific*, that is, "hard-wired" way of letting us know whether something is, or seems to be, helpful or harmful to our well-being. As such, it can, in principle, be reduced to entirely *rational* explanation — the bedrock of most of contemporary Western therapeutic psychology and social science.)

But, as G. K. Chesterton reminds us — and as we ignore at our peril —

A lunatic is someone who has lost everything *but* his reason.

On the other hand, we know exactly what the author means when we read in a summer beach book,

What I mean to say is, you mean *everything* to me.
Without you, life has no meaning!

In this example, that any reader can, or at least should be able to, easily understand, the term *meaning* only makes sense if the terms *heart* and *mind* have the same meaning. So, at least sometimes, we use the two terms in a way that presupposes that *heart* and *mind* refer to the same thing.

But still, many of us are of the opinion that mind does nothing but think, and that the expression "I can think of nothing but you! You mean everything to me!" should only be used in high school poetry clubs or romance novels. Outside such settings, anyone who can think only one person is usually considered to be obsessing, and in need of professional help. Likewise, when we hear someone soberly say that so-and-so means the world to him, we are often tempted to conclude that the person is suffering from an unhealthy reliance on the beloved in question — a condition that many of us we think can almost always be cured by self-confidence-enhancing techniques described in books to be found in the self-help section of bookstores everywhere.

In short, for many readers of Zen texts, heart and mind most often do *not* refer to the same thing: the term *heart* refers to an organ that pumps blood or the term refers to a non-scientific way of talking about our emotions when they have been overblown by an increased concentration of hormones in the blood — *precisely* Descartes' view.[31] Mind is what most of us use to solve day-to-day problems, and what industry's R& D specialists use to figure out ways for overcoming their daily research problems, and theoretical scientists use to figure out ways of constructing hypotheses that can be tested — and then, how best to test them.

But, what Zen refers to as *mind* is not quite what we mean by the term. Likewise with what we mean by the term *heart*.

Zen is certainly aware that it is *reason* that takes available evidence and leads us to where we can draw proper conclusions from that evidence, but that it is only *mind* that realizes those conclusions *as conclusions* — something reasoning cannot do. When someone says, "Ah! *Now* I get it!" that *it* does not refer to the last step in the chain of reasoning. After all, we sometimes have to go over and over a chain of reasoning, *including that last step*, before we get *it*. And, until we do get *it*, that last step is just the last step before the *it*. We don't get that *it* until we **get** *it*, or, to be more precise, until that *it* **gets** *us!*

In short, the Zen texts seem to consider reasoning, taken by itself, as being that activity of mind that either *helps* us as we look for ways to solve practical problems or *prepares* us to apprehend things and how they interrelate.

Consider a master builder building a house for himself and his family to live in: he draws up the plans he will follow in building the house; then he must go to various lumberyards and the like to pick out and buy just the materials he needs. Then he must choose a time of year when rain, snow, or cold will not interfere with his work. Then he builds and, when his wife and he have obtained the necessary furnishings and had them delivered, he is through building.

"And then?"

He *stops* building, cleans up the messes created by building the building, and, after the housewarming, he and his family *live* in the house he built.[32]

Another possibly useful way of thinking about this is to consider *thinking* as what *presents* a sort of smorgasbord of ideas, opinions, preferences, and the like; then mind is what notes that such-and-such is to eat and digest —

ignoring everything else.

That is, the Zen texts seem to say that the true appetite of Mind is for what it can truly "mind" — what it can find worth *caring* about; when it functions, it always chooses what is agreeable; that is, it never chooses to poison itself.

There is no
ORIGINAL SIN
in Buddhism,
so,
*mind's taste is **never** for*
JUNK FOOD.

Reasoning, carried on *prior* to caring/minding, is what a fisherman nets as he pulls his catch into the ship. But, he doesn't keep everything the net catches. Rather, he goes through his catch and *considers* which fish he feels he can sell. He throws the others back in. Sound reasoning is the net that catches; it is *mind* that leads us to decide to keep *this* fish and throw *that* one back.

But, perhaps that's not altogether accurate; it seems better to say that reasoning leads us to where we, who are reasoning, are prepared to stop reasoning. At that juncture, what we were searching for through our reasoning makes its appearance.

"*Why* then?"

Because then, and only then, do we stop flooding our consciousness with all manner of "thoughts" which, like bug-splattered windshields, hide what reasoning presents. (If we are "on the wrong track," reasoning doesn't present anything to mind.)

Even supposing all this for the sake of the argument, what are we to think about the likes of Fermi, Teller, and Oppenheimer, who developed the atomic bomb? They, after all, were not *intentionally* homicidal mass murderers. They most certainly could reason. But, at a certain point, when they were perfectly capable of seeing the truly inhuman consequences of what they were doing, what *did* they do?

N   O   T
H   I   N   G   !

Their thinking did not lead to their minding. They didn't "care," so, they stopped right before the "*it*." That is,

Look what WE can do!

Not,

LOOK
AT
WHAT
FOLLOWS!!!

If they had looked at what follows, perhaps they wouldn't have gone on to invent a new and efficient tool for mass slaughter. They might, rather, have become open to "minding" the consequences of their discoveries.[33]

"Well, okay; but 〵 is Heart-Mind and, if they are one thing, wouldn't the atomic theorists and scientists have *had* to mind? That is, if 〵 is both mind and heart, how is it even *possible* for living human beings with very powerful reasoning capabilities *not* to reason and *care* together?"

Well, it seems that reasoning only *presents* those matters about which we either care or do not care. "Mind the children," means "Take care of — ***care for*** — the children, using your *head*!" "I don't mind," can also mean "I don't care. Never mind."

"Is the human so schizophrenic as all that? And, if so, then what could it mean to say that ⌣ is a *unity* composed of heart and mind?"

Good question! But remember, even our hometown newspapers headline the news that:

RESEARCH SHOWS HEAD, HEART LINKED[34]

Still, all too often, we act contrary to that research's findings. But, it is at least consistent with the Zen texts' attitude toward our human sorrow to conclude that it views us sentient beings as having the power to undertake to reunite the *asymmetrical* pairs such as those composed of

ingenuity and intuition,
merely reasoning and not minding,
desire and longing,

and the like. The Zen texts seem to proceed under the presupposition that those pairs all have a single source, and it is the ordained labor of the Friends of Prince Siddhartha to realize clearly ⌣, or Heart-Mind, as being that one source. To do this, it seems that we must come to see, and then learn to value, asymmetry *infinitely* more than symmetry. As an article on the Japanese tearoom reminds us, concerning the cups,

sets come in threes and fives.

YES!
So,

ALWAYS choose
ODD
Over
EVEN!

"Why?"

Because,

Symmetry is DEATH —

a teaching that is surely one of the great teachings of Zen. Those of us who have completed courses in algebra and chemistry are aware of the central place of symmetry in them. In those and similar disciplines, we are constantly "balancing equations." Indeed, the very term *equation* makes no sense outside of the concept of symmetry.

As we have also seen above,

> "Abode of the asymmetrical" is also basically Zen, which is the philosophy of Becoming — a dynamic, endless process. Symmetry suggests completeness and the "aping of an abstract and artificial perfection." In the tearoom (sukiya) or in the Japanese house, the decorations are always off-center, the balance occult; sets come in threes and fives; one never finds the artistic representation of a man on display.

It seems that the work of the Friends is to reconnect that disunion into that oddity of oddities, the "indefinite Unity"[35]

WITHOUT REJECTING THE DEMANDS OF EITHER!

For, if we separate the two and set either of them loose from the other, then minding/caring disconnects from reasoning, and each goes its separate way.

When they are separated, minding and caring can then be enlisted in the service of sentimental feeling good. Sentimentality — which is nothing but brutality dressed up to look respectable — very often leads to an anger which, in turn, often leads to very dreadful things. Reason can be enlisted into the service of greed and anger — *and* to the invention of the atom bomb.

"And how did we separate them to begin with?"

Easy!

WE DEMANDED

S

Y

M

M

E

T

R

Y

!

It's that easy.

So *pretty*!

If we take it for granted that mind and heart are symmetrical,

and thus,

that EACH

can do the work of BOTH —

rather than, as Zen has it, that they comprise the manifestation of the Koan that is to be found in the origin of all things — heart and mind melt into one another, and we get such rational schemes as Stalin's starvation of millions of peasants as just one item in his list of *FIVE-YEAR PLANS*.

Time and time again, Zen practice demands that we learn to live within our Koan, by seeing clearly that

We are living Koans;
Living indefinite pairs that are
PAIRS NOT PAIRS.

And, what else is Zen practice but the attempt of sloppy, always-dying humans to clasp these two original terrors in an embrace that causes them to transcend themselves — and so transform the strife of the disunited pair into the infinitely caring of the crystal-clear vision of the Shepherd?

So, it might be helpful to think of '‿', *Heart* or *Mind*, when we meet with *either* of them in a Zen context as

**the immeasurably excellent union of
the two immense terrors.**

What the embrace of the separated two produces when Zen practice succeeds in gathering them together is something infinitely superior to what either of them is apart.

INFINITELY,

indeed, as superior as the technology leading to the manufacture of rice paper for calligraphy is to the technology leading to the manufacture of poison gases.

Well, even granting this, the perceptive reader might well wonder why, if we, as sentient beings, were so open to the world at our birth, did we subsequently distance ourselves from it by means of our intellectual constructs, our "concepts," and have to go to a great deal of trouble to return to that birth state. This account makes us into developmental

y   **os!**

y

o-

"The Zen Masters surely couldn't have meant *that*, could they?"

Well, something that makes the whole scene all the more strange is that, according to the Zen texts, we never, *ever* leave that primal birth state. Rather, our individual histories involve such tumults as the incomprehensibly violent commotions of puberty and the like, that powerfully tempt us to think that we are nothing but body and that nothing really exists except what helps or hinders our attempts to satisfy its cravings. Paradoxically enough, this disconnects us from our primal birth state, and we must use reason to *prepare* us to return to it.

But, however precious reason may be, it has its limits,

and we must *reason* we if we are ever to find the *limits* of reason.[36]

Zazen involves our wrestling with our reason until we have come to a place where ⌣, caring/minding, reveals to us what is *beyond* reasoning — revealing, for example, that no one can "figure out" a way to fall *in love* with someone, or, for that matter, a way to fall *out of love* with someone!

Furthermore, Lin-chi tells us that we can only realize that ⌣, "where things arise and disappear," is not accessible to us.

⌣ **is** truly a Koan!

NO!

⌣ is **THE** Koan!

But none of this seems to address the yo-yo development of the author. Why do we *start out* as Awakened Ones, and then slide into being Ego-centric concept constructors and then, if we practice correctly, yo-yo back into being Awakened Ones? And, as if that were not enough of a problem, how about those bizarre Ego-concentric constructs we sometimes entertain? For example:

> **If I kill enough of the Unbelievers, I will please the Deity in whom I believe. This will really make Him happy, because, although He created even those Unbelievers, they formed a group that somehow or other cooked up another Deity that — for obscure reasons of His own — our true Deity hates. (Why would He hate the creations of His creatures to the extent that he wants us to murder them? Don't know, but . . . well, He does!!**
> AND YOU'D BETTER NOT ATTEMPT TO DENY IT!!!)

Do Zen texts address this question of our insanity coupled with our wisdom in a manner that helps clarify our Western puzzlement?

Well . . . there's this wonderful Koan whose punch line is:

Sun-faced Buddha; Moon-faced Buddha,[37]

and there is Dharma-Bum Alan Watts's translation of Bassho's haiku,[38]

> The old pond,
> A frog jumps in:
> **_Plop!_**

"**_Old pond_**" and "**_Plop!_**" That pond may be old as taxes, but there's nothing old about "_Plop!_" Still . . . there you are —

"Plop!"

That's the kind of monster we are: as eternal as the sun and as appearing and disappearing as the moon. Old as ponds, new as **_Plops!_**

Listen to what Kyoko Okamoto, the contemporary koto musician and teacher, has to say about this:

> _Although the koto is ancient, we add to it with our_
> _lives when we play and teach. We contribute the_
> _dimension of the present to the past traditions of music._

"But, all that yo-yoing isn't fair! Why do we have to go through all that trouble to _un_-do what we were born to do!?"

Well, why not?

"It's not fair and it's not logical. It doesn't make any sense! _That's_ why!"

Talk about yo-yos shouldn't be serious. Let's relax a bit, rummage around in our children's toy-box, and dig up a yo-yo. Let's give it a few trial runs, untangle the string, and try again and again until we can "rock the baby," "walk the dog," and perform proofs of our recaptured mastery of the play. Then, let's look at that string. What does it do?

It connects

D

O

W

n

with

P

u

u

u

Up and down are not a simple pair made of two distinct elements; there's no such thing as a yo-yo that only "yos," it has to "-yo" too. All "yo" makers would go out of business; likewise any "-yo" makers. If up and down are considered as two *distinct* things, then, when my yo-yo is up, in the palm of my hand, then . . . *then* what? The string means nothing, and I merely look silly, standing there holding a "yo" that doesn't also "-yo"; or, if it has "yoed," but then sits down there at my feet, onlookers would wonder why I don't lean over and pick the thing up.

So, "up-and-down *both* make a pair and *don't* make a pair."

"That's *Zen*?"

Yes; look at what the contemporary Soto Zen Master Shunryu Suzuki has to say about pairs that are neither one nor two.

Speaking of why we cross our legs when doing Zazen, he says:

> *The position expresses the oneness of duality: not
> two, and not one. Our body and mind are not two
> and not one. This is the most important teaching:
> not two, and not one. If you think our body and
> mind are two, that is wrong: if you think they are
> one, that is also wrong. Our body and mind are
> both two and one. . . .* [39]

When he says,

"THIS IS THE MOST IMPORTANT TEACHING:

NOT

T   W O,

AND NOT

ONE,"

he means it! That is, we must practice ridding ourselves of our habit of making everything a matter of EITHER/OR, until we finally reach that Koan of Koans,

> the two which is one and not two,
> the one which is two and not one:
> The womb of all wombs.

Unless we do this, much of what we read in the Zen texts will be tiresomely puzzling.

So,

Master the guitar.

Next,

FORGET THE GUITAR

and

PLAY THE MUSIC,

and then, when we play the music, the guitar and the music-score are united within music, and that music is the musician's indefinite pair.

And ... and then, approaching the gate of Hell itself, Ikkyu's Koan scene appears:

The Gate of Hell / **Plum blossoms; Peach blossoms.**[40]

Likewise, if we wish to plumb the Zen depths of the character ⟨⟩, we must learn both to feel what we think and think what we feel — as we do when we say that we really *mean* something, or that someone *means* the world to us. Or even,

"But ... that means ..."

Yes!

No Old pond,

*no **Plop!***

No Sun,

*no **Moon.***

We really *are* Koans! And Koans begin on the far side of the misty, obscure Source of everything.

(Zen, again. ...)

Zen & Mu!

"MU!"
"What does that mean?"
"It means 'NO! NOT AT ALL!'"
*"Go on! You can't really **mean** 'No.' Are you serious?"*
"No! Not at all!"

Zen Master Hakuin informs us,

> *"What is this true meditation? It is to make everything:*

coughing,

swallowing,

waving the arms,

motion,

stillness,

words,

actions,

the evil and the good,

prosperity and shame,

gain and loss,

right and wrong,

into a SINGLE Koan."[41]

Many, and perhaps most, of us who are interested in Zen Buddhism follow Soto Zen's practice. Soto Zen, which is Rinzai Zen's relatively well-mannered sister, lays comparatively little stress on the usefulness of

Koans in meditation practice. In Rinzai Zen, however, Koans are often an important part of practice, but they are properly considered nothing more than exceedingly useful tools for making us tongue-tied, and thus "dumb" in the way that Zen practitioners aim to become dumb.

But, let it be said, Koan practice is by no means the only practice Zen admits as authentic. Dogen, the founder of the Soto branch of Zen, was a very great Master and a splendid poet. The Soto school founded by him does not, at least presently, stress Koan practice, and vast numbers of Soto practitioners have proven themselves to be outstanding Zen Buddhists. On the one hand, it is not true that all roads lead to Rome; some lead to Stalin's gulags and others to the much-less dramatic shopping malls and casinos of the West. On the other hand, as the examples of Thich Nhat Hanh and H.H. the Dalai Lama show, there are certainly a number of ways within Buddhism to lead practitioners to Awakening.

Still, since Rinzai is one of the major branches of Mahayana Buddhism, it might be useful to look once again at the role of the **MU!** Koan in (Rinzai) Zen practice. And those of us who find it particularly difficult to follow the old Chinese imperative to

Catch the Vigorous Horse of your Mind!

will find Rinzai Zen's Koans their especially useful lariat for catching that headstrong beast.

The **MU!** Koan has come to be known as "First Among Koans," but there doesn't appear to be anything even vaguely like it in our experience, so a few words about it might be helpful.[42]

As we have remarked earlier, **MU!** means *"No!"*, *"Nope!"*, *"Not at All!"* in Japanese. So, if we can shed light on why *that* particular Koan is so highly regarded in (Rinzai) Zen circles, we will also be shedding some light on an aspect of Zen's Koan practice that distinguishes it from other schools of Buddhism — as well as removing some of the obstacles Zen practice might present to interested readers.

First, it might be useful to note that saying *MU!* or *NO!* is an intensely *personal* act. ("**YES!**" is less personal; it means that the speaker accepts what is already present. *MU!* or *NO!* expresses the speaker's seemingly somewhat conceited *rejection* of something present.)

Furthermore, that exclamation point seems to be intended to show that the speaker really *means* what he or she is saying; it is a way of indicating that the writer is *shouting*. The "**!**" indicates that what the writer is saying is from the heart. But since in Zen, *heart* and *mind* have the same character, that is '◡', when we shout, we do so to show that we really *mean* it;

It's from the heart. I *mean* it!

Shouting **MU!** primarily manifests something about the shouter's Heart-Mind, about '◡', his or her living core, or, in Western terms, the shouter's *soul*. (All this also applies when we shout, **YES!** But, once again, **NO!** denies, whereas **YES!** affirms its subject, and denial is much bolder than affirmation.)

Now, **MU!** is **NO!**, and **NO!** negates something; it is negative. Isn't the act of negating something a way of saying, in effect, "You! You are inferior to me, and I obliterate you to satisfy myself?" In other words, isn't negation essentially egotistical? And, if so, doesn't this mean that MU!-ing is the work of Ego?

Well, as always, Zen's answer seems to be, "Yes *and* No!" To *mean* **MU!** is to use Ego to deny Ego.

"Not *again!*"

Look! The Zen texts seem to imply that the work of Prince Siddhartha's Friends involves them in undertaking a program of redeeming.

"Redeeming? Redeeming of what?"

Well, we, who negate, are certainly a part of the same world as what we negate. We have, so to speak, a common mother: that in me which spontaneously says "**NO!**" to this or that, is thereby rejecting something that "I" more or less spontaneously recognize as only a *counterfeit* of a true relative. (*Consider a mother thinking* **NO!** *when a distant uncle-by-marriage asks if he can play with her children.*

Whenever we say "**NO!**" — whether it is appropriate or not! — we are, so to speak, squabbling *both* with *the source* of our ability to say "**NO!**" *and* with what it is we negate. That is, we who squabble and whatever it is with which we take issue, belong to the same realm: we bubbles on the ocean of Being have taken that ocean to task!

These remarks concerning why the MU! Koan is known as the First among Koans shouldn't come as a surprise. After all, Zen Koan practice is designed to help the individual come to *Kensho*, that is, to *Self*-realization — and that realized Self is as close as we ever come to our living core, that is, to the ever-beating '◡'. (Only love grieves over the faults committed in its name; Ego merely shrugs them off. Ego is quite happy with what it thinks it is.)

It appears likely, then, that Zen's **MU!** Koan is designed to lead the practitioner to what he or she **IS** who practices by using it. As the Zen Masters instruct us time and time again, *"Seek the seeker!"* And, as Gita Mehta points out,

> *The Eastern Master, when asked "What is the answer?" traditionally answered,*

> *"Who is asking?"*

That instance of "Who is asking?" does not comprise a request for a name — as happens when I answer my phone and hear a perfect stranger ask me if they are speaking to someone with my name. (Like the Eastern Master, I answer the telemarketer, *"Who's asking?"*) Rather, Zen holds that when we know ourselves, then, and *only* then, are we truly open to this terrible, beautiful world around us, to this world that gave each of us our light of day and that will sooner or later withdraw us from ourselves.

For that matter, what is *any* question other than a

PRESENCE

mocking that

A B S E N C E

that is its

Answer?

And, so it seems, when we have **MU!-ed** everything during months or years of Zazen practice, then what?

Well, then that absence created by our **MU!**-ing leads us to an absence that presents answers to our questions —

EFFORTLESSLY!

(Imagine two lovers, where one asks the other, "Do you still love me?" The reply?

GIGGLING!

Giggling is so *easy*!)

At any rate, that "**MU!**" we say during Zazen is a sort of love-intoxicated chantey we bellow as we declare our dogged rejection of everything that hides our living world from us. The Zen texts seem to point to the conclusion that we sentient beings are a sort of living vessel containing, *and at the same time being contained by*, the living world of which we are both the whole as well as an oh-so-ambiguous, temporary, marginal, member — what Lin-chi refers to as "an echo." Our Zen practice aims at helping us realize this, and **MU!**-practice is an instrument to that end.

Nothing more!

"**MU!**" then, is the ardent heart's particular voice, and, to quote the Sufi Master Imam Ja'far,

> *The ardor of the heart is a fire that*
> *unexpectedly invades the depths of the*
> *heart and consumes all that is not*
> *the beloved object.*

Zen's **MU!** is the voice of the heart's ardor as it consumes anything that comes between the practitioner and the *really* real world that gave us to itself in our birth; its use in Zazen leads us to *realize* (active verb) the world given to us in our Sentience as what manifests the Living Mystery, "*Ku*", the "*living* Nothing" that is

WHAT EACH OF US IS
that
Everything-that-is
IS.

Imam Ja'far refers to "*The Living Mystery*" as "*the beloved object.*" And so we can properly claim that "**MU!**" is the single word libretto of ***the*** great beginningless and endless love song. (If you ever think otherwise, **MU!** that thought!)

"Wait just one minute, if you please! What's all this *love* talk in a book about Zen words? Sure; a couple of the great Masters fell in love with women, but that was the exception, rather than the rule. Zen is full of **MU!**-ing this and that, and saying **NO!** is hardly love talk. *'Do you love me?' 'No'* isn't *my* idea of love talk."

Fair enough. But Love shows itself in many ways, and . . .

"I know. *Love Is a Many-Splendored Thing*, and all that. Parents love their kids; kids love their puppies and ice cream. Sure. But Zen monks leave home and family, and they don't seem to have a lot of pets, and ice cream doesn't seem to be included on monastery menus."

True; all true. But, as we have remarked, Zen practice prepares us to collect what has been scattered, to join the parts of the heart that is broken by grief and loss; to work to persuade those in power to use their strength and resources to unite their people into a harmonious and healthy body of many parts.

In short, the principal work of the Friends of Prince Siddhartha is something like this:

To return

THE MANY THINGS

Into

The One

WITHOUT

Denying that the many <u>are</u> many.

And that, my friend, is what love seems to be to Zen: The love in

the love letters
sent by the wind and the rain,
the snow and moon.

The practice of Zen is the practice of love — even if most often, that

I love you!

is as silent as the sigh of a young woman when she first truly sees a man.

It might therefore be useful, when you meet with the word, *Zen* — in *or* out of a Zen context! — to say to yourself:

"!"

"But ... but, I can't actually *say* **"!"** "

Don't worry. Zen practice leads to that silence that contains all sounds. And

"!"

is one of those soundless sounds. (It means **NOW!** And it doesn't make any noise.)

An example of a sound that *does* make a noise is,

" ... Ahhhh!"

Well ... okay; but then the perceptive reader might wonder why our **MU!** practice doesn't lead us *away from* The Great Way and Prince Siddhartha's realm — which includes whorehouses, crack houses, courthouses, etc.? If we **MU!** everything, won't we end up in a cave on a mountainside somewhere? That isn't Mahayana's *Pastoral* Buddhism ... is it?

No. It certainly isn't. As the Zen jest goes,

> when you find yourself standing at the very top of
> the hundred-foot flagpole, you must still take

ONE

MORE

STEP.

That'll bring you down to this dirty, nasty Earth, down here where the Great Way leads us through the Capital with its

whorehouses, crack houses, courthouses, morgues, jails,
plum blossoms and peach blossoms.

"Okay. But, what makes us take that last step off the top of the flagpole? A hundred feet's a *looooong* way down."

Well, it's ⌣ that brings us down. After all, **MU!** is a *love* chantey; however pure the air is up there, one hundred feet above this dusty, dirty Earth, the Friend of Prince Siddhartha — the so-called "Bodhisattva" — only got up there in the first place by singing his or her love song. And, however rough the landing, Prince Siddhartha's Friends bring ⌣ back down to Earth with them.

This is what the Friends of Prince Siddhartha do. You'll never see one of *them* standing still at the top of a flagpole — just *standing* there! They'll take another step and sing all the way down.

And the song of Prince Siddhartha's Friends is:

it's high up here!
watch out below!!!
'cause here I come,
all *the way down*
singing,
MMM
   UUU
      UUUU
       UUUU!
      UUUU
      UUUU

(THUMP!)

        Now !

"NOW" What?
"NOW" is the moment you've *stopped*
    t
     h
      i
       n
        k
         i
          n
           g,

And START

             L

O

O

       K

         I

           N

G!

In short, unless Zen practitioners have an unwavering trust in their ⌣,
ten billion years of **MU!**-ing will only lead to a Zen Buddha-frog.

⌣!

Mu
uu
uuu
uuuu
uuuuuu
uuuuuu
uuuuuuu!
On
THAT!

Empty/Void

A snowy heron,
Unseen in the snow-covered field of winter grass,
hides itself in its own figure.[43]

Terms like *Empty* or *Void* have associations for Westerners that make it difficult for us to comprehend how Zen writers use them. We have been taught for the last two thousand years and more that the universe is ruled either by divine law as laid down by an all-powerful, all-knowing Creator who created the universe in a "Void":

1. In the beginning God created the heaven and the earth;

2. Now the earth was unformed and void, and darkness was upon the face of the deep; and the spirit of God hovered over the face of the waters;

or by all-powerful, blind laws of nature that act within some sort of an immense openness.[44]

When we come to either of the terms *empty* or *Void* in a Zen context, we tend to interpret them as if they to some extent mean what they mean in either science's account or that account found in that Verse 2 of *Genesis*. (What else *could* they mean!?)

But, as it turns out, our earlier relatives in the West did not understand these terms quite as we do today. In pre-Christian Latin, for instance, one of the words translated into English as void or empty is *capax*, from which we get our terms *capacity for* and *capacious* — that is, "having room for," "being able to take in." In English, echoing that usage, *capacity*, refers to the extent to which an empty container *can* be occupied by something. It does *not* mean merely empty — rather, always empty-for-just-so-much. As such, it involves anticipation of.[45]

But in the account of Creation found in the Jewish and Christian Bibles, the term *Void* seems to refer to a primal state of absolute lack, a lack of even any preparedness to be occupied by anything: otherwise, the Creator would be constrained to create in accordance with that preparedness, and the Void would only be a blueprint, and the Creator would be no more than a carpenter following an already existent set of directions for Creation — which is most certainly *not* how the West has understood that account of Creation. ("He saw it was good," *not*, "He anticipated that it *would be good*.")

In the Western understanding of the term *Void*, only the authentically un-mediated, *immediate* act of a Creator could populate it with subsequent creations that were not in the least anticipated by any characteristic of that Void. This involves

THE

THE EVERYTHING   &   THE NOTHING-AT-ALL

FACING EACH OTHER.

As a consequence, those latter-day creations are presented as comprising *negations* of that nothing-at-all that is the primordial, original Void — that anticipated nothing, and which most certainly did not anticipate true individuals. (The "empty" space of modern physics seems to contain echoes of this sterile view of the Void.)

So, we in the West have been taught from our earliest childhood that, *before* the Big Bang[46] or — if we are Bible-adherent Christians, Orthodox Jews, or Muslims — before the creation of individuals, the term *Void* has the meanings of "empty" and "lifeless," lacking any anticipation of being filled. In short,

for us in the West, that Void is to be considered as being absolutely passive, and by no means, in the least inviting.

So, when we human beings make our appearance, either as one of the kinds of creations or as one of those post Big Bang events — both of which view us *and* our universe as having been cast into the emptiness of a Void — our very existence is defined *in opposition to* that Void. Indeed, all things, but especially *living* beings, can be viewed as being intrusive *negations* of emptiness: *only* humans were told to "subdue" (!) the rest of creation, which is thus implied to be somehow "alien" to human life. (The West's Enlightenment science pretty much faithfully echoes this ecologically disastrous view, which *exactly* parrots one of the central teachings of what that very Enlightenment was created to replace!)

To the Western ear, therefore, the term *Void* refers to what lacks vitality — indeed, even as being positively *anti*-life — the lifeless members of Creation even making their appearance on days different from those on which living things were created.

In agreement this teaching,

Western Science is forced to view life itself as "emergent" from non-life.

(Now *that's* a trick!)

We are therefore likely to be only mildly surprised when we read in a Sunday supplement to our newspapers an article whose large, bold title provokes us to read it by asking:

MANKIND: ONE OF EVOLUTION'S MISTAKES?

One could be fairly expected to wonder precisely *which* PhD, also known as an "evolutionary mistake," is asking that question?

On its part, the central Buddhist terms the *Void* or the *Empty* (Shunyata) are used to mean something akin to the fundamental vitality of a womb — that is, as something akin to the Source of *the vital world*

that world present to us through the operations of our sentience.

The Zen texts seem to consider The Empty as a *vivacious* openness where no nanosecond of "events" is ever "frozen in time." In that emptiness, each and every *instantaneously* passing moment is simply complete in itself. As Dogen insists, there is

> no dragging what is **now** into any **next**.[47]

Indeed, Dogen tells us:

> See each thing in this entire world as a moment of time.
> Things do not hinder one another
> just as moments do not hinder one another.

and,

*In essence, all things in the entire world are linked
with one another as moments.*

Imagine, if you can, that a moment stopped: all the next moments would collide with it and Reality would be like a flute where a note got stuck and all the ones played after it were played together in the same moment. What racket! What a **Bang!**)

The Big Bang seems to me to be precisely a *Now*-like something that clogs up the torrent of time and produces a tidal wave of futures — or, better, perhaps, that *Now* is a cosmological dam that collects and stores the waters of ALL future times, a dam that has one small hole in it through which all the dammed-up *Nows* gush out in a never-ending stream of *nows*.

"Well, okay . . . maybe," our ever-vigilant **SHOW ME!** associate might reply, "but it's all too easy to sharpshoot at theories without suggesting a better alternative. Have you got one of those?"

Well, how about my song, **"BEFORE LIGHT"**?

*Before light was, it was your eyes that set the style for Heaven's stars;
And, Then, when light is gone from all the worlds,
Your face will save an image in that dreadful barrenness.*

*Before sound was, your mirth demanded music;
And so, when sound is silenced,
And the soft immensity of Nothingness is stilled in all its parts,
Then your merriment will measure still . . .
Why, some airs, some tunes, some melodies.*

*Before Time was, you quickened listless, languid, idle love with life;
And, when Time runs dry through all its long and tortured courses,
Your thrilling Now, never grounded in the killed stalls and stills
of Time's once roiling rivulets, streams and rills,
Will end Time's old end, and resurrect it in the meter
of your stirring heart.*

So . . . ?

"Whatever. . . ."

Okay. But, to continue, Zen Master Dogen seems to hold that it is as if the world present to us as sentient human beings is a world pregnant with itself, that is, pregnant with every next moment. No moment *causes* the next moment; each moment, *because* it *is what* it *is*, acts as a kind of "mother" to its successor. Indeed, the Zen texts sometimes speak as if the world, the *Now*, is the matrix out of which the next *Now* will spring.[48] Or, perhaps, we might picture each consuming-itself-*Now* as revealing the next *now*.

Nor should this be understood "rationally"; the great Zen Master Lin-chi tells us that

The place were things arise and disappear is
UNATTAINABLE.

He adds,

So that we are echoes answering the void.[49]

Zen teaches us that Awakening is achieving Emptiness, which means

WE,
YOU---AND----I,
BECOME
THE PLACE WHERE THINGS
ARISE AND DISAPPEAR.

That is, we Awaken, we become

FULLY SENTIENT,
which is precisely
to be
FULLY, VITALLY, EMPTY!

To repeat: to be actively receptive to everything, even to what seems to obstruct reception, is, for Zen, to be

truly empty,
which is to be
TRULY SENTIENT.

("I didn't hear you calling me; I'm afraid I'm somewhat preoccupied these days . . . what with Jen's problems at school and all.")

This view seems strange at first sight because it demands that only the human being who is truly *empty* is truly *open-to-be-filled-to-be-emptied.* ... For instance, fill in the blank,

Emptiness is _____.

See? What a blank *is*, is a something-to-be-filled! — a _____ that IS-to-be-filled or, perhaps better, it IS a to-be-filled Being. The Zen texts speak of *Being* as an activity, and not as a *defined* state — one of the most difficult things for us Westerners to comprehend. That _____ is infinitely *vital*! It demands to be filled.

For instance, Zen Master Hakuin tells us:

> *Form doesn't mask emptiness, emptiness is the*
> *essence of form;*
> *Emptiness doesn't break up form, form embodies*
> *emptiness.*
> *Form and emptiness are non-dual within the gates*
> *of Dharma,*
> *Where a lame turtle*
> *brushing his eyebrows*
> *stands in the evening breeze.*[50]

("A lame turtle brushing his eyebrows?" Indeed; *that* vital emptiness is the essence of form. We speak of someone having "a lively imagination"; isn't the expression *lively imagination* a way of referring to "_____"?)

At any rate, something like this seems to be what the terms *Empty, Void,* and the like refer to in the Zen texts.

But, since such central Zen Buddhist texts as The Heart Sutra make no sense to us without at least a beginning grasp of the difference between our usual understanding of Emptiness and Zen's understanding, something more might be in order.

It appears that *the* obstacle of obstacles to what Zen Buddhism refers to as *waking up* or *Enlightenment* is simply overcoming the subject-object duality. (Where can we *possibly* find that *subject/object* duality within works of the imagination? The works of so-called "non-representational" painters such as Kandinsky come to mind. His work doesn't seem to point to a subject-object duality between painter and painting.) Not only does Ego make it difficult for anyone — East *or* West — to overcome, but, on top of this, we in the West have been taught from our earliest days that we are creations in a created world — a world that is so "other" that our Creator first placed us in it to punish us, and then told us that we must "subdue" it in order to live in it. (The Big Bang world is just a stage for dogs to eat dogs on.)

It also appears that Ego demands that subject/object dualism. The "I" faces everything as being "for me or against me" in that alien world.[51]

Okay, but . . . well, it's curious; I sometimes quite spontaneously reject Ego's "Me-Them" demand entirely when, for instance, I look at the oak leaves on the ground: some of them are merely autumn's soft brown; others are the pale plum we see in our dreams of spring; all are carefully and ardently shapely, each one in its unique oak shape. In the moment we see it, they speak to us.

Really!

Their language is drawn from, and remains in, silence; but, for all that, it's crystal clear.[52] We both — we who perceive, no less than the leaf we perceive — relinquish our otherness-apartness as a response for each of our gifts of ourselves to the other.

This is *Zen*

SEEING.

This is the poet Bu-er's,

**A person looks,
The blossoms look back:
Plain heart seeing into plain heart.**

Nor is this "poetic" twaddle. It happens in the same world as falling in love; flu; heart attacks; the moon of August, and April's sweet welcoming.

So, reflecting on the texts, *the Empty* begins to appear simply as

the im-mediate,[53]

or, better, perhaps, as

*the-***nothing-***in-between* **we who perceive,** *and* **what it is we perceive.**

When I see that oak leaf clearly, there's nothing between it and me, and I'm not it, and it's not me. If the *least* thing were in between us, I couldn't see it clearly.

No?
Yes!
Whatever else it may signify, *Shunyata* seems to refer to

The-*nothing*-in-between.

Think of,

No matter what; *nothing* can come between us —

which means,

NOTHING is between us!

which, in turn, means:

The whole world is between us.
Each and Everything
Is
between us!

And, that Zen Enso,

identifies the one who paints it as an Awakened individual, a *living* Emptiness — even as an each-and-Everything all-embracing Emptiness.[54]

(But what is perhaps most difficult for us in the West is to entertain the notion that Zen's Emptiness is *vital*, and by *no* means inert.)

Finally, when we are really on the Great Way, Nothing does not stop us. (Once again, awful grammar; but *this* time, *perfect* Zen.) As our Zen practice more and more strips us of all those preferences and things to reject — finally leaving us with what the Masters term, "The formless Self" — we experience less and less to stop for. The ultimate goal is to reach the state where we can identify ourselves as:

the individual who is a

No -thing

which embraces

EVERY THING.

That exquisitely asymmetrical *No-Thing/Every-Thing* pair is what actively calls out to the musician to call forth flute-notes from his silent flute; it is the blank paper that actively calls to the painter to give what he or she "hears" it call for, and it actively calls to the poet to answer with his or her poem.

The empty flute **speaks** *to the musician to play it;*
the blank canvas **speaks** *to the painter to paint,*
and silence **speaks** *to the poet to compose a poem.*

In this view of things, free will/Creativity — terms that one seldom, if ever, meets with in the translations of Zen texts — are entirely replaced by the openness of the artist to respond to the demand of his or her medium — be that paper, canvas, the musical instrument, speech, and song.

It's that simple.

Listen again to Zen Master Tanchu Terayama speaking about Zen brushwork:

> Modern calligraphy is rated highly if the Kanji are well proportioned and pleasing to look at. In contrast, Hitsuzendo — the school of Zen calligraphy to which I belong and that I will introduce in this book — must demonstrate calligraphy that breathes with the energy and vitality of eternal life.

It almost seems as if the Master of Zen calligraphy views his or her paper as a definite *living* Nothingness, to which the definite *living* Nothingness of the calligrapher unites.[55]

But more.

Swept up by the peculiar glory of a breezy, sunny, color-streaked day in May,

I,
Richard Burnett Carter,
old, white-haired, heart-skipping;
i,

I!!

became one with that May day's glory!

This is the great asymmetry, the impossible contradiction, Zen's Koan of Koans.

> I — in all my here-and-nowness — I was absorbed
> into this May day's glory, leaving Nothing of that
> Me behind.

This is Zen Emptiness.

This is the life-blood of ⌣.

Source

LOVE

at

FIRST

S I G H T

What, in plain, everyday English, is the *Source* of the decision made by hard-working couples to adopt unwanted children when they are barely scraping by without them? Or what is the *Source* of the decision of a woman to live the life of a Mother Teresa? Or what was the *Source* of Bodhidharma's going west to China from Japan? What gets into them?

This whole concept of *Source* is basically puzzling. Anyone, East or West, finds it difficult to grasp what the word means. But, we in the West have our homegrown difficulty in finding a clear definition of it. That is, our notion of *our* Source is that of our Creator who is forever keeping tabs on us. That Source constantly watches over us, rewarding and punishing us for our deeds. This reward-and-punishment worldview of ours provides an added reason we Westerners find the term *Source* so difficult to grasp when we meet with it in Zen texts. Darwinian dog-eat-dog, survival of the "fittest," is just another version of the reward-and-punishment worldview: being fit is its own reward, and not being fit results in its own punishment.

For Zen, the Source of everything is non-grasping and non-judging.

Even so, our ever-present, indispensable **SHOW ME!** reader might be expected to object yet further that, if our Source is *entirely* non-grasping, how we can even *know* that there even *is* a source? After all, if a non-grasping Source does not keep hold of that of which it *is* the source, then, if we start from that of which it *is* the Source, how do we get *back* to it?

Furthermore, Zen Buddhism does not embrace the doctrine of Divine Revelation as it is understood in the West, and so we can justifiably ask how we even dream that there *is* a Source if that Source doesn't "reveal" itself to us. Our present-day Western concept of the ultimate Source of all things has been deeply influenced by the two-thousand-plus-year-old teachings of our Western religions, which teach us that there is an infinite discontinuity between the Creator and His creation, a discontinuity such that if the Creator had not revealed His presence, we would not even know that there ever *was* a Creator. If we worshiped anything, it might be some man-made idol or some generalized "force of nature." Many of us in the West feel that we need revelation through sacred scriptures to know that there is a Creator-Source, let alone any of the *details* of the intentions of our Maker in creating us.

This whole matter is even further complicated for us because the teachings of our Jewish and Christian holy books anticipate (even if quite unintentionally!) that stage of Western history in which European thinkers set about to *replace* what those books of revealed religion tell us about the meaning of Creation — and, by extension, the very need for a concept of *any* Creator. These thinkers taught that the very concept of a Creator is nothing but a pre-scientific anticipation of what our astrophysics teaches about the Origin of All Things.

That replacement consisted of a purely human, rational science of everything in the universe: our modern universal science of nature. That science requires us to go, step-by-step, logically, starting *down here* (where Faith once abided), with things whose properties are known quantitatively, through measurement and weight. We are then supposed to proceed without *any* discontinuities within our rational accounts — without any "leaps of Faith" — until we reach some humanly intelligible cause that can be considered to be the origin of each and every thing we can explain using those rational accounts.[56]

This, so the European Enlightenment thinkers projected, would constitute an *exact* rational, human replacement for Divine Revelation.[57] It followed from this that the Enlightenment's "Experts" would fill in the gap left between the Creator and His Creation: the professors of anthropology, sociology, and political science subsequently became the new Prophets to the Enlightened West.

The latest, most up-to-date version of this "rational" replacement for biblical accounts of our Source is the "Big Bang Theory" of the cause of everything. (Our **SHOW ME!** friend might sensibly ask, "Before the beginning of everything in the Big Bang, what was there to explode to make that Bang?") In this theory, the source of each and every thing in the universe can be traced back to that Big Bang and, so it claims, that Big Bang completely determines each and every subsequent event — necessarily including even the scientists' *theory* of the Big Bang! (The Zen Masters would likely clap, laugh, and roll around on the ground on hearing this!)

What could *possibly* lead Zen Buddhism to notions that seem to disagree with either of these points of view?

Well, some people really do reject one life for another — because of what they *are* and not because of any outside cause. In such cases,

what "brought about" the change is WHAT the changed individual changed into;

that is, in such cases,

the Source out-sources itself and so becomes an echo of itself.[58]

To be fair, the reader must admit that this statement is no more strange than the claim that the Big Bang ultimately led to the production of astrophysicists who, themselves!, then *produced* a Big Bang *theory* that includes *both* themselves *and* their Big Bang theory! Now, *that's* a Koan for you!

In Prince Siddhartha's case, it was his princely *being*, that is, his

BEING WHAT HE WAS,

that led him to reveal in his person what a true prince *really* is. The Buddha of this historical era was a man who, although born a prince, turned his back on his birth as a royal prince of a kingdom and *spontaneously*, that is,

through merely BEING what he was!

abdicated his claim to his father's kingdom in order to be the prince of begging Shepherds — thereby manifesting what it means to be a true prince, namely

a Shepherd whose teachings can even lead princes and rich merchants to become
begging Shepherds,
(or, at least, to honor them).

In Zen's view, nothing either in his past or in any prior event in the Universe prepared Prince Siddhartha to do this.[59] Out of the spontaneous generosity of his royal heart, out of its immense *vitality*, he left the palace and its luxuries in order to lead a life of poverty and deprivation. Out of the spontaneous illumination of his mind, he devised skillful means to help others purge themselves until they, too, were prepared to act upon the unborn (and thus uncaused, and so, im-mediate) generosity of their hearts and the unborn illumination of their unborn minds.

This book concerns the *language* of Zen, not Buddhist metaphysics. Still, the central concept of "the immediate/spontaneous" is central to Zen Buddhism, and the reader conversant with Zen texts will remember that all things present to us through our sentience are said to be contingent; none are true beings that are independent of any other beings.

How, then, can there be anything *spontaneous/im-mediate/un-mediated*?

Well, we meet the term *Tathagata* in the Zen texts. This is translated as "He who has thus come." The individual who has realized his or her Buddhahood has approached what each of us is and to some extent left that flickering temporality that, although defining humanity, is still almost always hidden behind the screen of its temporal mortality. Our work is to become what we were born to become; we are Koans that include what we are not and what we *are* — namely, what we are *not*.[60]

Zen again . . .

As we have seen above, Zen Master Lin-chi speaks of that Source in this particularly striking manner:

> *When in a moment of mind you find that the place*
> *where things arise and disappear is unattainable, so that*
> *you are like an echo answering the void, unconcerned*
> *wherever you are — this is called killing your father.*

That is to say, we realize our Source *only* to the extent that we know that what we are, *now*, **was** *before* our father was born. We are then "unconcerned wherever we are"; we then have no baggage to weigh us down, *no past and no future*. Only our

NOWs!

That's what *play* really means, isn't it? Watch two children playing and ignoring their mother's call to stop, come inside, and wash their hands for supper. They are not *disobeying* her; they simply don't know what it means to leave *their* play-*nows* for their *mother's* supper-*now!*

No *thens*. No *nexts*. Both collapse into a delightful *now*. Memories are only *then*s and *next*s that clutter those

Nows!

Ryokan echoes Lin-chi's thought elegantly when he tells us,[61]

> *Walking along*
> *I followed the drifting stream to its source,*
> *but reaching the headwaters left me stunned.*
> *That's when I realized that the true source*
> *isn't a particular place you can reach.*
> *So now, wherever my staff sets down,*
> *I just play in the current's eddies and swirls.*

Ryokan stops looking; he just sits and plays. Every moment is nothing but an

(EN-JOYING-ME) now!

Play!
Glorious Play!

Indeed, one of Zazen's great undertakings is to sweep away all that clutter and thus to prepare us to play —

Unconcerned,
wherever *we are*.

"Okay, okay! Enough of your Rinzai *word*play. What I want to know is: to what does the term *Source* refer in Zen texts? Is it animal, vegetable, mineral, person, place, or thing?"

Well, neither *animal, vegetable, or mineral* precisely captures what is referred to by the texts. But, how about,

The Pregnant Now-ness?

"Huh . . .?"

Well, then, how about looking at the term *Source* as referring to something whose meaning becomes at all clear to us only if and when, "in a moment of mind," we, and any this or that *Whatever*, really face one another: then, neither of us has a past or a future:

NOW!

shared

our

Just

When this occurs, Whatever is *present* to us — is *now* to us — is without baggage, without any **ME!** being dragged along with it. (A physician's medical school training never leaves him, even after many years have passed; it is always *now* — even when he is washing dishes and has no need of his education.) As the Buddha is quoted as saying, "By that [the Void] I mean the acquisition of the noble wisdom that is personal attainment being void of all inclinations toward the faults of others."

"What does *that* mean?"

Well, for instance, see that immensely fat man wearing that pink Speedo? It's just him. He and I are in this together. As Zen Master Ikkyu reminds us:

> ***All the people passing by,***
> ***To me, just as they are!***

He and I share the same before-our-Mother-Father-were-born. Ditto with that first moment that is the stunning split second it takes to realize that you have fallen in love. Grasping the truth that each and every *whatever* also has *our* Source, really *is* like falling in (universal) love. For then, we can also say,

"You mean the world to me."

"Hitler and bin Laden too?"

Yes; Hitler and bin Laden too, but not their demented fantasies. Our own pet fantasies are what we entered into Zen practice in order to purge. The world can give nothing to such men and their ilk; dead words have deafened them to the songs contained in

the love letters
sent by the wind and the rain,
the snow and moon.

As Zen teaches — and as Islam's own splendid tradition of mystical love poets such as Rumi, Attar, and Hafiz, echo time and time again in their Sufi way — the living Source of all things can be referred to by the Chinese character for the living, caring wisdom of the beating heart of the purged human being. That character, 心, points to the heart of Pharaoh's daughter, and thus to the heart of her adopted son, Moses, the recipient of the Law given to Israel by its God; to the heart of Prince Siddhartha, who turned his back on the luxuries of an Oriental court, entered the forest where he purged himself of all that was not clear and all-embracing, and then shared his Awakening with his Friends.

What soundless music lends its time to the beat of our unborn hearts?

Well, borrowing its time from the time of that soundless music, the beat of our 心 provides the rhythms of *both* the songs of spring's lovely flowering and the cries of our blood-drenched world's victims. Among Islam's one hundred beautiful names of God are "The Shaper of Beauty" and "The All-Compassionate, the All-Merciful." Such are some of the details of what Zen also refers to by 心, *our* Source.

So, the reader who despairs of ever understanding what the term *Source* refers to in Zen might think,

Have a heart! — 心!

(Know what I mean?)

But look; see this 心? It's *my* beating, **meaning**-fountain of a heart, too. I'm here and now, and my Source is before my 心 started beating and filled with meaning, and it still will be after *my* 心 no longer beats and provides meaning.

"So . . . ? What *is* beating and providing meaning!? 'Have a heart' doesn't mean my great grandfather should be more caring. How can *his* 心 and *my* 心 be the same Source of our minding?"

Well, how can that enormous full moon be up there and also in this dewdrop here and here and here . . . and here . . . ?

It is, you know? The same moon, countless different dewdrops . . .

Can't the moon in each dewdrop echo the way that the one moon in the heavens claims everything it illuminates? Isn't this an example of our Source claiming us, whose Source it is?

Like the moon in those dewdrops, the whole heavens and its moon are present too — in *each* of those tiny drops of water.

So, another possibly useful way of considering the term *Source* when the reader meets it in a Zen context is: what claims us

as
the moon in the heavens
claims
each and every moon
in
each and every dewdrop,
and,
as the moon in each and every dewdrop
claims
that moon in the heavens.

No?

And the moon is the *meaning* of the moon in each of those dewdrops.

Listen to the Zen Master Jakashitsu's poem concerning a song sparrow:

Deep in flower's shadow
You play your mystic song.
Its message present before you make the first sound. [62]

Void & Zen

You must not be contrary to the character of the bow,
And you and your bow must become one.
When it seems as though your spirit fills heaven and earth,
You draw the bow
And the distance between arrow and target
Is filled like an empty shell. ...
(Issai Chozanshi) [63]

The teaching concerning *Shunyata*, which translates to such English terms as *void, empty, nothing,* and sometimes as *clear,* is central to Buddhism, but is difficult to grasp for many reasons.

One of these might well be that we try too hard. In The Lankavatara Sutra, we find the Buddha quoted as saying: "What is the excellent Voidness [*Shunyata*] that constitutes the noble wisdom of ultimate kind? By that I mean the acquisition of the noble wisdom that is personal attainment being void of all inclinations towards the faults of [*others'*] views."[64]

For Zen Buddhism, even so obscure a term as *Shunyata* is understood in the context of us human beings,

DOWN HERE!!

acting as Shepherds toward other human beings who can benefit from their help. Buddhism, with its "never-despising heart," is ⌣; above all, it is

open to.

Likewise the Void: what is there to despise in a Void?

That "Nothing" can be understood as, ⌣, "what refers to the Awakened individual's reality which encompasses the whole universe perfectly,"[65] whose Source, in turn, is ⌣.[66]

Among its many oddities, Zen holds that true Awakening opens us up to Everything, and thus to Nothing, in particular — or better, to Nothing, *particularly.*

Reflecting on passages such as that one in The Lankavatara Sutra, it appears that what the term *Void* refers to is something akin to this:

When I bring nothing to things, they hide nothing from me.
In the case of the Buddhist Shepherd, he is entirely
open and comes to meet, rather than to judge.
That meeting, itself, has the characteristic of
being a cleared-out openness meeting a self-revealing
thus-and-not-otherwise-ness — Tathata — the *really* apparent.

According to Zen, only by following that Way which leads through the Capital can we entertain the great world in the ten directions, that is, can we

nurture our own source — *by returning to it.*

Isn't something like this precisely what we do when we nurture our children after we ourselves have become adults who have, themselves, been matured into adulthood by *their* nurtured parents . . . ? And when we become infirm, *they* nurture *us*.

When we set about to nurture our nature, then I! (**ME!**), am more and more "**MU!**-ed," "**NOT!**-ed," and each and every thing that sentience presents to us can be met with no preference for this over that. Then, all that those things present will arrange themselves as need be, and, when this or that one requires our small help — that is, we don't eat poison mushrooms, and we attempt to neutralize the bin Ladens of this world — we give it as easily as breathing.

NO WORK!

Desire and striving are replaced by comprehending the *Whatever* in its showing the Way as it leads to itself.

To grasp the message of Zen texts, we in the West must learn NOT to view ourselves as

ALIENS

deposited in this, our *birth world*. This may well be the single most difficult obstacle we face in our attempt to understand the language of Zen.

Zen Master Dogen has this to say about Buddhism and the Void:

To study Buddhism is to study the self. To study the self
is to forget the self. To forget the self is to be enlightened
by all things. To be enlightened by all things is to
drop off our own body and mind, and to drop off the
bodies and minds of others. No trace of enlightenment
remains, and this no-trace continues endlessly.[67]

That "no-trace" is Zen's Void.

"But, about that Void: is Zen Buddhism an Eastern form of Nihilism? And, if not, why not? It certainly sounds that way."

Fair question. Look at it this way. Let's begin with **MU!** and move on to *Void*.

What does **MU!/NO!** do? (If it doesn't do *anything*, it's just a noise.)

Well, to judge from the Zen texts, that **MU!/NO!** pretty much means what a policeman refers to when a crowd gathers around someone who faints on the street:

MOVE ON!!!!

Nothing more.

Look at Zen Master Hakuin's painting of Bodhidharma, the monk who brought Zen to China:

What's it all about?

EYES!!!
LOOKING!!!
SEEING!!!!

Seeing *what*?

Just what's in front of YOUR eyes!
NOW!
NOW!
NOW!

Look; if a single note of a flute song got stuck in the flute, what a racket the next notes would make when they hit it and got hit by the notes coming after them! It would be something like one hundred flutes playing all the different notes of a piece of music at the same time.

Or, if a single glance at a live wild turkey makes you think of how good he would taste come Thanksgiving, you won't see him, because you *can't* see *both* him in his feathered glory *and* him ready-to-eat at Thanksgiving. He could be the most elegant bird in the world, but you wouldn't really "see" any of that; you'd see him headless, footless, plucked, stuffed, roasted to a golden brown, and lying on a platter. *That* image obscures the sight of that turkey, there, in front of you.

True seeing requires us to "null-and-void" anything that is not right there, in front of us. And **MU!** aims to make "null-and-void" any thing that can in the least obscure that thing there, right in front of us.

M0000VE ON!!!!

(Then, only the form you *work* in remains along with you in that emptiness you *live* in.)[68]

Ah, but Ikkyu was right! What a heartbreak this beautiful, terrible world of full moons, music, poetry, beautiful young men and women, bin Ladens, earthquakes, and tsunamis. All of them.

There!
IN FRONT
of us!

Yes! What a heartbreak!

But hearts are tough. They are broken over and over and over again, only to be mended again and again and again, and no Buddhist practitioner will murder or counsel murder to prevent that heartbreak. All schools of

Buddhism instruct us to open our hearts to be wounded by this beautiful, terrible world, over and over and over again. Its beauty both enchants and saddens us, but the vision of Prince Siddhartha's splendid royalty shared by his Friends makes it all worthwhile, a thousand times over.

Before ending this thought, it should be stressed again that, when the term, *Buddhism*, or its derivatives occur in this book, they most often refer to Zen Buddhism, the branch of Buddhism whose followers have taken the vow to follow the example set by Prince Siddhartha, the Buddha of our age. That vow has two parts.

1. To purge our Selves of our selfishness by paying constant attention to our own responses to whatever occupies our attention. The practice that has proven very useful for this over the years is variously known as Sitting, Zazen, or Meditation. Once we have come to see what is really ours because we see what we really are (this is termed *Kensho* in Japanese), then, *and only then*, are we prepared for the second stage, which is,

2. Whenever we meet with someone who can benefit from our own experience of purging — through our own experience of Kensho — we must undertake to discover whatever skillful means we have at our disposal to help them purge themselves and thus attain Kensho as well.

"Well, okay; but, *why* do individuals undertake the work of the Friends of Prince Siddhartha?"

As we have seen above, Zen Master Dogen answers as follows:

> *All Buddhas' compassion and sympathy for sentient beings are neither for their own sake or for others. It is just the nature of Buddha-Dharma. Isn't it apparent that insects and animals nurture their offspring, exhausting themselves with painful labors, yet in the end have no reward when their offspring are grown? In this way the compassion of small creatures for their offspring naturally resembles the thought of all Buddhas for sentient beings.*

"What *causes* us to become Friends of Prince Siddhartha?"

No cause. It's just the way we are. *Why* did John fall in love at first sight with Jane? Because he is what he is, and she is what she is.

PERIOD!!

Purging, the work of Zazen, leads to that primary Koan, Mind-Heart — ⌣ — which eternally fills and empties the realm embracing all things. Zen looks at our practice involving our purgation as preparation necessary for the work of the Buddhist Shepherd.

In short, the Zen Buddhist Shepherds look to the Buddha of our age as the Royal Shepherd, and they are persuaded that each and every one of us was born a true prince, that is, was born to be a shepherd to all who can benefit by our efforts to help them. So, when we hear the term *Void* in a Zen context, it might help to remember Zen Master Hakuin's painting and poem, where this character means "middle."

Zen practice in the midst of activity is a million times superior to that pursued within tranquility.

Hakuin added:

Those who practice only in silence/tranquility,
cannot establish their [internal] freedom when entering
into activity. When they engage into worldly activities,
their usual Satori (Enlightment) will eventually
disappear without any trace.[69]

That is: the Zen practice of the Shepherds must involve comprehension of

dirty, "worldly"

concerns.

Here is a set of observations that might possibly help the reader grasp something of what that practice seems to refer to in Zen usage:

Zen is not a thing; it is an activity.

Likewise,

Human life is not a thing; it Is merely one of our Source's many manifestations of its vigor.
There is no end to our Source's vigor.
Nor is there any end to human heartbreak,
nor to Zen's vigorous collecting and binding together
the pieces of our broken hearts.
There is no end to sorrow,
for,
sorrow is only a shadow cast by a mended heart illuminated by Joy.
AND,

THERE IS NO END TO JOY.

Listen to Ikkyu again:

A wonderful autumn night, fresh and bright;
Over the echo of music and drums from a distant village,
The single pure note of a shakuhachi brings a flood of tears —
Startling me from a deep, melancholy dream.[70]

Zen is realistic, and so it has an aspect of deep sadness. But, if we work long and hard enough, any sadness, however chilling, can always be warmed by Joy.

Always!!

And then we can live our lives in a constant state of

SORROWFUL

JOY.

Like

A beautiful Love Song
Played
In a
Minor **Key.**[71]

Dharma & Karma

"NOT TWO, NOT ONE."

Although the terms *Dharma* and *Karma* are by no means considered exotic by many of us, their meanings in Zen contexts are all the more in need of discussion.[72]

As used in Buddhist contexts, Dharma often refers to the teachings of the Buddha, but in other contexts, the term resonates with the expression *the Way*, as in, "It's not the Democratic Way to bow to authority." In the expression *Buddha-Dharma*, it seems to refer to ways of living and acting that are in harmony with those of the Friends of Prince Siddhartha.[73]

Another meaning of Dharma for Zen is more or less closely allied to our term *Nature*, as in "Nature vs. Convention."

For example, the Athenians called Diogenes and his school "Cynics" ("Dogs"), because they coupled with their wives in the street, and defended the practice on the grounds that sexual desire was natural; the witty Athenians laughed at them and pointed out that coupling in the street was a *dog's* way, not a *human's* way. Turning the tables on Diogenes, they remarked that for humans to act like dogs was *un*-natural.

As for the term *Karma*, we find it used in a number of contexts, both in and out of Buddhism. Its root reference, however, seems to be something akin to: *the life you were born to live.* Thus, for example, some individuals with great mathematical or musical talents are born into families of teachers or musicians, and these might be said to have "good Karma"; others, who are equally gifted in mathematics or music, are often born into dirt poor families of peasants: "bad Karma."

As a matter of fact, some individuals really *do* seem to have been born with "silver spoons in their mouths," but the political regime of a Hitler or a Stalin can jerk those spoons out pretty quickly. So, in these and like instances, *Karma* and *Dharma* are closely intertwined. Indeed, Buddhism's Zen Shepherds could be said to act from the conviction that,

**there really is no good karma in a place where the Dharma
is such
that it chokes out the promise of individuals' karma.**

Let it be said, however, that many Buddhists — both in *and* out of the Zen schools — speak of something like "karmic pre-destination." Still, the great Zen Master Ikkyu, when he announces,

Buddhas are made, not born,[74]

appears to be in general agreement with this present treatment:

Where the Dharma is inhuman, a particular human being's karma means little.

If we answer that it is just a person's "bad karma" to be born in a Stalinist regime, then Stalin becomes a sort of karmic hero, providing a place for individuals with bad karma to live it out. That's just silly.

So, *Karma*, taken alone, doesn't seem to mean that much if taken to apply to someone considered outside of a wider socio-political or historical context — that is, when we consider it apart from good or bad Dharma.

Aside from all this, Prince Siddhartha's case at first sight seems to complicate how we should understand the term *Karma* yet further. He was born heir to a throne and all that such a birth involves; his life's work, his Karma, was apparently set out for him at birth as the eldest son of his loving father, the king. However, that king's son, the Prince Siddhartha, did not choose to live the life of the heir of an Oriental monarchy. Rather, he saw that his true life's work, his *true* Karma, was to be a different *version* of what every good prince truly is: namely, one who reveals to his or her subjects what the *truly* princely, royal life involves

SERVICE.

But, in leaving his father's kingdom, Prince Siddhartha in effect announced that the Dharma of the kingdom in which he had been born as prince was not the one in which his true Karma could be realized; he had to leave and found a *Sangha* — that is, establish a congregation — whose Dharma, whose rules guiding the day-to-day practice of the establishment, nurtured his Karma and that of his Friends.[75]

It is not unlikely that Hui-neng was reflecting on something like this when he told us to identify our faces as they appeared before the birth of our parents. Zen would say that the Buddha's face was Prince Siddhartha's face before his father, the king, was born. That face is timeless — *and featureless*!

Your face and *my* face: such faces are

MASKS.

Indeed, the deity of Greek theater, Dionysus, was characteristically represented as a mask *without* a face behind it: a mask that masks nothing!

That is to say:

that mask of Dionysus hides *by presenting* that infinitely fertile

Nothing

within which all true theater is conceived.

A mask that masks no face masks nothing
and so the Mask of Dionysus
is an image hiding Nothing.

For its part, Buddhist Awakening involves seeing clearly that what is in front of us is hidden from us by the masks-personalities we wear. Above all else,

Ego Masks & Blinds & Hides.

"Hides *what*?"

The Ego-mask hides that infinitely fertile

Nothing

that our *sentience* presents to us at our birth.

Prince Siddhartha's Great Realization under the Bodhi tree some six years after he had left the palace, could fairly be considered as being a thundering echo of his first, and perhaps most astonishing, Great Realization: namely, when he saw clearly his *true* princely life's work — that is, when he realized his true Karma. And, when he had realized his true Karma, he exchanged the trappings, the persona/personality of an

ORIENTAL PRINCE,

for the

ROBES OF A BEGGAR.

Doesn't this suggest that one's Karma is a future that can be realized following differing Ways? Thus, the *Prince*, Siddhartha, was Awakened to the fact that to activate (realize) his *true* future, he had to reject his past. And so, when he died, Prince Siddhartha died a splendid death because he had chosen to live out that true Karma — that is, a future involving a life's work that was as remote from the luxury of an Oriental court as imaginable.

One of Prince Siddhartha's titles is "The Dharma King," that is, something like the Master of the environment within which his Friends could best actualize their Karma. In Zen, both *Dharma* and *Karma* refer to elements involved in the *Way* of living; they are related to one another as soil is to the sort of plant that flourishes in it:

not all varieties of flowers or vegetables flourish in the same soil.

This Prince, Siddhartha, could see that his birth as the prince-designate of his father's small kingdom failed to adequately support his *true* lifework:

**to present the very model of the authentic Prince
for all peoples everywhere,
all of whom require a life-world
where they could live out their *futures* as Awakened,
compassionate, human beings.**

His own lifework, Karma, was thus a vastly magnified version of that of the monarch of a small kingdom in Northern India.

This, in its turn, led him to see that the reach of the Dharma of those who followed him as Friends of the Awakened Shepherd should extend far beyond his father's domains. He thus elected to leave both the luxuries and the personal guarantees of food, shelter, and clothing to be found in almost any political entity, replacing all of them with the incalculably extended, hugely simplified "life-world" — the Dharma-world — of the Buddhist monk. Then, as his Friends later realized, their friendship with this

DEFECTOR-PRINCE

required them to go out into the capitals of whatever worlds they found themselves to have been born in, and try to persuade its rich and powerful administrators to define and protect laws/Dharmas — that help their subjects to come to spiritual health, and where possible, to Awakening.

Something akin to this comprises the birth story
of
the Mahayana Zen Buddhism
of
Bodhidharma's line.

So, when the Sixth Patriarch, Hui-neng, told us that we should determine clearly what we looked like before our mother and father were born, he was, whatever else, directing us to distinguish between three things:

1. The *now*s (all that comprises our "personal settings," that is, our history: family, money, gender, government under which we live and die) — our "*life*-Dharma."

2. The what-we-were-born-to-do (our particular gifts *insofar as these relate us to the world we live in*) — our *Karma*.

3. The Source — our Buddha-nature, our unborn core, our ⌣.

During the later centuries following his death, Prince Siddhartha's friends came to see that, although the Great Realization under the Bodhi tree was surely great, still, it was essentially an echo of what was, arguably, a yet-greatest Realization:

that the Prince of princes was a teacher of Shepherds.

(Again, this could be looked at as the bedrock of Zen Buddhism.)

In profound loyalty to that insight, the great Zen Master Joshu would claim:

The Great Way passes through the Capital.

But more. Rinzai Zen also includes a vision of the Dharma that is *NO*-Dharma! Zen Master Huang Po — Lin-ji's *teacher!* — tells us:

The fundamental doctrine of the Dharmas is that there are no Dharmas —

Yet, that this Dharma-doctrine of no-Dharmas is, in itself, [also] a Dharma:

And, now that the no Dharma-doctrine of the Dharma-doctrine has been transmitted,

How can the Dharma-doctrine of the Dharma-doctrine be a Dharma-doctrine?[76]

"What could this *possibly* mean?"

Well, there is a sense in which Dharma refers to the hard-and-fast *rules* of any craft. Consider the art of surgery: there is a beginning, middle, and end to what the student of surgery must master to be recognized as an authentic surgeon. When medical students have mastered *all* the materials they are required to know in order to be certified as surgeons, then, if they exactly follow the rules they have learned, then they each become a *perfect* surgeon. There is nothing more *to learn* — except, of course, what they learn as they become more and more *experienced* surgeons. Such an individual has mastered the Dharma of surgery.

But, there is a stage beyond perfection, namely,

EXCELLENCE —

that is, excelling. As Zen Master Takuan remarks in his splendid book *The Unfettered Mind*, the true swordsman must first learn, *and then transcend*, everything there is to learn about the art. It is the same with the excellent in all the crafts as it is with the excellent tennis player — Björn Borg for instance, of whom a world-class rival remarked after he had been beaten by

Borg, "I don't know what he plays, but it isn't tennis." (Borg played *excellent* tennis — tennis-beyond-tennis, tennis-no-tennis.)[77]

Rinzai Zen claims that its teachings are *outside* the scriptures. This does not in the least mean that the great Rinzai Masters were not scholars of those scriptures and teachings; rather, it means that they had thoroughly digested them and then, but *then* and *only* then,

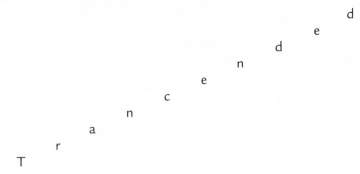

them.

In short, Mahayana Buddhism's Zen considers itself to be *excellent*, that is, *excelling* Buddhism, and it does not rest with the Dharma-teachings of other Buddhist schools. Rather, as Zen Master Hakuin insists, Kensho/Awakening (which occurs when the practitioner achieves clear and unobstructed vision of the world present to sentient beings), is *only the beginning*: next, the purged individual must connect with the world of whorehouses, crack houses, government houses, and temples, and see clearly the relationship of each of these to the others. He or she must become historical or, better perhaps, "sociological."

This, it seems, is the world of Huang-Po's Dharma–no-Dharma. It is the realm in which we find Zen's famous *Expedient Means*. These are fashioned *spontaneously* because the occasions for them cannot be prepared for, and so they are therefore excellent — beyond *any* conceivable Dharma, that is, *institutional* preparation. Thus, excellent judges practicing in wise political regimes apply the rule of *equity* when the Dharma appears to be insufficient for this or that case.

In short, for Mahayana Zen Buddhism, there seems to be *no* absolute Karma; the individual can, as did Prince Siddhartha, as it were, *un*-birth him- or herself.

So, when we hear or read the term *Dharma* in a Zen context, it might be helpful to think that Dharma refers:

most of the time,
To the ordinary,
the unexceptional;
but sometimes,
TO WHAT
SURPASSES
the merely perfect.

And, Karma,

**If you like violin music, have a perfect ear, the right fingers,
and enough money to attend The Juilliard, become a violinist —
if, that is, you don't live where violin playing is against the law.**

The historical fact that the *primal* pair, Dharma and Karma, seldom
effectively complement one another in the dismal history of empires and
states seems to manifest that terrible primordial Strife, that same

A-symmetry

we see so clearly in the case of thinking and minding or law and love —
a strife that Zen embraces as few other human institutions embrace.

The royal dimension of Zen is revealed in its willingness to follow the
Great Way until it arrives at the Capital, and then continue, only stopping
at farmers' houses to chat and, when asked, to give advice; at brothels, to
do likewise; at the mansions of the rich and powerful, to do likewise. Then,
and only then, can the Karma of the people be actualized to the extent possible for any given Friend of Prince Siddhartha.[78]

In short, the great commission of Prince Siddhartha to his Friends was
something like this:

**Labor to maximize the fit between the worlds *into which* individuals
are born, and the un-born gifts *with which* they are born, by
purifying the Dharma of those worlds.**

And, that purification of the Dharma enhances the opportunity human
beings have to actualize *their in-born gifts, both artistic and spiritual — that
is,* their Karma, their birthright.

In short:

Our Karma defines the actions that will save us from the bondage of

WORK

**because,
performing our true lifework,
our Karma,
is no work at all.
It is**

PLAY,

GLORIOUS PLAY;

but, still, make no bones about it: *finding* our Karma can be *very* hard *work!* (What if Dad is a fighter pilot, and his son wants to be the drummer in a rock band?)

All well and good; but the term Dharma also seems to refer to what we in the West consider as the realm of the laws of nature. Isn't the Buddhist understanding of Dharma only a pre-scientific version of our Western natural law theory?

There are reasons to think, "Not really."

When it is used to refer to what we consider as "natural" events, that term *Dharma* does not suggest anything *imposed* upon them. However much as European thinkers wished to replace the concept of the world around us as a creation constantly ruled by its Creator, and they seemed to have dispensed with the Creator/Ruler, to be sure, but they then replaced that Being with . . . what? Apparently with a set of Rational Commandments that apply to every activity of abstractions such as *mass, velocity, mathematical space, time,* and the like.

For its part, viewing the world in which the Dharma is to be found, we find a world in which individual things act as they do because they are what they are: that is, it is a world in which there *can* exist Zen Masters because there *do* exist individuals who both *can* and *have* mastered *themselves.* Likewise, the rising and setting of the moon and the sun are understood in terms of what the sun *is* and what the moon *is.* If the light of the full moon leads poets to sing, this is because the light of the full moon is the light of the full moon and the poets are what they are.

Prince Siddhartha became the Prince of Beggars because Prince Siddhartha was what he was, and those who learned from his *silent* example were what they were.

Under our Western analysis, we might find something like the following explanation of Prince Siddhartha's "odd"behavior:

When the Prince married, he replaced his Mother figure with his wife and this resolved his Oedipal yearning to take his Father figure's place in her bed. But, when his wife died, he had to become his Father figure to men outside his nuclear family, etc., etc. He just *had* to![79]

But Zen's view of the Dharma is not a view involving wish fulfillment![80]

Still, won't someone be likely to ask, "Okay . . . but, how is it that we experience **any** things to begin with? If they are merely just what they are, how could they also be anything **to** anything else? What's in it for oxygen to combine with hydrogen to become H_2O? Are the elements nothing but 'able-to-combine-with' sort of things? And, if so, they would not really **be** anything; they would then be entirely defined by the things they can combine with. But something has to be what it is while it is still un-combined in order to be able to combine with anything. Sure; a flower's blossom is to some extent defined by that about it which tempts insects to itself; but it is also simply a blossom. Flower lovers might like to have vases filled with flowers in their houses, but they don't want to include the honeybees with them!"

Perfect! The Zen texts seem to address this question if we take the term *Dharma* to refer to that aspect of things that permits them to be shared — that is, Dharma seems to include reference

TO THE VITAL GENEROSITY,
&
INTERRELATEDNESS,
OF THE THINGS
PRESENT
TO SENTIENT BEINGS.[81]

It's the Dharma of oxygen and hydrogen that is manifest in their combination as water; it's the Dharma of flower blossoms that is manifest in their attractiveness to honeybees *and* their loveliness to humans; it's the *Dharma* that unites us living, sentient humans to the world that gave us to itself, and itself to us in that sentience.[82]

So, perhaps it might be helpful for readers to think of the following sort of thing when they meet with the term *Dharma* in Zen texts:

The **moonshine** *of Moon;*

The **wetness** *of water;*

The "you" of "I love you"

&

the "too" of "I love you too";

....

etc., etc.

Yes?

But, still, a last word on Dharma, which to our Western ear is likely to sound so unrelentingly like, "You must behave just so, and not otherwise. Follow the straight and narrow path."

That sounds pretty boring. Anyone full of love and its ardor would reject that vision of life along with its Western no-love, no-laughter versions. Such teachings embalm; they certainly don't vivify. To our ears, there is an essentially *tyrannical, uncompromising* resonance to the term and all that is attached to it.

No?

Well, the Zen Masters speak of "*Dharma-joy!*"

"Oh? How can there be any joy in a life lived following a set of regulations that are in effect from dawn to dusk — *and* thereafter? Death would seem to be a release!"

Let's see.

When the Masters, several of whom were masterful poets, others, theater directors, and yet others, painters, speak of *Dharma-joy*, they are likely referring to our living our lives in an infinitely open emptiness in which we are entirely free to practice within the forms of our life's work — be that banker, home-maker, painter, checkout person at the supermarket, poet, policeman, musician . . . whatever.

That imperative, *Live in Emptiness, Work in Form*, refers, it seems, to a way of life where we are so freed from the chains of prejudice and other people's Ego demands that our life's work becomes a sort of high playing. As Ryokan relates,

> ... **wherever my staff sets down,**
> I just play in the current's eddies and swirls.

Indeed, even helping others whose follies have led them into very terrible thickets of confusion and pain is effortless: after all, those who are truly free do not *expect* any reward for what they do, and thus they face the needs of others without anticipating any reward. Even if their efforts don't result in any substantial improvement in those they are trying to help, they have done what they saw needed doing, and the rest is up to what the Masters refer to as "the Great Law of the Universe," to "the Dharma-Wheel" — that, for instance, manifests itself in the *too* of "I love you, too."

In short, Dharma-joy is the plum blossom in the core of each of us; all we have to do is work in form so that the eternal sun of spring can warm us. Joy then blossoms in us without effort — just by following the Dharma to Joy.

Meditation/Zazen/Sitting

Zen Master Dogen, founder of the Japanese Soto Zen branch of Zen Buddhism, said that even the most advanced practitioner should keep up Zazen. But, many of us who have been practicing Zen Sitting/Zazen for just months, or even those of us who have been practicing for years, sometimes come to a point where the practice:

1. simply bores us;

2. becomes a habit that we miss whenever we skip several days;

3. we become self-conscious — that is, we feel estranged from ourselves as we sit there like bumps on a log, doing nothing, thinking of as little as we can for as long as we are able.

We just *sit* there! Why aren't we acting like living, breathing, busy human beings who *do* something? All that talk about Sitting being good for your health sounds as if we humans were born just to act as if we were bumps on a log, as if merely *doing* things is unhealthy.

But, we humans are sociable animals and we live and thrive being around other humans — talking, fighting, loving, planning, building, tearing down. All that.

So ...?

Why Sit?

Well, to begin with, Zen Sitting does, in fact, involve actively *doing* something; namely, *actively* tearing down the barriers constructed by Ego and self that separate us from what is *really* going on in that busy world of talking, fighting, loving, and the like. However, although the Zen texts warn us against using Sitting to "figure out" things and solve problems, this is not because Zen has a negative view of thinking; rather, what it aims to do by telling us to clear our mind of thoughts and concepts is to help us *actively* reject our mental act of replacing our grasp of *this* and *this*, and *this* with concepts and thoughts — that is, with convenient groupings of individuals that blot out the *what-ness* of each of them. We tend to collect them together once and for all, and generalize.[83]

We stereotype.

Versions of the following Zen story illustrate an example of stereotyping.

> An old monk, a good and kind man, was return-
> ing to his temple from his travels when he was
> overtaken by a fierce autumn storm. A cold rain
> soon soaked him to the bone, and then a chill wind
> made his teeth chatter with the cold. He looked
> for shelter, but all he could see was one house set
> somewhat back from the road. He approached it,
> knocked on the door, and a young woman opened
> the door. When she saw the monk she said,
>
> "Venerable Monk, this is a brothel! Why are you
> knocking at the door?"
>
> "I am cold and getting sick; can you let me come
> in, warm up, and stay until I am warm and dry?"
>
> "No! It would be terrible for business and, besides,
> a holy man ought not even be in a place like this,"
> and shut the door in his face.

All well and good; but a cold, wet, old man is a cold, wet, old man, even if he is wearing a monk's robe; a warm, dry house is a warm, dry house, even if it is a brothel.

Generally speaking, monks *don't* belong in brothels; cold, wet, old men *do* belong in warm, dry houses — even if a particular one happens to be a brothel. The *concept* of a monk in a brothel might be viewed as a scandal; the need of an old, wet monk seeking shelter in the first house he comes to, even if it is a brothel, cannot properly be viewed as a scandal.

Grouping is, to be sure, useful for calculating statistics: gender gaps, age groups, tax brackets, professional interests, etc. Under certain circumstances, these can be very useful tags, but they are never useful in the search for our knowledge of ourselves and our world, because, if for no other reason, groupings only comprise useful illusions.

That's all!

The grouping-term *Asians* may be useful for calculating immigration statistics, but it can also blind us to what makes the individual from the Far East standing in front of us what he or she happens to be — just a particular human being. Denying shelter to a cold, wet monk because he is a monk illustrates this quite well.

Just because he was a holy man!
What a *prig* that prostitute was!

The monk had no problem with spending the night in a brothel; a warm, dry place to sleep is nothing more than a warm, dry place to sleep — brothel or no.

The prostitute couldn't handle it because she was

too full of

G

I

I

I

I

I

I

B

ideas

But in the real human world, there are brothels and there are temples and there are cold, wet, old men who need shelter. When we Sit properly, we are working to enter a real world that includes all these. As Zen Master Joshu reminds us,

The Great Way passes through the Capital,

and Zen Sitting, Zazen, is designed to help us find what the Masters called "the Gateless Barrier" through which we must pass in order to enter onto the Great Way to the Capital.

That Barrier is Ego, self-centeredness. If we purge ourselves of it, we will find "the never-despising heart of the Bodhisattva" as we travel along toward the Capital.

But, once again, Zen makes clear that we will certainly find *both* brothels and temples scattered all along the Great Way.

We should despise *none* of them.

This is the path, the Great Way, of Zen Buddhism, and it directs us to let wet, cold visitors spend the night:

even **monks**,
even in whore-houses.

"But... I don't know what Zen's Path is! That's one of the reasons I'm reading all this, to find out!"

It's easy. Zen's Path is simply

*where no one **ever** has to ask,*
"What's next?"

After all, it is not the *traveler* who decides what's next when he or she is on The Path; it's *The Path* that leads the traveler to what's next. That is what a path does.

Nothing else.

All we must do is follow our path. Okay?

But more. Zen Master Hakuin goes on as follows about Zen Sitting:

"When the moon reaches the summit,
Shadows disappear *from the wall."*

That is, according to Zen Master Hakuin, the goal of Zen Sitting is to have "the shadows disappear from the wall" so that the clear light can reveal everything, brothel and temple alike — and some of (but, by no means, *all* of) what that moonlight reveals is a stitch!

What's so funny?

"The idea of that old wet monk asking the girl to let him bed down in a whorehouse is hilarious; and one of its girls refusing on the grounds that it would be *improper!* is a stitch — that *she*, in *her* line of business, should undertake to instruct an old monk about *respectability*! . . . now, *that's* a stitch!"

At any rate, the terms *Meditation, Sitting, Zazen* primarily refer to our quiet *activity* of clearing out of our minds all traces of our own stereotypical concepts. To the extent that we have succeeded, the things present to us as sentient beings can then mean *themselves* to us

in all their *immediacy*!

and those meanings will replace their counterfeits — our *concepts* of them.

So, when the reader comes across any of the terms *Meditation, Sitting*, or *Zazen*, it might help to think:

No more fishing!
*The **jewel-encrusted***
HERE-AND-NOW
Fishes
gladly jump out of the water
into my frying pan.

All we have to use as bait is to keep clearing out all that "*serious*" stuff, those

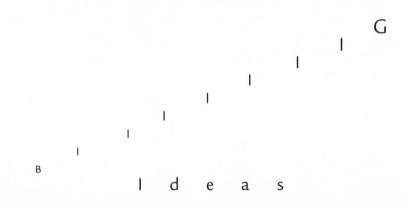

But even if Zazen is considered as nothing more than our interior house-cleaning — an *all-season* spring housecleaning! — it is still a very effective way of letting go of whatever it is we pick up during our travels along the Great Way — such as:

Dust.

CONCEPTS.

W

    O

        M

            E

                N . . . .

A Zen tale about picking up women while traveling along the Great Way:

> Two monks, one old and the other young, came to a muddy road with a lovely young woman standing and weeping at the side of it because she couldn't cross it without getting her silk gown filthy. The old monk, seeing this, scooped her up, crossed over the road, and deposited her on the other side.
>
> The two monks walked back to the monastery in silence. Finally, as they approached the temple gateway, the younger monk said:
>
> "You are a monk. You're not supposed to even touch a woman, and you ***picked her up***!"
>
> "Yes. I picked her up, but I've put her down!"

Moral:

IT'S NOT WHAT YOU PICK UP THAT MATTERS,
IT'S WHAT YOU CAN'T PUT DOWN!

So when the reader comes across any of the terms *Zazen*, *Meditation*, or *Sitting*, it might be helpful to think,

**Zen detachment doesn't refer to *not* picking up,
it refers to letting go of whatever it is that
you have *already* picked up.**

If you come across something you *know* will addict you — something you *know* you cannot put down if you pick it up — why, ***don't pick it up***!

Zazen practice is an *excellent* way of practicing how to let go — and even of practicing to learn what *not* to pick up to begin with! And this, perhaps, is one of the central reasons we in the West find Zen obscure: we expect "Sitting" and all those other Eastern practices to relax and refresh us — valued because they enable us to cope with a difficult world.

Well, Zazen is designed *precisely* to prepare us

not to cope!

That is, it is designed to

O

P

E

N

us up to the world, and absolutely ***NOT*** to enable us to cope with it. For Buddhism in general, and certainly Zen, we are not "co-dependent" on this world;

OUR BIRTH INTO IT IS NOT VIEWED AS THE BEGINNING OF PUNISHMENT!

For Buddhism, we live in this world fully **NOT** by acting like pigs, barnyard roosters, or alley cats, but by learning to read the letters sent by wind, rain, snow, and the moon.

But more.

The Zen texts say *both* that:

if we seek Awakening, we will not achieve it,

as well as

we will *not* achieve it if we do *not* seek it.

Doesn't it logically follow that we should not practice Zazen in order to achieve the Awakened state?

"But . . . but, don't we *seek* Awakening when we do Zazen? And if we never sit, will we just *trip* over it?"

This highlights a huge problem for us beginners, namely, the words of the Zen Masters are often spoken for monks who have years of practice, and often spoken to beginners.

In the Zen texts, there is

ZEN-SPEAK,

and then there is simple, everyday,

Zen-speak.

"Oh, oh! Now we're in for it!

*Secret code-messages for **those-in-the-know!**"*

Well, look at it this way. You tell your kids about the birds and the bees — without going into all of the details of what *really* happens: a scientific textbook's illustrations highlighting details of human reproduction might be seriously damaging to a seven-year-old boy. Wise parents stick to the birds-and-bees account because

what the child will find out later is *in no way*
obscured by such an account.

Many an excellent scientist's first acquaintance with the whole idea of human reproduction almost surely involved *some* version of the birds-and-bees account.

And so it is with Zazen practice: it begins with our practicing to wipe our consciousness clean of everything we have ever intentionally *or* unintentionally pasted on it. No more "All Asians are . . . ," "All white Europeans are . . . ," or other such clichés. For most of us, the first months of this practice are unpleasant, hard humiliating work; only the ardor of our ‿ keeps us going, and many of us feel that we are just too busy to continue. We feel we just *have* to occupy ourselves with pumping up our Egos so that we will continue to think that we appear ten feet taller to *other* people than we appear to ourselves.

But not all of us. Some of us are just so tired of our swarm of **ME!**s that we stick with it. Bored, tired of the whole business, and humiliated by it as we feel, we may stop our practice for a while; but we find that we are sick and tired of our swarm of those **ME!**s which, oddly enough, seem to have gained in number and offensiveness during the period in which we didn't practice!

So, we start again, but, at each stop-and-start episode, we find that we feel less and less tired and humiliated, and, after a while,

VOILA!!!

We actually feel refreshed after kicking those damned **ME!**s around.

But then, sometimes after a long spell of this stopping-and-starting, we see clearly why the Masters say in their Zen-speak that we must neither try for Awakening nor *not*-try for it.

For then . . . well, there is a story told about Hakuin that, when he met a gang of sword-carrying tough guys who said they were going to cut him open to find "that-there *heart*" Zen priests are jabbering about all the time, he more or less answered,

Cut away;
***But you will no more likely find my heart** that way,*
Than you would find cherry blossoms
When you cut open the branch of a cherry tree in January.[84]

The tough guys ran away. Hakuin was too strange.

"The point of your story being . . . ?"

That, since Awakening is nothing the practitioner *reaches*, it is therefore nothing to be *reached for*. Being fully Awakened is *in* us as the cherry blossom is in the branch of the cherry tree. (After all, at the end of *every* pilgrimage the true pilgrim finds him- or herself.)

So, for Zen practitioners, Awakening takes place in a sort of not-*now* that is like *just before* the first little sign of a bud at the end of a cherry twig; it grows, assumes new sizes and shapes, and, at last, opens to reveal the lovely cherry blossom —

That was

NEVER

NOT

in that twig.

Ikkyu's Joy in those blossoms at Hell's Gate; our sorrow as we view that terrible Gate; all that: these are in

OUR BEING ALWAYS IN OUR **NOW**!

in the way the cherry blossom is a is-not-*now* "in" the Winter branch of the cherry tree. It's like in the magic shows,

NOW

You don't see it,

NOW

YOU DO!

True Zen Sitting leads to that **NOW** that is *neither* what-was *nor* what-will-be, and Awakening forever lurks in that

a-t e m p o r a l

NOW

exactly as the cherry blossom lurks in the twig during the biting cold of January.

(Zen again . . .)

Oh! One last word on Zazen.

Whatever else Zazen is good for, it helps us learn how to

KEEP OUR MINDS ON WHAT WE'RE DOING!!

Subject/Object

As the Chinese founder of Soto Zen counsels us,

If you use your ears to listen, you'll never understand —
Only when you hear in your eyes will you know.[85]

As an Iranian Sufi counsels us,

... *not [do not]* to apprehend the world as an object or an idea, but as an unveiling. Not to see the world as an object, is also not to represent it as something out there, laid out in front of us, but to discover it as something opening spontaneously, suddenly before us, like the unveiling within ourselves of a flower in blossom.[86]

We read time and time again in Zen texts that distinguishing between subject and object obscures reality from us. But what's so objectionable about distinguishing between subject and object? Not only do we learn subjects in school, we also see objects all around us. The *subject* of a sentence, what it's *about*, it's what you had in mind before you said it — or, in many cases, before you were even conscious of it. When words don't just "pop out of our mouths," the *object* of speaking them is to make known to someone else what the *subject* of the sentence means to you who say it. So, the sentence's *subject* is its meaning to the speaker; its *object* is to share what the speaker had in mind before he or she uttered or wrote the sentence. (We lie when we wish *not* to share what we had in mind before we utter or write the sentence.) All of this seems so simple and straightforward that Zen's rejection of the distinction between subject and object might very well present a real problem for anyone interested in learning more about it.

But ... you know? We often say that this or that *"means"* something to us — as if the *this* or the *that* had an *object* in merely being what it is — namely, its object is *to*

Mean-itself-*to*-us.

Thus, to take an instance of this, some animals scent their territories to let other animals know to keep away or, in some cases, to tell them to keep on coming; the scent itself *means* something to the animals who smell it — and that's why it was deposited. That scent is a

CALLING CARD

and calling cards are presented to *actively* announce a presence; such calling cards *actively* mean something. The animal who smells a scent knows what it means — the animal doesn't make up what it means; if it did, then it wouldn't be effective.

Likewise, when we say, "But *that* means . . . !" it isn't *we* who mean something; it's the "that."

Doesn't this provide at least some grounds for thinking that at least one of the things that "things" do is

**actively *mean* themselves to someone,
JUST IN MERELY BEING WHAT THEY ARE ?**

A story illustrating this: I once knew a very reserved, frosty psychiatrist whom I had never seen smiling or heard laughing. On one occasion I was invited to dinner at his house and, while I was eating, his fat, ill-tempered cat jumped up onto my lap from under the table. I reached down to pet her and she bit me. Hard! I yelped and roughly pushed the beast from my lap with one hand while I licked the other hand to stop the bleeding. The only expression of sympathy I got from my host was that I shouldn't have upset the cat.

Psychiatrist and cat made a perfect pair. He was gloomy and his cat was ill-tempered.

One day several months afterward, he telephoned me out of the blue and asked me if I would go to the zoo with him. I had never particularly enjoyed his company, but I was so astonished that I said yes. He knew I loved animals, and when we got to the zoo he burbled about how interesting and beautiful animals were. (In light of his pet cat, this particularly amazed me.) Then he told me:

HE WAS
HEAD
OVER
HEELS,

T
  O
     P
S
Y-

T

   U R

  V
Y

IN

      V

O
  E!!!

     L

"She means the world to me. She is beautiful. She is everything any woman ever was to any man."

For the first time in his fifty-plus years, the world meant something to him, namely,

Itself!
And
it meant itself
TO HIM!

And so he carried on and on, smiling and laughing, and was never anything but delightfully lighthearted.

It was a very pleasant afternoon.

That expression *She means the world to me* can be accurately recast as *Because of her, the world she inhabits means itself to me*. It has meaning, and that meaning is addressed *to* me!

To **ME!**

This doesn't mean that the world was merely "full" of meaning for him because of her; rather, he now took *his* meaning from the *world's* meaning, and he was filled with the joy of his having the world mean himself to him.

That gloomy psychiatrist had really changed. Before her, the dead and uninteresting world was just

There. . . .
DEAD AND UNINTERESTING.

It had only been something he had to be careful not to bump into. Things that he had hardly even noticed in the past now existed actively and "made him happy," or, if the reader will pardon the strange grammar,

*They **in-Joyed** themselves in-to him.*

It wasn't so much that he enjoyed them as it was that *they in-joyed him.* Literally!

He was realized

within
their Joy.

And just what did those formerly mute and meaningless objects mean when he fell in love?

They meant *himself* to him! The world was alive with itself, and now he was alive with *its* life.

He could join Zen Master Ikkyu and, for the first time in his life, read

**. . . the love letters sent by the wind and rain,
the snow and moon.**

Or, as Zen Master Dogen has it:

*When you see forms or hear sounds fully engaging
body and mind,*

You grasp things directly.

Now! At long last! He was finally alive — *alive with the meaning of his world.* He became the world's intention in a way similar to the way a long-awaited child is the intention of its parents. Sometimes, a child is said to be a mistake. Before the psychiatrist fell in love, he felt as if he were a mistake in the nature of things.

Well, I saw him several months later and he was his old gloomy, frosty self.

HE HAD

F

A

L

L

E

N

OUT

OF LOVE . . .

The world stopped meaning himself to him. She had brought it about that the world meant himself to him, but now that she was no longer in his life, his world stopped meaning him:

It had no meaning that was <u>also</u> *HIM*.

It was just

THERE:

THE WHOLE WALLFLOWER UNIVERSE.
THE HOMELY GIRL NO ONE WANTS TO DANCE WITH;
THE SKINNY BOY WITH THE BAD SKIN.

He was no longer that in-love him. After her, he was just another psychiatrist, alone with an ill-tempered cat — both of whom were *full of* objections to the world around them rather than *filled by* and *realized in* its meaning. Psychiatrist and cat were once again subjects of their inner demons that ruled over them as tyrannical kings rule over their subjects.

Isn't this a good reason for Zen to object to the subject-object distinction? That is, if we manage to get rid of our habit of making distinctions between subject and object, then it's like being in love all the time. It's like having the world mean *ourselves* to us without ceasing. Think of what the Broadway musicals try to do:

MEAN THE AUDIENCE TO ITSELF

If it *doesn't* succeed in this, it soon closes.

So, when we meet with passages in the Zen writings that urge us to work with all our might to overcome our sense of the subject-object duality, it might be helpful to think,

AH! HOW GOOD OF THE WORLD
AND ALL THAT IS IN IT
TO MEAN ITSELF TO ME —
TO
ME!

When that happens, what had appeared as objects surrounding us are no longer "out there." I now know they are there because they **tell** themselves to me.

And, if this sounds too fancy, think: mustn't scientific researchers work to jockey themselves and what they study until they have no secrets from one another? All those scientists who are caught fraudulently reporting results are really just being *unfaithful* to their material —

PRECISELY AS WHEN WE ARE UNFAITHFUL TO SOMEONE WE LOVE!

So, it might be useful when we come across Zen arguments against the *subject-object* distinction, to remember that cats and dogs "naturally" *object* to one another, don't they? That is, they look at one another as objects — for cats, dogs being *objects to avoid*, and for dogs, cats being *objects to chase* — until, that is, they become like the psychiatrist and his girlfriend and fall in love with each other.

Just *look* at what happens then!

Ah! But we who feel such sorrow at this world's madness and its diseases perhaps are just as sorrowful, or even more so, when we have grown up. But we are still astonished by beautiful young men and women as they laugh in their thrill at being so young and lovely; by those late winter insinuations of a spring — soon to come, but now feeling infinitely remote; by the loveliness of the perfect day as it draws to its close; by our sorrowing wonder as we finish reading a splendid book, knowing its author is long dead and so shall we never meet him or her.

You.
I.
We.
Sun-faced Buddhas, Moon-faced Buddhas all.

We, the

NOWS!

in Eternity.

We the

PLOPS!

in the old pond.

For Zen, there are no nouns;
only stop-frames catching
ACTIVITY
&
FLOW.

Or, as Heraclitus tells us,

> *All things flow onwards, nothing lingers.*

> (τα παντα ρει και ουδεν μενει)

In the particularity of our existence, we are all to some extent forever estranged from the things we most love. Here *we* are, and here *they* are, clasping us in the infinitely intimate embrace of their very presence to us as sentient beings; still, although our meaning is inextricably intertwined with theirs, they are in some ways inaccessible to us. Our hearts should break, but they are held together by the bands of our tuneful laughter, in our longing, by our delight at the very gift of being humans who can both wonder and sorrow together.

Longing's sugar lends its sweetness to suffering and reduces it to sorrow. And those whose suffering cannot be sweetened by that sugar are the monsters of history — the bin Ladens; the Hitlers; the Stalins. ... They are vandals who destroy what is beautiful — to avoid their bitter sorrow in comprehending it, and thus to avoid their being comprehended *by* it.

The catalog list of these vandals' names goes on and on without end.

WHAT dwarfish cowards **THEY ARE!**

But, no murder for those who follow Zen's practice. Rather, they follow Ikkyu and "read the love letters sent by the wind and rain, the snow and moon."

Or, as one contemporary love-besotted Zen writer has it,

Look!

P

u

u

u

u

U

THERE!

At that **moon,**

drifting through the radiant Autumn skies,
feeding itself on the longing of lovers.[87]

The Fox

Perpetual movement!
Endless change!
You are all that is left to be enlightened about.
Ah, ten years of study — all for nothing.[88]

The reader who has gotten this far may think that some of what Zen seems to offer is really preferable to the fare listed on the spiritual menus of two of the West's principal watering holes. The one seems to offer what is, in effect, only different versions of the following fare:

He sees you when you're sleeping,
he sees you when you're awake
He sees you when you're good or bad

SO BE GOOD FOR GOODNESS SAKE!

And the other offers gems such as:

> The modern gentleman may prefer blondes. But new research has found that it was cavemen who were the first to be lured by flaxen locks. According to the study, north European women evolved blonde hair and blue eyes at the end of the Ice Age to make them stand out from their rivals at a time of fierce competition for scarce males. The study argues that blond hair originated in the region because of food shortages 10,000–11,000 years ago. Until then, humans had the dark brown hair and dark eyes that still dominate in the rest of the world. Almost the only sustenance in northern Europe came from roaming herds of mammoths, reindeer, bison and horses. Finding them required

long, arduous hunting trips in which numerous males died, leading to a high ratio of surviving women to men. Lighter hair colors, which started as rare mutations, became popular for breeding and numbers increased dramatically, according to the research, published under the aegis of the University of St. Andrews.[89]

"Sure; but Zen, for all its talk about the Capital and its worldly-wise Way leading to it, is detached from this world. The world of Zen is . . . well,

UN-REAL!!!

"It's just as unrealistic as those products of something like extreme sensory isolation, writing from St. Andrews about blondes. How can I live as a tax-paying, nine-to-five worker with a mortgage, kids, insurance, and medical bills to pay . . . all that, and *also* take Zen, Zazen, and that talk about seriously playing around? How's this Zen so different from Timothy Leary's advice to

turn

on,

tune

in,

d

r

o

p

out?

"I don't do drugs and, except for weddings and New Year's Eve, I don't usually drink too much. And, still; I don't see *any* of those plum blossoms, peach blossoms lining the path to

MY HELL.

"Eh?"

How to answer soberly . . . ?

Well, to begin, Zen Master Ikkyu's Hell gate was no less infernal than ours. The civil wars that took place when he was nearing eighty slaughtered thousands and burned down his beloved Kyoto — including the beautiful temples, among them the one to which he had belonged. After the civil wars, he collected funds to rebuild his temple and he oversaw its construction while he suffered from bouts of severe diarrhea. Still, he found blossoms at that gate — in part, at least, *because* he had spent his last years rebuilding what the folly of others had led them to destroy.

How did he manage to do this?

Hard to say, but there is a very strange Zen Koan known as Hyakujo's Fox that might shed some light on an answer.

This Koan relates that a monk who was cursed to live in the body of a fox for many lifetimes because, when he had been the Master of a monastery, a monk had asked him, "Does the Awakened man **fall under the yoke of** causation or not?" and he had answered "No."

Well, he asked Zen Master Hyakujo the same question, and was answered, "The Awakened individual does not **ignore** causation." The monk was immediately awakened and was released from further punishment.

Our reader might well be expected to respond with,

> **Of *course* I am forced to "fall under" the
> laws of cause and effect. *If* I don't pay my income
> taxes and get caught, *then* I will "fall under the yoke of
> causation" and the judge will cause me to go to jail.
> Isn't that *cause* and effect at work?**

Of *course*! Pay your income taxes. But, maybe the *real* reason for you to pay your taxes is *not* to keep out of jail. They are YOUR taxes. Dr. Leary's advice to drop out was another way of saying, "The with-it don't fall under laws of cause and effect."

Well, Dr. Leary was the Peter Pan who never grew up. Not the Zen Masters. His mind-altering drugs only prepared the taker to live in Never Never Land where you don't even *have* a life; those drugs take you out of

the life-world
that
gave you
to
itself!

AND

itself

to

you.

So, exactly *what* have the druggies dropped *out* of?

"My stinking *old* life! That's what . . . *to get* a **new life!** *Get It?*"

But, *that* new life isn't the life that gave you to it and it to you. It's a sort of *counterfeit* of living, and that makes those drop-outs

Z

O

M

B

I

E

S!

But look: this book concerns Zen's *language*; it isn't written to get people to stop doing drugs. It's written for those of us who *know* we have a real life, but still have a deep and abiding sense that something is missing about it, namely, we aren't

In-Joyed

by our real life. It's **real**, all right, but we feel that the reality of our real lives

isn't really *our* reality!

It's only an

OUT
THERE

reality.

What might Zen say to us?

Probably that, if our world doesn't *belong* to us, that's because we feel we don't *belong* to it. If we *crave* this or that, rather than really and truly *seeing* it, we feel that we don't really belong to the things of this world. And, if we don't let *our* world speak to us, it will flee us, and leave us with our endless, restless hunger.

"Well, maybe . . . but what about that Zen saying that claims that before we begin Zen practice, a tree's just a tree, a mountain's just a mountain; when we get into it, trees are no longer trees and mountains are no longer mountains; BUT, when we Awaken, trees are just trees again, and mountains are just mountains again. Eh? What about that? Even if I've gone far enough to be Awakened, I'll still be in the same world — and that same world is certainly the world of cause and effect, cigarettes, cancer, war, and all that. No?"

Yes . . . "and all that."

Still, Ikkyu's song comes to haunt us:

at the very gate of Hell, plum blossoms, peach blossoms.

Those blossoms weren't there *before* we returned to this world where mountains are just mountains and trees are just trees; at least, we didn't *see* them if they *were* there.

"So . . . ? What's going on? What's changed?"

Yeah. What *has* changed?

Well, *What* is one of the oddities in the Zen experience is that the very *world* of Zen:

IS THE SAME CRAZY WORLD,

but now, there are

Plum Blossoms, Peach Blossoms,

Even leading to

the gate of Hell.

It really *is* a different world, but with *all* the same things in it; only Zen helps us to *be in* this world *as our own*, in this world that gave us to itself, and itself to us. When we can observe the world in this way, then,

I *HAVE* to do it!

is transformed into,

I *HAVE* it to *DO*.

I do it be-*cause* it's *mine to do*! Causation has been transformed into real-i-zation.

To the extent that there is a fundamental dualism for Zen in the world as we experience it, it would seem to be between

THIS world before we began our Zen practice,

and

THIS *same* world
After we have achieved our Awakening!

"I still don't get it. How can the same world with the same things in it be different? Are we talking about science fiction's *parallel universes* here?"

No! Parallel lines, universes . . . whatever . . . never *meet*! What we are talking about here are two worlds never *separate*, so how could they be parallel?

"What? How can there be *two* worlds that are never *separate*?"

Well, look at the story of the two monks, one young and the other old. They come across the *same* beautiful young woman dressed in silk, weeping at the side of a muddy road because she can't cross without spoiling her gown. The old man scoops her up, crosses over, and puts her down. The two monks continue on back to the monastery.

Just as they arrive, the younger says, "You're a monk. We aren't supposed to touch a woman, and you had that one in your arms."

"Yes. And I put her down —

back there."

Well, let's compare the worlds of the same two monks, and the same lovely girl.

OLD MONK	YOUNG MONK
"That *poor* lovely young thing! All dressed up and afraid to cross the muddy road because she'll get dirty. *'Here! Upsy-daisy! Okay. Now, down you go. That's it. Glad to be able to help.'* Hmm. It's getting cloudy. Hope we get back to the monastery before the storm breaks!"	She looks so good. but I'm a monk. I'm not supposed to even get near her, and here I am watching him with her in his arms. ***Damn!*** I'll be dreaming about her for the next month. Damn! Why did he pick her up? I don't care if she gets her silken gown all muddy! Do I? ***Damn!***

**EXACT SAME BEAUTIFUL YOUNG WOMAN
THE SAME TWO MONKS.
BUT
BUT
BUT
but
but**

. . . .
. . . .

**Same girl.
Same world.**

No . . . ?

"Well . . . Yes *and* no. But about that cause and effect?"

Oh, yeah; the beautiful young woman the old monk picked up?

"What about her?"

She didn't cause anything as far as the **old** monk was concerned. But that poor young monk?

**SHE MAAADE HIM WANT HER.
HE DIDN'T WANNA DO IT!
HE DIDN'T WANNA DO IT!
SHE MAAADE HIM WANT HER**

. . . and she didn't even know *he* existed!

Poor man! He'd better sit down, breathe slowly and deeply until he

GETS A LIFE!

No?

Both Bull and Self transcended.[90]

That Zen symbol ⭘, to what does it refer in Zen calligraphy, or on the wall hangings we see in walls of Zen temples?

The Star of David, ✡,

the cross, †,

the star and crescent ☪;

these refer to three "life-worlds," worlds that, in certain ways, are essentially different from one another . . .

"I don't get it. All humans in possession of their five senses live in the same world. How can there be *different* 'life-worlds'? What would that mean? The same birds, the same sun and moon . . . All those. What's so different in them?"

Ah! But remember:

OLD MONK	YOUNG MONK
"That poor lovely young thing . . ."	**"Damn!** *SHE'S GORGEOUS! AND, SHE SMELLS SO GOOD.* **DAMN!** *. . ."*

And, remember this?

> *A futures trader in, say, hog-bellies, walking to his car*
> *and thinking about his last bid, might answer a secretary*
> *in his office who says, "Mr. Jones! Look at that moon!"*
> *with, "Yeah. Nice. Did you finish typing tomorrow. . . ."*

He didn't even really see that moon! That moon doesn't exist for him. He was preoccupied with hog bellies, and this left no room for **moonshine.**

The secretary's life-world includes wonderful full moons; the futures trader's life-world includes no such thing — only

> *"something sometimes shiny up there after the sun goes down."*

The life-world in which that old monk *saw* the girl was not the same life-world the young monk lived in; the old monk lived in a world containing "damsels in distress"; the young monk lived in a world of desirable young females who he might have to hold in his arms.

"Okay; maybe those life-worlds referred to by
the Zen circle, ◯
   the Star of David, ✡,
     the cross, †,
and the star and crescent ☾ are really, *really* different from one another in many ways. But, still; aren't there numbers of Jews, Christians, and Muslims who would see the same young woman as the old monk, and the same full moon as the secretary? You don't mean to claim that *only* Zen practitioners live in that world? It's not likely the secretary to that futures trader lives in a Zen temple after office hours."

True! But, once again,

Zen **is not** *a religion!*

It is

A WAY,
A PRACTICE,

that *anyone* can choose to follow. And, there have been countless men and women over the ages who have followed *their* different ways along *their* pilgrim routes and who have arrived at

THEIR UNBORN, UNDYING SELF.

Seen in this light, it seems that the vital, living, empty!, world referred to by ◯ is what the Zen Masters consider as that world in which "things" don't *strike* the Zen practitioners' senses but, rather, they announce their presence by

$$G$$
$$N$$
$$I$$
$$L$$
$$B$$
$$B$$
$$u$$
$$B$$

up in them.

As such, they are a sort of calling card,

ANNOUNCING THE PRESENCE

OF

WHATEVER

TO

WHOEVER

IS

WIDE

AWAKE!

These cards announce the presence of birds, cats, clouds, and everything else embraced by what the Zen symbol, ◐, refers to.

Isn't the FORM of that image ◐ a perfect expression of the union of

E   m   p

t   i   n   e   s

s

and

FORM

?

"Well, I think I understand what it means to work in Form; but *live in Emptiness* sounds like a sentence to life in solitary confinement."

Not at all! Remember just what Shakuhachi Master Fuyo Hisamatsu says about it:

> *A good player of shakuhachi is one who makes*
> *the bamboo shaft alive. A master naturally and*
> *effortlessly brings forth something inconceivable.*
> *However, without study it is impossible to enter the*
> *boundaries of mastery.*
>
> *You become the bamboo. The bamboo becomes you. A*
> *master lives in emptiness while working in form. . . .*[91]

Hisamatsu insists that, "without study it is impossible to enter the boundaries of mastery."

It is those "boundaries of mastery,"
and ONLY those "boundaries of mastery"

that make it possible for us to live in Emptiness. (Reaching Zen's goal is hard work — no less than ballet.)

In the course of perfecting whatever particular undertaking defines our life's work, we submit to the limits that those "boundaries of mastery" impose upon us, and it is precisely *those* boundaries that define that Emptiness in which we live and work.

Just go to the supermarket and watch the checkout personnel. Some are sullen and obviously discontented with their work; their lives are cluttered with things they just "*gotta* do"; when they are at work, they are wishing they were elsewhere; when they are elsewhere, they are dreading going back to work. Others are cheerful and are completely "into" their work. When they are done for the day and go home, they don't have to give work a moment's thought.

Only those of us whose work "has" us have no work to do —

because, as the reader may remember from high school science classes, *work* is defined as

"EFFORT DIRECTED TOWARD OVERCOMING AN OBSTACLE."
No obstacles in Emptiness.
So,
No work in Emptiness.

As the Shakuhachi Master continues on to say,

> *A master naturally and **effortlessly** brings forth*
> *something inconceivable.*

No effort required in that Empty realm, and thus *no work* — although anything can come to seem like work when we become physically tired! (But, after all, we're only fragile humans.)

Whatever else it may signify, the Zen symbol

refers to those humans living in that realm of the emptiness embracing all those forms in which everything proceeds to function — including even those forms of folly in which so many of us live and work. That ◯ reveals the strength of our Zen.

"But, isn't that just another version of the Taoist, yin-yang circle ☯? So, why not use the Taoist yin-yang circle?"

Well, perhaps it's *too* perfectly circular and symmetrical to express Zen. The Zen Masters often paint the Zen Enso roughly! For example:

"Well . . . okay, so why do the Zen painters, who are *very* good!, seem to be sloppy sometimes when they draw their Zen circle? You'd think that then, of *all* times, they would show their skill, but often they don't. In many instances, a Master seems to be trying to outdo other Masters in his crude painting of the circle. What's going on? You never see the Taoist yin-yang circle drawn any way but perfectly round and symmetrical."

Good! *Very* good. "" is the symbol of the world that is, somehow or other, ultimately self-contained. Sure, there are myriad contradictions in it, but the symbolizes a world in which all these can be composed into a unified whole

WITHIN

A

PERFECT

CIRCLE.

But Zen doesn't view things that way. For Zen — and especially the Zen of Bodhidharma's line! —

is *both* the source of the world of moonlight and roses, *and* the world in which that beautiful moon is captured within the dewdrop on the mercilessly sharp beak of that great night hunter, the crane. It is Zen Master Ikkyu's world of Hell's gate framed within the blossoms of plum trees and peach trees. And *that* terrible world can best be symbolized by Zen's rough, crude Enso. By

not by

 captures the immensely asymmetrical character of the endless productions of , and it could be seen as being painted in that way as a reminder to Zen practitioners that their life's work is to labor *endlessly* to do what cannot be done.

Redeem the primal transgression of *'s unity*
as it
out-sources
itself.

Zen would lighten this dark sentiment somewhat by reminding us that,

when you are really *into* your life's work,
it's not work,
After all,
a master musician doesn't
work
the instrument.
He or she uses it to
Play the music!

In short, as Zen Master Tanaka reminds us:

The so-called "One Round Shape" (Ichi-enso),

,

that is the eighth stage of "Drawings of Ten Bulls,"
means "forgetting both the bull (Buddha-nature)
and self" and the shape refers to ultimate reality
that encompasses the whole universe perfectly.

The rough way of painting of Enso is not so
important.

In the vital power of writing we can recognize the
"True Man without any rank."

Or:

In original nature
There is no this and that.
The Great Round Mirror
Has no likes or dislikes.

(Zen Master Seung Sahn)

So, the Masters tell us to forget all about Buddha-nature and Self.

But, although our **SHOW ME!** overseer might fairly be expected to be unhappy with this whole section devoted to the Zen symbol ◯, still, it has been used to identify its peculiarity by the Zen community for more than a thousand years. So it seems appropriate to examine it closely to help the reader get a clearer sense of that peculiarity — and thus get a better sense of Zen's odd approach to things.

To begin with, that ◯ obviously resembles a full moon, and the Zen Masters often refer to the full moon as the Illumination that occurs in Awakening.

Why?

Well, perhaps because the full moon's gentle light illuminates without burning:

Zen's Compassion!

Furthermore, the *absolutely unique* aspect of Zen's view of that symbol, painted in a style known as *Zenga*, is this:

given any example of the ◯, it makes absolutely no sense unless it has been painted
by

A ZEN PRACTITIONER!
NONE!

"Why?"

Because this Zenga style of painting, including paintings of ◯, has one and only one aim:

to reveal the living truth of Zen as each painter thrives within it.

In short:

each and every example of Zen painting was painted
to reveal the extent to which the eye of its painter is
the unborn eye of his or her original face:

the very essence of Zen.

The Language of Zen

Speech and silence — absolutely the same:
Extremely subtle and profound.
(Zen Master Dogen)[92]

The secret of the receptive must be sought in stillness.
(Sun Bu-er)[93]

Parents tend to be more careful about what their little ones put into their mouths and swallow than what they take in through their ears. But although today's strained spinach will leave no trace of its former presence years from now, hateful angry words can burrow into the child's living substance, occupy it, and fester there for years. Indeed, I knew a middle-aged psychiatrist, a fine and generous person, who had immigrated to America as a young man from Germany just after the war; when he was twelve years old, he had been enlisted by his parents into a Nazi Youth camp during the year the war ended. He confided in me that he was nightly haunted, even forty years later, by the words he had listened to during that year.

The Zen Master Bassui (1327–1387) speaks eloquently and at length about the difference between "living" words and "dead" words in his book *Mud and Water*. Dead words make it difficult for us to entertain anything except our hard and fast ideas concerning what is desirable or not where we are concerned. This creates an opaque screen of theories and prejudices. This screen, in turn, makes it extremely difficult for us to recognize that the world of which we are aware as sentient beings is the same world that originally included us within itself when we were born into it.[94] Then, instead of the clear, bright presence of that vital world, we are forced to entertain nothing but the flickering forms of our fantasies.

But our living, receptive core always remains ardent, endlessly seeking to perceive clearly and without any hindrance what our sentience presents to us living human beings. Words aimed at helping us as we seek to see the living world are what Bassui refers to as *living* words.

This view of words can be said to begin with the Buddha himself.

The man we now know as *the Buddha* was born a prince some 2,500 years ago. He was named *Siddhartha Gautama*. The details of his story relate that, having been raised in the lap of luxury, married, and having become a father, he came upon an old man, a sick man, a corpse, and an ascetic. His response? He left the palace grounds, went into the forest and practiced terrible austerities for six years under the guidance of ascetics — to subject himself to the agonizing task of opening himself up to the receptivity of his ardent core. This early-middle-aged prince, a husband and the father of a young son, left his father's kingdom and, when he had succeeded in recapturing that original, all-embracing receptivity that is the birthright of all sentient beings, he realized that it was his mission to encourage us to follow his example. Those who have attempted to follow Prince Siddhartha are known as *Buddhists*.

And those austerities, what led him to undergo them? The records in no way suggest that he did so to recover from an addiction to sex, drugs, or any of the pleasures readily at hand at his father's court. Then why his rejection of his life as a prince?

It is not unlikely that when the prince saw the old man, the sick man, the corpse, and the ascetic, *he simply did not know what to make of them*. He saw them, but saw that he didn't really *see* them. He was unable to entertain their existence as being as authentic to him as was his own; he was unable to *view* them as true members of his kingdom, and this alerted him to his failure to realize in his person a true prince's essential definition. Many of us would likely have shrugged off his experiences of these four, but, in him, seeing them aroused his wonder.

Wonder lies at the heart of Zen Buddhism — and what is wonder other than our spontaneous human response upon being presented with two events, each of which we see clearly, but that we also clearly see cannot exist together? There these men were: old man; sick man; dead man; ascetic. They were *there*, in front of him — all of them subjects in his father's kingdom which also included ceremonial elephants with gold-tipped tusks, white stallions with jeweled saddles, silk coverings for his bed, and scented, warmed waters for his baths. All these he doubtlessly knew what to make of: they were his to enjoy. But sick men? Old men? Dead men? Ascetics? It seems that these were foreign to him, that they made no *sense* to him.

He saw that he didn't see them.
That is,
He saw his *not*-seeing.

At least a possible setting which might make sense of this is that, rather than shrugging all this unpleasantness off, he wondered at his seeing of **not**-seeing, and that it was his *wonder* that led this Prince Siddhartha to spend the next six years cultivating himself to prepare himself to see both seeing and not-seeing.

When he had succeeded in his quest, he realized the splendor of clear and unobstructed sight in sentient beings *as* sentient, and his message was that we, too, should undertake to cultivate ourselves until we become open to the world that presents itself to us as *sentient* beings. When we have succeeded in this enterprise, then each of us can realize that clear and un-obstructed seeing of our world's wonders. That "clear and un-obstructed seeing of our world's wonders" is Zen Buddhist Enlightenment, which claims that *only* when we are Awakened in this way can we can be truly active participants within that world given us through our sentience.

One of the central goals of the Zen Buddhism discussed in this book is to really *sense* the world as it presents itself to us, and thus to be part of it — or, better perhaps, to be truly included *within* it.

But the drama of that story is perplexing. What sort of man was this Prince Siddhartha, who, when faced with these "alien" individuals, freely elected to leave his palace and all that it had to offer? Was he the less princely in turning his back on his kingdom when he realized there were individuals in it for whom he, the kingdom's prince, could not account? If so, why would that shake him so deeply?

As we have remarked, upon looking into himself when he realized that he, the prince, *could not make sense of these four individuals*, this man, Siddhartha, saw that in order to *be* a true prince, he must recognize and care for *all* his people.

Unless stated otherwise, the expression *Zen Buddhism* in this book has referred to that branch of Buddhism that holds that the Buddha of our age was a true prince. This means that his followers' practice requires that they too recognize and care for all sentient beings who can benefit by their care — and, as Bodhidharma pointed out to us, that Buddhism is vastly empty, nothing holy!

This man, Prince Siddhartha, saw that, whatever his birth, he was only a man, and that it was therefore of the essence of merely being human to recognize and care for all living things. In short, he saw that to be truly human was to act like a true prince: forever *care-filled*. That is, he realized that seeing — *true* seeing — involved, something like,

seeing the thing as meaning something merely in presenting itself.

In leaving the palace and subjecting himself to six years of intense seeking, Prince Siddhartha sought Enlightenment, which, to judge from the Zen texts, is something like the state in which the one who sees and the one seen share the same meaning. When this happens, *"See what I mean?"* becomes much more than a request for someone to understand what he or she said. Rather, it then involves a kind of loss of separateness on the parts of the hearer and the speaker, and in losing their separateness, they become *fully* sentient. Otherwise, each is nothing more than an incident, an "event," to the other.

This is the root of the Zen Buddhism which teaches that our true practice as humans only truly begins when we are entirely open to the world presented to us as sentient beings. Then, *and only then*, are we prepared to respond appropriately to whatever is present to us as sentient beings — including other humans we can be of help to. As Prince Siddhartha is quoted as saying:

> *In first establishing himself in what is proper,*
> *And only then teaching others,*
> *The Sage will not be stained.*[95]

This present book considered certain words, *not* doctrines, that are centrally important to Zen. There are *no* doctrines in Zen — only signposts and tools for self-purging, along with a certain kind of silence. Its goal is not the mastery of any doctrine or teaching, and its practice is only designed to help practitioners discard whatever tends to obscure the clear vision of all those things that are present to them through sentience.

Above all else, Zen Buddhism seeks the
SENSIBLE!

As the old saying goes,

Though gold dust is valuable, when it falls in the eye, it blurs the vision.

Zen practice leads to *seeing* and not to *theories* or *doctrines* — however "golden" those doctrines might truly be.

Still, although there are no Zen words that communicate Zen doctrines and truths, there *are* Zen words that can be used as signposts and tools of purgation. These words are nothing but tools that Zen uses to help its practitioners see what is right there in front of them. They are the kinds of words that Zen Master Bassui referred to as *living words*, and they are, strictly speaking, "words *not*-words." That is, when the Masters spoke them to particular individuals at particular moments, these living words were most often intended to be understood in a way that was quite different from their usual meanings.

As we have already remarked, we often meet with words in the Zen texts that we are tempted to take as having the same simple, clear meaning as they have in our own day-to-day usage. This book gave a number of examples where we might misunderstand terms found in Zen texts if we assumed they meant the same thing as they did in different contexts. For example, *Compassion* and *Ego* — words whose usage in our contemporary speech is usually just similar enough to their Zen meaning to mislead us in our attempt to understand their Zen usage. (This book has also included a few terms such as *Dharma* and *Karma* that have entered mainstream usage.)

In short, I've chosen a list of the Zen words for discussion that seemed to me to be particularly liable to misinterpretation. But, once again, each of these terms is merely one of many Zen tools used to help us uncover that in us which unites us to what is present to us merely as sentient beings.

A final word about Zen words.

The Buddha himself is quoted as saying toward the end of his long life of preaching that he had never uttered a single word. What he seemed to intend by that perplexing statement was something like this: to experience a spontaneous act of kindness or to experience the moon floating in a dewdrop is to experience the song of life as it hums through that thicket that is our humanity; and, except for the lyrics of such songs, there is *no Zen Language*.

Or, as the great love poet of Islam, Hafiz, reminds us:

We are rich with need, and have no tongue to ask.[96]

This is the language of the heart.

About This Book

A Butterfly
Resting upon the temple bell
Asleep.
(Buson)

That butterfly **wakes up!**

It Stamps!

The temple bell RINGS.

Its sound?

This book.

(Its Author)

Endnotes

1. *Wild Ways: Zen Poems of Ikkyu*, trans. John Stevens (New York: White Pine Press, 2003), 26.

2. Nur Ali Elahi (1895–1974), Kurdish Iranian mystic and master of the Ahl-e Haqq Sufi order, as well as an outstanding tanbur player.

3. This drawing is a gift from Kato Shoshun, arranged for by my roshi, Zen Master Kanju Tanaka. The painter is Fuugai Ekun (1568–1654), who belonged to the Soto sect of Zen.

4. "The Recorded Sayings of Lin-chi," trans. J. C. Cleary in *Three Chan Classics* (Berkeley, Calif.: Numata Center for Buddhist Translation and Research, 1999), 3. This quote is taken from the preface of 1297, written by Linquan, abbot of Baoen Zen Temple.

5. Samantha Sinnayah, "Cloud Gate Dance Theatre of Taiwan: 'Cursive II' and 'Wild Cursive,'" *Japan Times*, September 7, 2006.

6. *Dewdrops on a Lotus Leaf*, trans. John Stevens (Boston, London: Shambhala, 2004), 56.

7. *Ryokan: Zen Monk-Poet of Japan*, trans. Burton Watson (New York: Columbia University Press, 1977), 29. (Those "Three Worlds" are past, present, and future.)

Part I

1. Scott Wilson, *The Unfettered Mind, Takuan Soto, Writings of the Zen Master to the Sword Master* (New York, Tokyo: Kodansha, 1987), 27.

2. Stephen Berg, *Crow with No Mouth* (Port Townsend, Wash.: Copper Canyon Press, 2000), 67.

3. Ibid., 36.

4. Lucien Styrk and Takashi Ikemoto, *The Penguin Book of Zen Poetry* (New York: Puffin, 1977).

5. Berg, *Crow with No Mouth*, 26.

6. The reader who would care to pursue this issue further in the context of classical Zen texts will find much food for thought in *The Five Ranks of Tozan* (San Diego, New York, London: Harcourt Brace, 1965, 1993), 63–72.

7. David Schiller, *The Little Zen Companion* (New York: Workman, 1994), 124. This book is a must-have.

8. Matisyahu is a contemporary Hasidic rapper from Brooklyn. This lovely thought of Matisyahu can be found on this A Fe Me Page Dis Iyah blog entry about Jamaica:

"Him Nuh Look Jamaican" http://iriejamaica.blogspot.com/2006_09_01_archive. html (accessed January 5, 2009).

9. In the *Republic*, 518d, Socrates is presented as saying that the beginning of true insight is a *turning around,* periagoge. This expression captures precisely what Buddhism refers to by "awakening" or "kensho."

10. Watson, *Ryokan: Zen Monk-Poet of Japan*, 90.

11. John Blofeld, *The Zen Teaching of Huang Po* (New York: Shambhala, 1994), 161.

12. It should be pointed out, however, that Islamic mysticism, even nurtured as it is on Islam's Holy Koran, often speaks of this world and we humans who inhabit it in a far different way. Likewise, so it would seem, with Saint Francis of Assisi. (Within the West's great religions, there are several figures whose thoughts are by no means altogether incongruent with that of Mahayana Buddhism.)

13. Once again, Christianity's Saint Francis of Assisi is a magnificent exception to this rule.

14. Not surprisingly, even those scientists who consider themselves too sophisticated to believe in the Creation story refer to the living thing's ability to respond to changes in the environment as its "irritability." Even to be *aware* of "others" is to be *irritated* by them! Nor should this be taken as mere wordplay. For these thinkers, the sentient being's sentience is its evolved way of maximizing its survival by being able to anticipate food or enemies.

15. It's like those Klein bottles of topology; they have no outside distinguishable from inside. Likewise, but less dramatically perhaps, with the Möbius strips.

16. The book *Theogony* by the great Greek poet-philosopher Hesiod (c. 700 BCE) presents a world in which there are exceedingly evil immortals who, *because* they are immortals!, *cannot* be killed; their ruling deity, Zeus, either imprisons them or assigns them to exceedingly unpleasant jobs in Hades — a fact of which all the other immortals were very aware.

17. I was told by a Rinzai Zen monk that one of their vows was not to kill, even if this involves themselves or others dying. But this book is not the place for discussing the pros and cons of killing under any circumstance. And this book is not written for individuals preparing to become Zen monks.

18. The Marine Corps Gen. Samuel B. Griffith's translations and notes are superb. They are published by Oxford University Press. Sun Tzu's dates are given as c. 544–496 BCE and the Buddha's as c. 563–483 BCE.

19. Title of the French philosopher Descartes's 1641 book:

Meditations
Touching
the First Philosophy
in Which
the Existence of God

and
the Distinction Between
the Body and the Soul
Are
Demonstrated

With few exceptions, all Western-oriented philosophy has been based on that book— either agreeing with it, disagreeing with it, or further developing points made in it.

20. Katsuki Sekida, *Two Zen Classics: Mumonkan and Hekiganroku* (New York, Tokyo: Weatherhill, 1996), 147. (I have been advised by Jeff Shore, professor of International Zen at Hanazono University in Kyoto, that this phrase is better rendered into English as: "Not one single thing within or without.")

21. Once again, the reader who would like to pursue this question further should read "The Five Ranks of Dong Shan," which can be found in translations of Hakuin; for example, in Isshu Miura and Ruth Fuller Sasaki, *The Zen Koan: Its History and Use in Rinzai Zen* (San Diego, New York, London: Harvest Books, 1969, 1993).

22. John Keats's splendid poem "Lamia" vividly presents our oh-so-human inclination to rest easy with our delightful counterfeits. And as the philosopher Ludwig Wittgenstein points out in his delightful book *On Certainty*, "The walls support the foundations": We accept amazing theories and "belief-systems" because we are so charmed by what has been built on them, thereby removing them out of our sight by that age-old sleight-of-hand trick of getting the audience to look away from where the illusion is being created.

23. Zenkai Shibayama, *Gateless Barrier: Zen Comments on the Mumonkan*, trans. Sumiko Kudo (New York, Evanston, Ill., San Francisco, London: Harper and Row, 1974), 91.

24. The following is taken from a transcription of a talk given by Yamada Koun on May 9, 1975, at San-un Zendo in Kamakura, Japan. This article is a copy of the transcription appearing in Maria Kannon Zen Center Newsletter 4, no. 2 (Winter 1995): 5. "I am often asked by Christians, especially Catholics, whether they can practice Zazen, and still preserve the beliefs of Christianity. To that question, I usually answer that Zen is not a religion, in the same sense that Christianity is a religion."

25. Dharma Communications, from The Monastery Store Web site: http://www.dharma.net/monstore/index.php?cPath=83_44_72 (accessed January 5, 2009). Although this site is maintained by a monastery store, it makes some interesting points, and the reader can benefit from reading it.

26. Julia V. Nakamura, *The Japanese Tea Ceremony* (New York: Peter Pauper Press, 1965), 29–30.

27. The original version of this story can be found in James Green's *The Recorded Sayings of Zen Master Joshu* (Boston: Shambhala, 2001), 53.

28. This Zenga (painting by a Zen Master) is an icon for Zen practitioners both in the East as well as in the West.

29. Kabir Edmund Helminski, *Love Is a Stranger: Rumi* (Threshold Books, 1993), 35.

30. Bill Buford, *Heat* (New York: Alfred A. Knopf, 2005), 272.

31. The *shakuhachi* is the Japanese bamboo flute. It is quite similar to the Middle Eastern *ney*.

32. Robin Hartshorne and Kazuaki Tanahashi, "The Hitori Mondo of Hisamatsu Fuyo," *Annals of the International Shakuhachi Society* 1.

33. I owe this insight, as so much else in this book, to my roshi, Kanju Tanaka.

34. Green, *The Recorded Sayings of Zen Master Joshu*, 108–109.

35. "Klein bottle." Wikipedia. http://en.wikipedia.org/wiki/Klein_bottle (accessed January 5, 2009).

36. In the writings of the great Roman poet Virgil we find, "*sunt lacrimae rerum et mentem mortalia tangunt,*" which can be translated as: "these are the tears of things, and our mortality cuts to the heart" (*Aeneid*, I, 462). Virgil does *not* go on to say that there is any *end* to the tears at the heart of things. This great poem is largely an account of the ability to bear sorrow as an elevating human virtue. Indeed, Virgil seems to think that suffering is a vice to be avoided at all costs.

37. As Saint Paul reminds us in Ephesians 4:7, "But unto every one of us is given grace according to the measure of the gift of Christ." Salvation, the great gift of grace, is a *gift*, and not anything to be earned by our deeds.

38. The "super-ego" of Freudian psychiatry seems to be a Western version of that judging, unborn self. For Freud, however, the super-ego is profoundly shaped by the environment, which consists of our childhood shaping by the teachings of our family's religion and by their own psychopathologies.

39. Lucien Stryk, *Zen Poems of China and Japan* (Auckland: Evergreen Books, 1994), 81.

40. Robert Conquest's *Reflections on a Ravaged Century* (New York, London: W. W. Norton, 2000) lays out this scene with the grave dignity it requires to do it justice.

41. Readers conversant with Plato's Socratic dialogues will recognize this as an example of what we in the West know as "Meno's Paradox."

42. Kazuaki Tanahashi and Tensho David Schneider, eds., *Essential Zen* (San Francisco: Harper San Francisco, 1994), 130.

43. This exquisite poem is by Paul Reps, Zen painter, poet, and translator (from Kazuaki Tanahashi, *Essential Zen*, 129.) Reps sees that, for Buddhism, dying involves that act of *returning*.

44. The death poem of the Zen nun Ryonen. From Paul Reps and Nyogen Senzaki, *Zen Flesh, Zen Bones* (Boston, London: Shambhala, 1994), 84.

45. In the legislative year 2005 the state of Maryland, with somewhere near 2.7 million citizens, passed into law 363 new laws — in one year (a new law for every 74,380 men, women, and children).

46. Hozoin (c. 1560) was a Buddhist monk of the Kofuku-ji Temple in Nara, Japan.

47. John Stevens, *Three Zen Masters* (Tokyo, New York, London: Kodansha, 1999), 33.

48. Although this saying is often attributed to Hakuin, he is actually quoting the earlier Zen Master Dahui Zhonggao (1089–1163).

49. The expression "That monk Gautama" refers to Prince Siddhartha *after* he had left the kingdom to become a prince of beggars. (Saint Francis would have understood this easily; born into a rich family of merchants, he gave all that up and became the monk who preached love to beggars and to the very birds who flew to his feet to hear his words.) This expression is taken from the *Ten Directions* by Eihei Dogen Zenji translated by Yasuda Joshu Dainen roshi and Anzan Hoshin sensei (excerpted from the forthcoming book *Dogen: Zen Writings on the Practice of Realization*).

50. For example, in the "Simile and Parable" (third) chapter of the Lotus Sutra, Prince Siddhartha says, "I am the Dharma King, free to do as I will with the Law. To bring peace and safety to living beings — that is the reason I appear in the world."

51. Stevens, *Three Zen Masters*, 47.

52. The translation goes: "One, two, three — but where, my dear Timaeus, is the fourth. . . ." That *where* translates "*pou*." Where, indeed! Plato's silence is every bit as full of meaning as that of the Zen Masters.

53. Exodus 3:14 (English-Hebrew Bible, Mechon-Mamre edition).

54. The Christian teaching of the Incarnation of the Word (Logos) of the Creator in the "person" of Jesus Christ presents that event of God-Become-Man as taking place in the Creator's own good time — and certainly not in response to something done or said by any creatures. Luther's Protestantism — which, along with Calvin's teachings, can be said to provide the basis of present-day American Evangelical teachings — is summed up by Luther when he attributed Divinity's choice of whom to save or not to the unsearchable will of God alone (see Romans 11:33), together with his illustration in *"De servo arbitrio"* that every person is like a beast of burden who is ridden either by God or the devil.

55. As the endnote immediately above is meant to make clear, Christianity's view of this matter is much more complex on the surface, but, as Saint Paul and Martin Luther point out, even God the Son who Christians believe was sent to redeem His creation, is ultimately known only through His *self*-revelation.

56. Aristotle says that we make mistakes because, like bats who are blinded by the light of day, we are blinded by the light of truth.

57. Cleary, *Three Chan Classics*, 43.

58. Zen Master Torei, Hakuin's great successor, is recorded as saying:

> *Shinto is the root,*
> *Confucianism is the trunk,*
> *And Buddhism is the flowering and sweet fruit.*

59. Gita Mehta, *Karma Cola* (New York: Vintage, 1994), 187–88.

60. Christianity's great beggar-monk, Saint Francis — along with his friends, would, I think — both have understood and agreed with this sentiment.

61. Aristotle tells us in his *On the Heavens* that, outside the All — what we call "the Universe" — there was "Not even Nothing." It might be interesting to consider the Void of the three great religious texts of the West in that way to see if they fit.

62. To be fair, in Science's view, "empty space" is something akin to an "information field." For instance, the equivalence of mass and energy, their transformation following strictly the laws of mathematical physics, implies that all that really "exists" in that emptiness is something akin to "information," *i.e.,* what can be stated mathematically by formulae such as "$E = mc^2$." (It almost seems as if that field is the reason that one thing follows another in a necessary way — *i.e.,* everything in it is actively "in-formed" by the always-present informative power of that information field! All very confusing, but interesting!)

63. Watson, "Waking from a Dream of My Younger Brother," *Ryokan: Zen Monk-Poet of Japan*, 23.

64. Camille Paglia, *Break, Blow, Burn* (New York: Vintage, 2005), xvi.

65. Arthur Braverman, *A Quiet Room: The Poetry of Zen Master Jakushitsu* (Boston, Rutland, Vt., Tokyo: Charles E. Tuttle, 2000), 14.

66. Thomas F. Judges and John Stevens, *Zen Brushwork, Tanchu Terayama, Focusing the Mind with Calligraphy and Painting* (Tokyo, New York, London: Kodansha, n.d.), 33.

67. "The Song of the Grass Roof Hermitage," *Zen Brushwork,* 33.

68. Zenkai Shibayama, *Gateless Barrier: Zen Comments on the Mumonkan*, trans. Sumiko Kudo (New York, Evanston, Ill., San Francisco, London: Harper and Row, 1974), case 29.

69. In Homer's Greek, we find a pairing of *fren* or *boule* with *thumo*s, "Mind/Intention" with "Spirit/Ardor," which parallels the use of the character '⟨⟩ in Zen Buddhism. (See, for instance: *Odyssey*: III, line 128; VII, line 75).

70. "Figuring out" seems to involve what Western cognitive scientists, starting as early as Descartes in the 1630s, say it is: namely, a process involving following constructs that are only anticipations of our present-day "neural pathways" in the brain. Cognitive science in the West tends to be based on the study of brain structures. To the extent that this is on target, we can say that figuring-out is to "minding" what knowledge of the mechanics of a watch is to telling time. Computers cannot compute; they only follow pre-etched connections according to the input of the keystrokes. It is the human using the computer who computes, *i.e., makes sense of*— what is presented on the screen. Computers don't ever blurt out, "Ah! *now* I see!" Do they?

71. The reader who knows German might compare this expression to the term *Urquell.*

72. Watson, *Ryokan: Zen Monk-Poet of Japan*, 104.

73. David Hinton, *Chuang Tzu: The Inner Chapters* (New York: Counterpoint, 1998), 25. Lao Tzu is often identified as the author of the *Tao Te Ching*, but several very careful scholars feel that Chuang Tzu might be a better choice. David Hinton is one of them.

74. We find a particularly clear example of this procedure in Plato's dialogue *Phaedo*, where Socrates is giving his intellectual autobiography. Up until the Christian Scholastics modified this Socratic view of the scientific method, it was considered to be the firm foundation of scientific method. But, it must be stressed, what we consider a truly scientific method to consist of is basically a modified version of the Socratic/Platonic view — which, itself, has deep roots in the Pythagorean use of analysis and synthesis.

75. Strictly speaking, it is the unity, Mind/Heart, which grasps meaning.

76. Hartshorne and Tanahashi, "The Hitori Mondo of Hisamatsu Fuyo."

77. Timothy L. O'Brien, "Are U.S. Innovators Losing Their Competitive Edge?" *New York Times*, November 13, 2005, Business sec.

78. Descartes's early work, "Regulae ad Directionem Ingenii" — universally *mis*-translated as "Rules for the Direction of the Mind" — can be accurately translated as: "Directions for Engineering the Solution of Problems."

79. Isn't an opinion a sort of shape that defines a number of experiences as belonging together? For example, after 9/11, we tend to group all Muslims together, and when we meet a Muslim, we experience him or her as identical to Muslim terrorists. If so, then an opinion is a sort of box into which we throw a number of experiences and then consider them as interchangeable.

80. This is implied in Zen Master Hakuin's book *Poison Words for the Heart*, where he speaks of the five *skandhas* — something like "forms of possible experience." (The earlier Zen Master Ikkyu appears to think this way as well.)

   Those *skandhas* prepare us to experience our human world, which is the gift of our sentience. And, make no bones about it, for Zen, the originating source of those *skandhas* is exactly the source of what we experience by means of them!

81. Zen Master Kanju Tanaka, given to me by him.

82. The following is taken from Joel Achenbach ("Can We Stop the Next Killer Flu?" *Washington Post*, December 11, 2005, W10) in an article concerning contemporary researchers' discovery of, and the subsequent publishing of, the details of how to re-animate the 1918 Spanish flu, which killed millions.

83. If this seems either far-fetched or merely some Oriental mysticism, readers with a background in ancient Greek philosophy might care to compare what I've described as Zen's view of redeeming and Aristotle's remark in *Metaphysics*, 1074 b: 35, where he says of Mind, "And Mind's activity is Minding mind," *noesis noeseos noesis*.

84. This contradicts Pascal's famous *Pensées*, "Reason has reasons the heart knows not of." For Zen, there *are* no such "heartless" reasons or reasons inaccessible to the heart.

Part II

1. *Wild Ways, Zen Poems of Ikkyu*, trans. John Stevens (Buffalo, N.Y.: White Pine Press, 2003), 51.

2. Kazuaki Tanahashi and Tensho David Schneider, eds., *Essential Zen* (San Francisco: HarperSanFrancisco, 1994), 104. There is an aspect of the Rinzai "Mad-caps" that is quite reminiscent of the great Sufi mystical poet Hafiz's "Rends."

3. Shibayama, *Gateless Barrier: Zen Comments on the Mumonkan*, trans. Sumiko Kudo (New York, Evanston, Ill., San Francisco, London: Harper and Row, 1974), 141.

4. Kazuaki Tanahashi, *Moon in a Dewdrop: Writings of Zen Master Dogen* (New York: North Point Press, 1985), 217. (In Dogen's time, there was apparently relatively little difference between the practice of Soto Zen and Rinzai Zen.)

5. "We admit that in different countries there are differences with regard to the life of Buddhist monks, popular Buddhist beliefs and practices, rites and ceremonies, customs and habits. These external forms and expressions should not be confused with the essential teachings of the Buddha." Source: Walpola Rahula, *The Heritage of the Bhikkhu* (New York: Grove Press, 1974), 137–38. The reader for whom such questions represent obstacles to understanding Zen Buddhism in its peculiarities would do well to consider reading Ngawang Zangpo's splendidly well-balanced, intelligent *Guru Rinpoché: His Life and Times* (Ithaca, N.Y. and Boulder, Colo.: Snow Lion Publishers, 2002), especially the chapter "Buddhism, History and Truth," pages 27–48.

6. This claim is widely disputed, both by Buddhist practitioners as well as by secular scholars of Buddhism. While studying in Kyoto, I asked both my roshi (a Rinzai Zen Master) and another Zen Master who is the president of Hanazono University, the only Rinzai Zen university in the world, if my understanding concerning this was accurate. They both agreed strongly that it was. Still, what other schools of Buddhism hold as true is beside the point — as long as those opinions don't stand in the way of the practitioners' progress toward Awakening!

7. In Latin, "*Neca eos omnes. Deus suos agnoset*," reputedly said by the leader of the attackers, an armed Christian abbot.

8. S. Palosaari, *Japanese Buddhism: A Short History* (Kyoto: Yamada M. Ryukoku University Translation Center Shichijo Omiya, 1980), 600.

9. Shibayama, *Zen Comments on the Mumonkan*, case 24.

10. *Dharma* could be translated here by "it's just the Path Awakened individuals follow!"

11. Tanahashi, *Moon in a Dewdrop*, 35.

12. J. C. Cleary, "The Recorded Sayings of Lin-chi," in *Three Chan Classics: The Recorded Sayings of Linji* (Berkeley, Calif.: Numata Center for Buddhist Translation and Research, 1999), 43. In this passage, Lin-chi is largely restating Hui-neng's injunction saying that we must seek the face we had before our parents were born. (Neither master was suggesting patricide!)

13. Arthur Braverman, *Mud and Water: A Collection of Talks by Zen Master Bassui* (San Francisco: North Point Press, 1989), 98.

14. Ibid.

15. Once again, in *any given instance* of a painted Zen Circle, that Emptiness is the Emptiness of the Living Truth of the painter of that Zen Circle — ◖.

16. Shibayama, *The Gateless Barrier*, case 5.

17. Gil Fronsdal, *The Dhammapada: A New Translation of the Buddhist Classic* (Boston, London: Shambhala, 2005), 21.

18. Descartes' great war cry was: **Ego** cogito; ergo **ego** sum — I think; therefore, I am.
    And ninety-eight years after Descartes' death we find the 1748 book *The Spirit of Laws* by Montesquieu, where he tells us that money is a symbol of *everything and anything that can be bought*; in his *Persian Letters*, he points in the direction of *quantifying* sexual desire — how much will you pay for satisfying it? — which in turn ends, presently, in prostitutes as being defined as "sex *workers*," as *wage earners*.
    For the European Enlightenment, everything becomes a commodity. *Everything!* And "a commodity" can be defined by its ability to satisfy some desire of a potential purchaser — indeed, as *defining* human beings as consumers. (Economics is truly the "dismal science," but it is at the heart of the West's Enlightenment.)

19. In the case of real estate, before a sale can occur, the property must be "free and clear" so the buyers know that there are no prior claims on it.

20. Kabir Edmund Helminski, *Love Is a Stranger*: *Rumi* (Brattleboro, Vt.: Threshold Books, 1993), 69.

21. "The Elimination of Colour in the Far East," from Adolf Portmann and Dominque Zahan, *Color Symbolism: Six Excerpts from the Eranos Yearbook 1972* (Woodstock, Conn.: Spring Publications, 1972), 167–95.

22. Elaine Woo, "Frank Okamura, 94; Expert Took Spiritual Approach to Bonsai," *Los Angeles Times*, January 29, 2006. http://articles.latimes.com/2006/jan/29/local/me-okamura29 (accessed March 20, 2009).

23. In this translation, I have replaced *desire* with *ardor*. Rumi, I am certain, would wholeheartedly concur. He, along with all the great poets of Islam, would understand desire as counterfeit longing. (In Arabic, the term *Islam* means *submission*. True submission does not countenance desire — only longing.)

24. These observations were made by Salley Vickers during her interview with Jane Wheatley, in the April 1, 2006 issue of the (London) *Times*. http://entertainment.timesonline.co.uk/tol/arts_and_entertainment/books/article699733.ece (accessed March 20, 2009).

25. Helminski, *Love Is a Stranger*: *Rumi*, 35.

26. "The Recorded Sayings of Lin-chi," *Three Chan Classics*, 12–13. In BDK English Tripitaka 74-I, II, III.

27. Jennie Yabroff, review of *A Plea for Eros*, by Siri Hustvedt, SFGate.com, January 1, 2006.

28. This I know — not because Zen taught it to me, but, because it was that experience that led me to seek Zen's sugar. It was "the tears of things. . . ."

29. William Shakespeare, *The Merchant of Venice*, act III, scene 2.

30. Tanahashi, *Moon in a Dewdrop*, 70.

31. This is not meant disrespectfully to Descartes. Rather, it is one of his central teachings, which makes it so difficult for Westerners to grasp what Zen is saying; so his teachings are *entirely* appropriately considered in this book.

    His influence is difficult for Americans, especially, to gauge accurately. Thus, for instance, we find in *Democracy in America* by Alexis de Tocqueville, bk. 2, chap. 1: "Philosophical Method Among the Americans":

    > I think that in no country in the civilized world is less attention paid to philosophy than in the United States. The Americans have no philosophical school of their own; and they care but little for all the schools into which Europe is divided, the very names of which are scarcely known to them. Nevertheless it is easy to perceive that almost all the inhabitants of the United States conduct their understanding in the same manner, and govern it by the same rules; that is to say, that without ever having taken the trouble to define the rules of a philosophical method, they are in possession of one, common to the whole people. To evade the bondage of system and habit, of family maxims, class opinions, and, in some degree, of national prejudices; to accept tradition only as a means of information, and existing facts only as a lesson used in doing otherwise, and doing better; to seek the reason of things for one's self, and in one's self alone; to tend to results without being bound to means, and to aim at the substance through the form; – such are the principal characteristics of what I shall call the philosophical method of the Americans. But if I go further, and if I seek amongst these characteristics that which predominates over and includes almost all the rest, I discover that in most of the operations of the mind, each American appeals to the individual exercise of his own understanding alone. America is therefore one of the countries in the world where philosophy is least studied, and where the precepts of Descartes are best applied. Nor is this surprising. The Americans do not read the works of Descartes, because their social condition deters them from speculative studies; but they follow his maxims because this very social condition naturally disposes their understanding to adopt them.

32. In the Attic Greek of Plato, *nous* was "mind," and *dianoia* was "reasoning, thinking."

    As we see in Plato's *Republic*, the task of reason was thought to be building "scaffolds" — "hypotheses" — to permit us to see over intellectual obstacles and, when those scaffolds are high enough to permit us to do so, we get rid of them. Zen is in essential agreement with this view. That activity of Minding was, in Attic Greek, *noesis*, or "intellectual intuition." Descartes, one of the principal architects of our European Enlightenment, goes out of his way to deny that there even is anything such as intuition; for him, Minding only involves "reasoning" about cause and effect and the like.

33. Professor Philipp Frank, Einstein's personal biographer and lifelong friend, told us in a graduate class he held, which I attended, that Einstein was horrified when he realized what had developed from his $E = mc^2$, and remarked to him, "I wish I'd been a plumber."

34. Dr. Daniel Ford, "Research Shows Head, Heart Linked," *Baltimore Sun*, June 30, 2006, sec. D.

35. This "Indefinite Unity/Pair" comprises a couple or pair whose constituents are not a simple number like, for instance, a couple of socks is a pair. In this present case, the members are "bound together" *in spite of — or, perhaps more accurately, because of — their dis-similarity.* It might also be termed "the asymmetrical," or even something like "the odd."

36. Finding the limits of reason was the primary undertaking of the philosopher Kant (1724–1804). But, to his mind, the task involved determining the exact limits of reason in order to locate a sphere of personal freedom, outside the reach of Newton's mathematical laws of nature — and not, as in Zen, to reveal the sphere of human joyful sorrow and the Shepherd's compassion.

37. Case 3 in *Two Zen Classics: Mumonkan and Hekiganroku*, Weatherhill, 152.

38. The literal translation of the Japanese is:
Fu-ru (old) i-ke (pond) ya,
ka-wa-zu (frog) to-bi-ko-mu (jumping into)
mi-zu (water) no o-to (sound)

Bassho seems to be contrasting the no-sound of the water in the old pond and its *now*-sound as the frog jumps into it — the *always* with the *now*. What is more, we find Hakuin remarking that the huge temple bell makes no sound until it is struck. Each seems to be saying that true sound is the child of true silence. (Hakuin, who created the Koan "What is the sound of a single hand?," relates that his Great Awakening occurred upon his hearing the sound of a distant temple bell.) Zen again. . . .

39. Tanahashi, *Essential Zen*, 26.

40. John Stevens, *Three Zen Masters: Ikkyu, Hakuin, Ryokan* (Tokyo, New York, London: Kodansha, 1999), 49.

41. Philip Yampolsky, *The Zen Master Hakuin: Selected Writings* (New York: Columbia University Press, 1985), 58.

42. We English speakers are fortunate to have a splendid introduction to Koan practice in Isshu Miura and Ruth Fuller Sasaki, *The Zen Koan: Its History and Use in Rinzai Zen* (San Diego, New York, London: Harcourt Brace and Company, 1965, 1993).

43. Tanahashi, *Moon in a Dewdrop*, 214.

44. That is, in the *pre*–Big Bang there was nothing to modify or in any way qualify the effects of that primal commotion. The way was clear, open. (However, modern mathematical cosmology almost surely requires that the pre–Big Bang openness possessed mathematically defined regulations, according to which *subsequent* events "in space" could act; otherwise, there could not even be a mathematical physics to trace events from today's cosmologists *back* to that Big Bang. Like it or not, those cosmologists presuppose something like Buddhism's unborn/eternal Dharma, and Greek philosophy's Logos.)

45. The following list of derivatives of the Ancient Greek *stereos* ("solid") may be of interest to readers who know Greek. The range of these derivatives is strikingly reminiscent of the ambiguities of Void in the Zen texts.

Στερεὸς, ἀ, ὸν / Στὲρεω

Στερεὸς, ἀ, ὸν	=	"Firm; solid"
Στὲρεω	=	"Deprive of; Bereave; Rob of"
Στερὲωμα, τὸ	=	"Solid body"
Στὲρημα, τὸ	=	"Privation; Loss"
Στὲρησις		
Στεριϕὸομαι	=	"Become hard, solid"
Στὲριϕος, ἀ, ὸν (= Στερεὸς, ἀ, ὸν)	=	"Firm; solid"

The Latin of the Christian Bible translated the beginning of the Hebrew Verse 2 of Genesis as *Terra autem erat inanis et vacua*. The Classical Latin authors used *inanis* to refer to what had been abandoned, and so was emptied of what was there, and as "empty," as in an "empty" grave — a grave which did not have in it what could be expected to be in it. On its part, *vacua* was usually used to refer to what had not been occupied but could be inferred as *properly* being occupied.

In both the pre-Christian Latin and in the Ancient Greek, terms such as *empty* and *void* seemed to imply that what was referred to by those terms was something that anticipated being changed by being filled.

At the very least, we can say that the pre-Christian usages seemed to imply something *not yet completed*. The Christian holy books appear to intend a much more absolutely negative intent.

46. We can only wonder where that Big Bang took place.

47. "Moon in a Dewdrop: The Time Being," *Uji*, 76–83.

48. We find this both in the writings of Zen Master Dogen and in those of Zen Master Huang Po. Also, the Lotus Sutra speaks at length of the Tathagatagharba, "The Womb of The Enlightened One."

49. "The Recorded Sayings of Lin-chi," *Three Chan Classics*, 48.

50. "Zen Master Hakuin's Poison Words for the Heart (Dokugo Shingyo)," *The Eastern Buddhist* 13, no. 2 (Autumn 1980): 73–114. A less clear translation can be found in Norman Waddell's translation of *Zen Words for the Heart*, 31.

51. I was once told by a friend of mine — a scholarly Christian pastor — that without the concept of ego, Christianity has no meaning.

52. The reader is reminded of what is said in endnote 14, Part I.

53. I owe this, as well as many other things in this book, to remarks I've read in essays of Jeff Shore.

54. The reader who has read Plato's dialogues the *Sophist* and *Parmenides* might here be reminded of the formula, "Other is other than other," out of which Plato seems to derive the "*community* of the Forms/*eide*."

55. Tanchu Terayama, *Zen Brushwork: Focusing the Mind with Calligraphy and Painting*, trans. Thomas F. Judges and John Stevens (Tokyo, New York, London: Kodansha, 2004), 14.

56. For example, Gödel's theorem (1931) was designed to demonstrate that there is no single universal mathematical formula — Leibniz's "Universal Characteristic" — from which we can deduce all possible mathematical/rational accounts for what happens in this world.

57. As early as Saint Anselm of Canterbury (1093–1109 CE), we find the expression "*Fides quaerens intellectum*" (Faith seeking knowledge). Revelation was from Creator to creature; the seeking of knowledge beginning with faith was from creature to Creator. The European Enlightenment replaced "faith" with "scientific hypothesis," and, as we see with the so-called "Big Bang" theory, scientists today feel that such theories lead to a replacement of a Creator with an immense cosmic event. In this account, the beginning involved no *Father* of Everything but, rather, the *Mother* of All Rackets.

58. This, of course, is reminiscent of Aristotle's "Final Cause" — the "*to ti en enai*" ("the that which it was to be").

59. There are, to be sure, many branches of Buddhism that reject this and say that the historical Buddha was anticipated throughout the ages. On their part, many of the Zen Buddhist Masters make great, sometimes not altogether charitable, sport of this teaching, and say that *Buddha* is a name. Each of us is Buddha. The rituals and temples, according to these Masters, are nothing more than means of helping others focus their attention before they are ready to discipline themselves fully by Zen practices. As Prince Siddhartha himself is quoted as saying, "It is like stopping a child's tears by telling him that the golden leaf is a gold coin." Zen tells us, "If you meet the Buddha, kill the Buddha." The essence of Zen Buddhism is to replace the texts with "happenings" — the what-he-said — with Nows!, with what-you-are.

60. As noted previously (note 54), the reader conversant with Plato's writings will detect echoes of the arguments of his *Parmenides* and *Sophist* here. (Jacob Klein's

"Plato's Trilogy," which includes close interpretive readings of *Theatetus, Sophist,* and *Statesman,* is incomparably useful to readers interested in these matters (Chicago, London: University of Chicago Press, 1977). That Klein treats these three dialogues as a trilogy ending with *Statesman* suggests that he thinks the Socratic schools such as Plato's also thought, as did Zen of Bodhidharma's line, that ⌣ leads us to the capital. This sort of note is appropriate to *The Language of Zen,* because it is largely our post-Classical metaphysics that nurtures the West's views, which most powerfully obscure Zen's Way from us.

61. Ryuichi Abe and Peter Haskel, *Great Fool: Zen Master Ryokan: Poems Letters and Other Writings* (Honolulu: University of Hawaii Press, 1996), 44.

62. Arthur Braverman, *A Quiet Room: The Poetry of Zen Master Jakashitsu* (Boston, Rutland, Vt., Tokyo: Charles E. Tuttle, 2000), 27.

63. Issai Chozanshi, *The Demon's Sermon on the Martial Arts,* trans. William Scott Wilson (Tokyo, New York, London: Kodansha, 2006), 100.

64. Gishin Tokiwa, *The Lankavatara Sutram/A Jewel Scripture of Mahayana Thought and Practice/An English Translation/A Study of the Four-Fascicle Lankavatara Ratna Sutrum* (Osaka: Privately published, 2003). Gishin Tokiwa, 4-17-1, Nishi-awaji, Higashi-yodogawa-ku, Osaka, 533-0031, Japan. The author, who is professor emeritus, Hanazono University, Kyoto, kindly presented me with a copy during my stay at the International Research Institute for Rinzai Zen Buddhism, Hanazono University, Kyoto, Japan.

65. This definition of ◯ is a gift to me from my roshi, Zen Master Kanju Tanaka. (However, once again, any hand-painted occurrence of it also refers to the condition of the painter who painted it. *No one who is not awakened can successfully paint that* ◯!)

66. The association of ◯ with ⌣ is discussed at some length in the last entry.

67. Tanahashi, *Moon in a Dewdrop,* 70.

68. If this treatment of Void seems to present a misunderstanding of what Zen concludes on the subject, I can only respond that it is firmly based on Hakuin's "Zen Words for the Heart." In particular, the development to be found on page 31 of Norman Waddell's translation (Shambhala, 1996), along with his stress on the strange ambiguity of the *skandhas* — they are a sort of bridge between the unborn/undying and our *sentient(!)* mortality. There, Hakuin seems to be stressing the correctness of Zen's outreach in preparing its practitioners to be Shepherds — Friends of Prince Siddhartha. (My own scholarship over the last forty-five or so years has involved a great deal of reflection on modern medicine's modulations of Descartes' neurophysiology of sensation. Hakuin's treatment of it in his commentary on The Heart Sutra is, *far and away,* the deepest, most intelligent and clearest I have come across — only rivaled by that of the Swiss zoologist Adolf Portmann. I am also deeply indebted, in this as in so many other points, to my roshi, Zen Master Tanaka, who alerted me to the radical importance of appreciating the place of Shinto to my progress in grasping Zen's conclusions on this point.)

69. Although this saying is often attributed to Hakuin, he is actually quoting the Chan master Dahui Zhonggao (1089–1163). The reader is urged to obtain a copy

of *Penetrating Laughter: Hakuin's Zen and Art* by Kazuaki Tanahashi (New York: Overlook Press, 1984), 93. It presents this Zenga, together with Hakuin's calligraphy and Tanahashi's commentary. This is an important book.

70. Stevens, *Wild Ways: Zen Poems of Ikkyu*, 69.

71. One of the aspects of Sufism that struck me most forcibly was its music, much of which presents wonderfully joyful sound in deeply purple minor keys.

72. Gita Mehta's take on the West's misuse of these terms in her book *Karma Cola* is well worth reading. See especially "Forked Tongues," 98–100. Indeed, reading that book might well be an excellent partner for someone reading this present book.

73. The Ancient Greek use of the term *Music of the Spheres* is reminiscent of the term *Buddha-Dharma*. The Latin term *Mos-mores* echoes the sentiment exactly: "It's not our American way to bow to authority."

74. Stevens, *Three Zen Masters*, 35.

75. The fact that there are so many branches of Buddhism reveals how important it is for Buddhism to articulate Rules/Dharmas; each branch seeks to provide the best possible environment, Sangha, for its practitioners to realize their Karma as Buddhist practitioners.

76. The literal translation from the Chinese is: "Dharma original Dharma not Dharma, Not-Dharma Dharma also Dharma, Now transmit not-Dharma Dharma, Dharma Dharma how can be Dharma?" This can be found in John Blofeld, *The Zen Teaching of Huang Po* (Boston: Shambhala, 1994), 110–11, and note 52, 241–242.

77. The reader might find the following *Scientific American* article by Philip E. Ross on July 24, 2006: "The Expert Mind: Studies of the mental processes of chess grandmasters have revealed clues to how people become experts in other fields as well." Zen's response to the conclusion of this article — "practice, practice, practice" is the only way to perfection — is likely to be something like: "Okay; but practice only leads to perfection; Zen practice also aims at perfection, but in such a way as to constantly remind the practitioner that beyond perfection there lies Excellence." Björn Borg's opponents were no less "practiced" than Borg concerning the ins and outs of professional tennis; he, however, was excellent — because he became, so to speak, his tennis. He lost himself in tennis, and tennis manifested itself through him as does the bamboo in the hand of the master painter.

78. The great Orientalist Henry Corbin has pointed out that Ismaili Sufism is to Islam what Mahayana Zen Buddhism is to Buddhism.

79. The reader who is interested in Ancient Greek thought might enjoy comparing Heraclitus' use of Law/Logos with Zen's use of Dharma. (Kathleen Freeman's translation of the fragments of Heraclitus in her *Ancilla to the Pre-Socratic Philosophers* [Cambridge, Mass.: Harvard University Press, 2003] presents them all.)

80. Probabilistic mechanics and, to speak generally, quantum physics, seem to be moving in the direction of the Zen view of Dharma. There are certain elements in these branches of theoretical physics that dissolve "cause and effect" into something like

"adjacent probabilities of occurring in sequential time." This opens the door to a less deterministic view of what underlies events. But the theoreticians have not as yet reached an understanding of "probabilistic events," which involves an understanding of what it means *to be*.

81. In pre-Christian — that is, Greek — thought, the term *Logos* approximated the meanings of the term *Dharma*.

82. The reader who has read Plato will perhaps be reminded here of the so-called "community of the Forms," a teaching that was presumably an outgrowth of Pythagorean Number Theory — which, centuries later, led to algebra via Diophantos' book *Arithmetic*, which appeared in the second half of the third century CE.

83. John Locke's "Essay of Human Understanding" (1689) goes to great length to define all our ideas as abstractions from experience. They are boxes into which we throw a number of ideas gained by experience — an idea, for Locke, being a perception.

84. This story is also told of Ikkyu, in *Zen Masters*, 33. It is also related as happening to Hakuin centuries later!

85. Tozan Ryokai (806–869), first Patriarch and founder of Soto Zen (Chinese Tsao Dong Ch'an) lineage.
    The complete verse is:

    How wonderful! How wonderful!
    The inanimate expounding of Dharma is inconceivable;
    If you use your ears to listen, you'll never understand —
    Only when you hear in your eyes will you know.

86. Elizabeth T. Gray Jr., *The Green Sea of Heaven* (Ashland, Ore.: White Cloud, 1985), 30. This quote is from the book's introduction, "The Visionary Topography of Hafiz," by Daryush Shayegan. Shayegan would, I think, feel very much at home with Rinzai Zen. (He has lived and taught in Tokyo, and, since he knew Henry Corbin personally, he surely knows Mahayana Buddhism and its similarity to the Ismaili branch of Islamic mysticism — *i.e.,* that spiritual temperament shared by Mahayana Buddhism's Zen in Bodhidharma's Pastoral line.)

87. The author.

88. By the contemporary Korean Buddhist poet Ko Un in Gary Gach, "Pointing Beyond Words," *Buddhadharma* (Fall 2006): 63.

89. Roger Dobson and Abul Taher, "Cavegirls Were First Blondes to Have Fun," *Sunday Times*, February 26, 2006.

90. *The Ten Oxherding Pictures*, by Kakuan, stage 8: "Both Bull and Self Transcended."

91. Hartshorne and Tanahashi, "The Hitori Mondo of Hisamatsu Fuyo," *Annals of the International Shakuhachi Society* 1.

92. Tanahashi, *Moon in a Dewdrop*, 218.

93. Chinese Zen-Taoist woman poet (1246–1304).

94. Something like this is one of the principal teachings of Zen Master Hakuin's commentary on the Heart Sutra.

95. Gil Fronsdal, *The Dhammapada: A New Translation of the Buddhist Classic* (Boston: Shambhala, 2005), 42.

96. Gray, *The Green Sea of Heaven*, 51.

Index